A Longman Cultural Edition

DR. JEKYLL AND MR. HYDE
Robert Louis Stevenson

THE SECRET SHARER
Joseph Conrad

TRANSFORMATION
Mary Wollstonecraft Shelley

THREE TALES OF DOUBLES

Edited by

Susan J. Wolfson and Barry V. Qualls

PEARSON
Longman

New York   San Francisco   Boston
London   Toronto   Sydney   Tokyo   Singapore   Madrid
Mexico City   Munich   Paris   Cape Town   Hong Kong   Montreal

Editor-in-Chief: Joseph Terry
Executive Marketing Manager: Joyce Nilsen
Production Manager: Denise Phillip
Project Coordination and Electronic Page Makeup: TexTech International
Cover Designer/Manager: John Callahan
Cover Photo: Pach Brothers, New York, *Richard Mansfield as Dr. Jekyll and
Mr. Hyde* (ca. 1885 and 1990)
Senior Manufacturing Buyer: Dennis J. Para

Library of Congress Cataloging-in-Publication Data

Dr. Jekyll and Mr. Hyde, The secret sharer, and Transformation : three tales of
doubles / Robert Louis Stevenson, Joseph Conrad, Mary Shelley ; edited
by Barry V. Qualls and Susan J. Wolfson.
     p. cm.—(A Longman cultural edition)
     ISBN 978-0-321-41561-5
  1. Doppelgdngers—Fiction.   2. English literature—Psychological aspects.
3. English literature—19th century—History and criticism.   I. Qualls,
Barry V. II. Wolfson, Susan J., 1948–   III. Stevenson, Robert Louis,
1850–1894. Strange case of Dr. Jekyll and Mr. Hyde.   IV. Conrad, Joseph,
1857–1924. Secret sharer.   V. Shelley, Mary Wollstonecraft, 1797–1851.
Transformation.
  PR1309.D67J45 2009
  823'.80927—dc22   2008003352

Copyright © 2009 by Pearson Education, Inc.

All rights reserved. No part of this publication may be reproduced, stored in
a retrieval system, or transmitted, in any form or by any means, electronic,
mechanical, photocopying, recording, or otherwise, without the prior written
permission of the publisher. Printed in the United States.

Please visit us at www.pearsonhighered.com

ISBN-13: 978-0-321-41561-5
ISBN-10:   0-321-41561-2

3 2020

Contents

List of Illustrations

Cover: Detail of Mr. Mansfield as Dr. Jekyll and Mr. Hyde

About Longman Cultural Editions

Reading always vibrates with the transformations of the day—now, yesterday, and centuries ago when presses first put printed language into circulation. So too, literary culture is always open to change, with new pulses of imagination confronting older practices, texts transforming under new ways of reading and new perspectives of understanding, canons shifting and expanding, traditions reviewed and renewed, recast and reformed. Inspired by the innovative *Longman Anthology of British Literature,* Longman Cultural Editions present key texts in contexts that illuminate the lively intersections of literature, tradition, and culture. In each volume, a principal work gains new dimensions from materials that relate it to its past, present, and future: to informing traditions and debates, to the conversations and controversies of its own historical moment, to later eras of reading and reaction.

The series is designed for several kinds of readers and several situations of reading: the cultural editions offer appealing complements to the *Anthology,* as well as attractive resources for a variety of coursework, or for independent encounters. First-time readers will find productive paths to investigate, while more seasoned readers will enjoy the fresh perspectives and provocative juxtapositions. The contexts for adventure vary from volume to volume, but the constants (in addition to handsome production and affordable pricing) are an important literary work, expertly edited and helpfully annotated; an inviting introduction; a table of dates to track its composition, publication, and reception in relation to biographical, cultural, and historical events; and a guide for further study. To these common measures and uncommon enhancements, we invite your attention and curiosity.

Susan J. Wolfson, General Editor
Professor of English, Princeton University

About This Edition

Joseph Conrad originally planned to title *The Secret Sharer* "The Second Self," or perhaps "The Other Self"—Englishing the Latin phrase *Alter Ego*, to describe an intimate relation of self and other. The three tales of transformation in this volume—Conrad's *The Secret Sharer*, Mary Shelley's *Transformation*, and Robert Louis Stevenson's iconic *Strange Case of Dr. Jekyll and Mr. Hyde*—are all adventures in transformation, wherein an uncanny other turns out to be a second self, a sharer (and bearer) of intimate anxieties, repressed energies, dark impulses.

No wonder all three tales seem so dreamlike, as if their landscapes were of the mind, a map of the unconscious. To illuminate this terrain, we supplement the tales with excerpts about the subconscious from the land of individual dreams and repressions, to cultural anxieties about the social and political unconscious. Mary Shelley's retrospective introduction to *Frankenstein* tells us that her tale came not just from fragments of other tales and waking conversations, but also from the strange and anarchic assimilation of this material in a horrific dream. Stevenson's haunting essay, *A Chapter on Dreams*, links dreamwork to writing-work: "The past is all of one texture—whether feigned or suffered—whether acted out in three dimensions, or only witnessed in that small theatre of the brain which we keep brightly lighted all night long," he begins, with *texture* joining memory, dreaming, and writing.

As Stevenson's texture of "the past" suggests, this is a rich and frightening terrain. Some of it already gestates in the excursions, both playful and anxious, of childhood. We include a clutch of poems from Stevenson's *A Child's Garden of Verses*, in which the world of children and their dreams and nightmares, cultivates the materials out of which tales such as *Transformation, Dr. Jekyll and Mr. Hyde,* and *The Secret Sharer* grow. The past is also biological, anthropological. With the rise of new sciences—from the 1790s (the decade in which Shelley sets the scientific experimentation of *Frankenstein*) through the 1910s, fraught with treatises and theories not only about the advance of knowledge and civilization, but also about an underlying tug of degeneration—civilized subjects confronted the proximity of primitive origins and impulses in every human being. Charles Darwin's account of the Fuegians of South America in his record of *The Voyage of the Beagle* vacillates between recognitions of common humanity and shocked registers of savage otherness; his conclusion to *The Descent of Man* hopes that human capacities for kindness and generosity will ensure community and civilization in the face of primitive instincts. Max Nordau's *Degeneration* worried that devolutionary elements were already pervasively and perilously at work—not only in the primitive cultures of humanity, but in the strata of civilization from which we might expect the utmost refinement: artists, intellectuals, spiritual leaders. Even in the ultra-refined, ultra-erudite fiction of Henry James, Conrad could see a primitive agon: "From the duality of man's nature and the competition of individuals, the life-history of the earth must in the last instance be a history of a really very relentless warfare. Neither his fellows, nor his gods, nor his passions will leave a man alone." Other supplements to our tales of "duality" include a revealing report on the key words, *Strange* and *Case*, that precede *of Dr. Jekyll and Mr. Hyde*, in Stevenson's title, a sample of reviews and reactions to Stevenson's and Conrad's tales (including the authors' own letters), and a bibliography for further reading.

In developing our edition, we are grateful to Princeton University for material resources, and for expert advice, to our second selves at Longman (David Damrosch, Andy Elfenbein, Talia Schaffer, William Sharpe, and Heather Henderson), as well as Vance Smith and Louise Barnett. Susan Wolfson gives special thanks to her lively seminar at Princeton (English 401, fall 2006) for sharp, adventurous discussion of the contents of this edition, and much much more.

Susan J. Wolfson
Barry V. Qualls

Table of Dates

MWS: Mary Wollstonecraft Shelley

RLS: Robert Louis Stevenson

JC: Joseph Conrad (we are indebted to David Damrosch's Longman Cultural Edition of Conrad and Kipling)

1797   March 29: Mary Wollstonecraft and William Godwin marry; August 30: daughter Mary born; September 10: Wollstonecraft dies from septic poisoning incurred during childbirth.

1798   *Lyrical Ballads,* including S. T. Coleridge's *The Rime of the Ancyent Marinere.* Godwin, *Memoirs of the Author of a Vindication of the Rights of Woman;* scathing attacks on Wollstonecraft in the reactionary press.

1799   Napoleon's coup makes him first consul. Godwin, *St. Leon* (the novel's hero makes two discoveries: how to transmute base metals into gold; and the elixir of life, granting immortality).

1800   Napoleon crosses the Alps with 4000 men to attack Austria. Alessandro Volta produces electricity from a cell, and creates first electric battery. Humphry Davy publishes studies in chemistry.

1802   Georges Cuvier's lectures on comparative anatomy, Davy's *Lectures on Chemistry.*

1803   John Aldini, *An Account of the late improvement in Galvanism . . . an Appendix, Containing the author's Experiments on the body of a Malefactor Executed at Newgate.*

1807   Napoleon invades Spain and Portugal, and British troops support the opposition. Parliament abolishes British slave trade (colonial slavery still legal).

1808   J. W. von Goethe's *Faust,* part I.

1809   Napoleon beaten by the Austrians. Jean-Baptiste Lamarck's *Philosophie Zoologique* theorizes evolution.

1811   Prince of Wales becomes Regent, after George III is deemed incompetent.

            Charles Bell, *New Idea of the Anatomy of the Brain.*

1812   Mary Godwin meets Percy Shelley.

            Napoleon's Grand Army invades Russia in June and retreats from Moscow in December, with catastrophic losses (500,000 of 600,000).

1813   Napoleon loses key battles all over Europe and is forced into retreat.

1814   Mary Godwin becomes pregnant by Percy Shelley; elopes with him and her stepsister Claire Clairmont in July; they travel in Europe until the end of the summer.

            Allies invade France; Napoleon abdicates and is exiled to Elba; Bourbons restored.

1815   February 22: premature birth of Mary and Percy's baby, who dies March 6.

            Napoleon escapes Elba, enters France, is defeated at Waterloo, and exiled to St. Helena; restoration of European monarchies.

1816   January 24: William born to Mary and Percy; they travel to Europe in the summer, make Lord Byron's acquaintance in Geneva. Mary gets the idea for *Frankenstein* in a dream.

            December 30: Mary and Percy marry and Mary becomes pregnant again.

            Coleridge's *Christabel* is published.

1817   Coleridge's new version of *The Rime of the Ancient Mariner* is published. *Blackwood's Edinburgh Magazine* founded.

1818   January 1: *Frankenstein* published.

1819   March: Shelleys go to Rome; June: son William dies. November: Percy Florence born, the only of their four children to survive into adulthood.

        Birth of Queen Victoria.

1820   MWS writes poetic dramas, *Proserpine* and *Midas*.

        Death of George III; Regent becomes George IV.

1822   Percy Shelley drowns in a storm at sea (July 8).

        Thomas De Quincey, *Confessions of an English Opium Eater.*

1823   February: MWS publishes her novel *Valperga,* quarrels with Byron (for whom she was doing secretarial work) and returns to London. Stage versions of *Frankenstein,* including one at the Lyceum, increase her fame as "The Author of *Frankenstein.*" August: second edition of *Frankenstein,* managed by Godwin and now with MWS's name on the title page, is published. MWS receives a £100 annuity from Percy Shelley's father. Byron becomes involved in the War for Greek Independence.

1824   Byron dies in Greece in April.

1825   Annuals craze begins with *Forget-Me-Not.*

1826   MWS's novel, *The Last Man,* published. When Percy's eldest son (by his first wife) dies, Percy Florence becomes heir.

1828   MWS begins to publish in the annuals, with a tale in *The Keepsake.*

1830   *Transformation* **appears in** *The Keepsake for MDCC-CXXXI.* MWS's novel *Perkin Warbeck* published.

        Opening of Liverpool and Manchester Railway.

1831   October 31 (Halloween): a new edition of *Frankenstein* with "Introduction" is published.

        First Reform Bill, which would have given the vote to some of the unpropertied working class, defeated, in the midst of often violent debates.

1832   Second Reform Bill passed, with more liberal terms for property ownership.

1833   Emancipation of slaves in the British colonies.

1835   MWS's novel *Lodore* published.

1836   First railway in London. Charles Dickens begins *Pickwick papers*.

1837   Victoria becomes Queen.

1838   William Hazlitt Jr. asks to publish *Frankenstein* in his series, *The Best Works of the Best Authors*.

1842   Robert Browning, *Dramatic Lyrics*. Chartist riots.

1847   Charlotte Brontë, *Jane Eyre;* Emily Brontë, *Wuthering Heights*.

1850   Robert Louis Stevenson born, November 13, in Edinburgh. William Wordsworth, *The Prelude*. Alfred Tennyson, *In Memoriam*.

1851   February 1: Mary Shelley dies in London.

        Crystal Palace Great Exhibition of science, technology, industry.

1857   December 3: Józef Teodor Konrad Korzeniowski (later Conrad) born in Poland.

1859   Charles Darwin publishes *On the Origin of Species by Means of Natural Selection*. George Eliot, *Adam Bede*. J. S. Mill, *On Liberty*.

1860   Charles Dickens, *Great Expectations*.

1862   Christina Rossetti, *Goblin Market*.

1864   Lewis Carroll, *Alice's Adventures in Wonderland;* Robert Browning, *Dramatis Personae*.

1865	Jamaica Rebellion.
1867	RLS enters Edinburgh University to study engineering.
	Karl Marx, *Das Kapital* published.
	Second Reform Bill.
1868	Opening of the Suez Canal.
1869	When Jósef Korzeniowski's father dies, he is adopted by his uncle.
	J. S. Mill, *The Subjection of Women* published.
1871	RLS gives up engineering for law. Darwin publishes *The Descent of Man.*
1872	RLS passes the first round of examinations for the Scottish bar.
	George Eliot, *Middlemarch*.
1874	Józef K. runs away to sea, joining the French Merchant Marine.
1875	RLS meets poet and editor W. E. Henley and passes the bar exam. Józef K. attempts suicide.
1876	RLS meets (a married) Fanny Osbourne.
1878	Fanny Osbourne rejoins her husband in San Francisco. Józef K. joins the British Merchant Marine, serves until 1894.
	Thomas Hardy, *The Return of the Native.*
	Electric streetlights in London.
1879	With Henley, RLS writes *Deacon Brodie*, a play about a double-life, a secret self with a nighttime life of crime. Fanny Osbourne's marriage fails, and RLS goes to California, riding west on the railway, experiences he recounts in *Across the Plains* (1892) and *The Amateur Emigrant* (posthumous, 1895). When Fanny's divorce is finalized, they go to London.

1890   RLS settles in Samoa; JC becomes a riverboat captain for the Belgian Corporation for Trade in the Upper Congo. Henry Morton Stanley publishes *In Darkest Africa*. Wilde's first version of *The Picture of Dorian Gray* in *Lippincott's Monthly Magazine;* William James, *Principles of Psychology,* 1890.

              First subway line in London.

1891   Richard Garnett publishes a collection of **MWS's tales,** including ***Transformation.***

              The Picture of Dorian Gray, revised and with a cheeky preface on the amorality of art; Thomas Hardy, *Tess of the Durbervilles;* Arthur Conan Doyle, *Adventures of Sherlock Holmes.*

1892   RLS, "A Chapter on Dreams" republished in *Across the Plains.*

1894   December: RLS dies in Samoa.

              Edward Carpenter publishes *Homogenic Love.*

1895   February: Wilde's *The Importance of Being Ernest* (a comedy of male double-lives) a stage success in London. Wilde arrested and tried for "gross indecency," sent to prison for two years of hard labor. Max Nordau's *Degeneration;* JC's *Almayer's Folly.*

1896   JC marries Jessie George, publishes *An Outcast of the Islands.*

1897   JC's *The Nigger of the "Narcissus";* Bram Stoker's *Dracula.*

1898   JC's son Borys born.

1899   JC's *Heart of Darkness,* in *Blackwood's Magazine;* Sigmund Freud's *The Interpretation of Dreams.*

1900   JC publishes *Lord Jim.* Death of Wilde, in Paris.

1901   Death of Queen Victoria, succession of Edward VII.

              Havelock Ellis's *Studies in the Psychology of Sex* and Freud's *The Psychopathology of Everyday Life* published.

1902   *Heart of Darkness* published in book form, with another novella, *Youth*. Also published, JC's *Typhoon*.

1904   JC's novel *Nostromo* published.

1905   Wilde's *De Profundis* (his letter from prison) and Sigmund Freud's *Three Essays on the Theory of Sexuality* published.

1906   JC's son John born.

1907   JC publishes *The Secret Agent*.

1910   Joseph Conrad publishes *The Secret Sharer*.

1912   JC publishes *Under Western Eyes*.

1913   JC's novel *Chance* is a best-seller.

1914   World War I begins.

1915   JC, *Victory*. D. H. Lawrence, *The Rainbow*. Virginia Woolf, *The Voyage Out*.

1918   World War I ends.

1922   James Joyce, *Ulysses*.

1924   August 3: Conrad dies.

Mary Wollstonecraft Shelley 1797–1851

"My husband was, from the first, very anxious that I should prove myself worthy of my parentage, and enrol myself on the page of fame. He was for ever inciting me to obtain literary reputation," writes Mary Shelley in a retrospective introduction to her page of fame, *Frankenstein,* when it was republished in 1831 (first, anonymously in 1818). If by the 1830s she had become a professional writer, this was hardly her design when she eloped as a teenager with the charismatic, transgressive, idealistic poet Percy Bysshe Shelley. Her parentage was no small burden. It was not just that William Godwin and Mary Wollstonecraft were leading intellectuals of the 1790s, writers whose social and political views, as well as premarital cohabitation, made them both famous and infamous. It was also that her mother died giving birth to her, a tragedy that made little Mary a monster in her father's eyes, later evoked in the story of a creature spurned and despised by his creator from the moment he first drew breath.

Though she was passionately attached to him, Mary Godwin never felt loved by her father. He even sent her off, when she was 14, to live with another family in Scotland, feeling that he could not support her along with his family by his second wife, Mary Jane Clairmont (who also wanted to distance Mary from her father). On a visit home in 1812–13, Mary met Percy Shelley, when he came to call on his hero Godwin. Mutually charmed, they renewed the acquaintance when she returned in spring 1814. She was 16; he was 21 and unhappily married. They fell in love, trysted secretly, and Mary was soon pregnant. At the end of July they eloped to France. Godwin was furious, and scarcely warmer when they returned a few months later and married at the end of 1816, even as he continued to pester Percy for loans. The journey across the natural beauties and war-ravaged terrains of Europe were recorded in Mary's first book, *History of a Six Weeks' Tour,* published anonymously in 1817.

Mary's life with Percy was exciting, tempestuous, and fraught with pain. Percy had lost custody of his two children by his first wife in consequence of his blasphemous publications. His first child with Mary, born prematurely, died within weeks; Mary had a dream of bringing her back to life. From 1814 to 1822, Mary was almost continuously pregnant or nursing. Their second child, William, born in 1816, died in 1819; their third, born in 1817, died even sooner, in 1818. Mary suffered a nearly fatal miscarriage in 1822, and a few weeks later Percy, who had been growing distant from her, drowned in a storm at sea. Devastated, impoverished, and with one surviving child (Percy Florence) to support, Shelley returned to London at age 24, longing for anonymity and propriety. Wollstonecraft was notorious; Godwin, declined from his 1790s celebrity, was regarded as an eccentric radical; Percy's life and opinions, and her life with him, were still scandals. Writing augmented the small annuity (£100) from her father-in-law that was contingent on her not publishing a biography of her husband. Working in whatever genres promised income, Shelley produced encyclopedia articles, essays, reviews, travel books, five more novels, a mythological drama, poems, and some two dozen tales, most of them published in a new, popular, and lucrative venue, the annuals.

Transformation and *The Keepsake*

Flourishing from the mid-1820s into mid-century, these ornate anthologies of poetry, fiction, essays, enhanced with engravings, were a hot fashion. Among the most popular was *The Keepsake* (1828–1857), edited by Frederic Mansel Reynolds. Across the 1830s, Shelley published more than a dozen tales herein, including *Transformation.* Our text is from *The Keepsake for MDCCCXXXI* (pp. 18–39), signed "By the Author of 'Frankenstein,'" her routine pen-name.[1] Originating in France and Germany, the annuals proved so popular that German-born London printer Rudolph

---

[1] In this *Keepsake,* Shelley had two poems and another tale, *The Swiss Peasant* (rpt. *The Longman Anthology of British Literature,* vol. 2).

Ackermann brought the product, along with the technology of lithography, to England. He launched *Forget Me Not* in 1822, "expressly designed to serve as tokens of remembrance, friendship, or affection." In 1824, Alaric Watts brought out *The Literary Souvenir, or Cabinet of Poetry and Romance,* which he edited from 1825 to 1835. It debuted in an inexpensive print-form, dressed up with pastel-board binding, gilt-edged pages, and engraved illustrations by noted artists. Priced at 12 shillings, it sold 6000 in its first two weeks; the 1826 *Souvenir* sold 10,000. In his preface to *The Keepsake* for 1829, Reynolds boasted in italics that eleven thousand guineas had been spent on the production, and across the 1830s *The Keepsake* sold 15,000 every season. Bound in silk, morocco leather, or decorated leather, edged in gold, valued as much as objects of display as for the contents, the annuals were published at the end of the year, timed for gift-giving (*The Keepsake for MDCCCXXXI* in late 1830)—especially to female recipients, whose names could be inscribed on sentimental presentation plates. The titles proffered little treasures: *Affection's Gift, Book of Beauty, Bijou, Gem, Cabinet of Literary Gems, Amethyst, Emerald, Pearl, Cabinet, Jewel, Amulet, Keepsake, Friendship's Offering, Love's Offering, Forget Me Not, Literary Souvenir, Talisman, Wreath, Cameo.*

For female writers, the annuals were hospitable and lucrative, and for Shelley, the "polite" venue helped dispel clouds of scandal trailing from her past. For men of letters, the compensation trumped the taint of female culture and commercialism: poets Coleridge, Wordsworth, Lamb, Moore, Hood, Clare, Scott, Tennyson, and even Poet Laureate Robert Southey appear in their pages. Though Southey blamed the annuals for the slow sales of his own books, he joined up, listed as "The Poet Laureate" in the Table of Contents. "The world . . . seems mad about 'Forget me Nots' and Christmas boxes," Scott exclaimed in 1828 when he was offered £800 a year to edit *The Keepsake.* He declined, but not without selling a tale for £500, enough to support a middle-class family for five years. Even as Wordsworth blasted these "ornamented . . . greedy receptacles of trash, those bladders upon which the Boys of Poetry try to swim," he, too, published in *The Keepsake.* The engravings, by some of the major artists of the day (J. M. W. Turner, E. Landseer) were a major attraction—not typically as embellishments of writing already in hand, but as its anchor and occasion. *Transformation* was probably commissioned for the illustration of Juliet that appears near the end.

Transformation was among the *Tales and Stories by Mary Wollstonecraft Shelley* that Richard Garnett collected in 1891 (London: William Paterson & Co.) for a world excited by such alter-ego tales as Stevenson's *Strange Case of Dr. Jekyll and Mr. Hyde* and the first version of Oscar Wilde's *The Picture of Dorian Gray* in *Lippincott's Monthly*. *Transformation* entertains a literal question: what would it be like to exchange one's bodily form, or feel split into two beings? "Transformation" may also suggest a spiritual change in character and condition. And there is always a question of artifice: is this transformation genuine or theatrical? In *Hamlet*, guilty King Claudius is more than a little concerned with his suspicious nephew: "Hamlet's transformation: so call it, / Sith neither th'exterior nor the inward man / Resembles that it was" (2.2.5–7). The narrative frame of *Transformation*, a retrospective confession of sin and redemption, also raises a question about form and transformation, inner and outer. The genre is both sensation and reform. Is the teller completely penitent? Are there hints of gloating or boasting? How much does the summary "lesson" govern the sensational entertainment of the story?

As Shelley's title may suggest, she was mindful of Byron's unfinished drama, *The Deformed Transformed* (1822), which, as his secretary, she prepared for his publisher. This play also involves a diabolic exchange, in which the devil offers a hunchback a fair form, and after the transformation, hangs around as a dark double. Shelley's internal echoes index still other tales of alter-egos in monstrous bodies, chief among these Coleridge's *Christabel* and her own *Frankenstein*. Her epigraph is from a late point in Coleridge's supernatural ballad, *The Rime of the Ancient Mariner* (1817 text: 578–85). Returning from a horrific sea-voyage, the Mariner appeals to a shore-dwelling Hermit to "shrieve" him—hear his confession and re-integrate him with the Christian world. "What manner of man art thou?" the Hermit cries out; the epigraph verse follows.

On the same page as the conclusion of Shelley's tale (in *The Keepsake*, p. 39) appears a poem, *Absence*, "By the Author of 'Frankenstein.'" That it is not listed in the Table of Contents may be an oversight (perhaps it was a late insertion to fill up some empty page space), but thus unmarked, it has the look of a coda to *Transformation*—an enigmatic bookend to the prefacing verse by Coleridge.

Transformation

By the Author of "Frankenstein"

Forthwith this frame of mine was wrench'd
With a woful agony,
Which forced me to begin my tale,
And then it set me free.

Since then, at an uncertain hour,
That agony returns;
And till my ghastly tale is told
This heart within me burns.

COLERIDGE'S ANCIENT MARINER.

I HAVE heard it said, that, when any strange, supernatural, and necromantic[1] adventure has occurred to a human being, that being, however desirous he may be to conceal the same, feels at certain periods torn up as it were by an intellectual earthquake, and is forced to bare[2] the inner depths of his spirit to another. I am a witness of the truth of this. I have dearly sworn to myself never to reveal to human ears the horrors to which I once, in excess of fiendly pride, delivered myself over. The holy man who heard my confession, and reconciled me to the church, is dead. None knows that once————

Why should it not be thus? Why tell a tale of impious tempting of Providence, and soul-subduing humiliation? Why? answer me, ye who are wise in the secrets of human nature! I only know that so

---

[1] Necromancy: in general, sorcery; specifically, raising the dead to hear a prophesy or beg influence on events.

[2] The situation of addressing a listener invites a pun on *bear* (convey).

it is; and in spite of strong resolve—of a pride that too much masters me—of shame, and even of fear, so to render myself odious to my species—I must speak.

Genoa! my birth-place—proud city! looking upon the blue waves of the Mediterranean sea—dost thou remember me in my boyhood, when thy cliffs and promontories, thy bright sky and gay vineyards, were my world? Happy time! when to the young heart the narrow-bounded universe, which leaves, by its very limitation, free scope to the imagination, enchains our physical energies, and, sole period in our lives, innocence and enjoyment are united. Yet, who can look back to childhood, and not remember its sorrows and its harrowing fears? I was born with the most imperious, haughty, tameless spirit, with which ever mortal was gifted. I quailed before my father only; and he, generous and noble, but capricious and tyrannical, at once fostered and checked the wild impetuosity of my character, making obedience necessary, but inspiring no respect for the motives which guided his commands. To be a man, free, independent; or, in better words, insolent and domineering, was the hope and prayer of my rebel heart.

My father had one friend, a wealthy Genoese noble, who in a political tumult was suddenly sentenced to banishment, and his property confiscated. The Marchese Torella went into exile alone. Like my father, he was a widower: he had one child, the almost infant Juliet, who was left under my father's guardianship. I should certainly have been an unkind master to the lovely girl, but that I was forced by my position to become her protector. A variety of childish incidents all tended to one point,—to make Juliet see in me a rock of refuge; I in her, one who must perish through the soft sensibility of her nature too rudely visited, but for my guardian care. We grew up together. The opening rose in May was not more sweet than this dear girl. An irradiation of beauty was spread over her face. Her form, her step, her voice—my heart weeps even now, to think of all of relying, gentle, loving, and pure, that was enshrined in that celestial tenement. When I was eleven and Juliet eight years of age, a cousin of mine, much older than either—he seemed to us a man—took great notice of my playmate; he called her his bride, and asked her to marry him. She refused, and he insisted, drawing her unwillingly towards him. With the countenance and emotions of a maniac I threw myself on him—I strove to draw his sword—I clung to his neck with the ferocious resolve to strangle him: he was obliged to call for assistance to disengage himself from me. On that night I led Juliet to the chapel of our house: I made her touch the sacred relics—I harrowed her child's heart, and profaned her child's lips with an oath, that she would be mine, and mine only.

Well, those days passed away. Torella returned in a few years, and became wealthier and more prosperous than ever. When I was seventeen, my father died; he had been magnificent to prodigality; Torella rejoiced that my minority[3] would afford an opportunity for repairing my fortunes. Juliet and I had been affianced beside my father's deathbed—Torella was to be a second parent to me.

I desired to see the world, and I was indulged. I went to Florence, to Rome, to Naples; thence I passed to Toulon, and at length reached what had long been the bourne of my wishes, Paris. There was wild work in Paris then. The poor king, Charles the Sixth,[4] now sane, now mad, now a monarch, now an abject slave, was the very mockery of humanity. The queen, the dauphin,[5] the Duke of Burgundy, alternately friends and foes—now meeting in prodigal feasts, now shedding blood in rivalry—were blind to the miserable state of their country, and the dangers that impended over it, and gave themselves wholly up to dissolute enjoyment or savage strife. My character still followed me. I was arrogant and self-willed; I loved display, and above all, I threw all control far from me. Who could control me in Paris? My young friends were eager to foster passions which furnished them with pleasures. I was deemed handsome—I was master of every knightly accomplishment. I was disconnected with any political party. I grew a favourite with all: my presumption and arrogance was pardoned in one so young: I became a spoiled child. Who could control me? not the letters and advice of Torella—only strong necessity visiting me in the abhorred shape of an empty purse. But there were means to refill this void. Acre after acre, estate after estate, I sold. My dress, my jewels, my

---

[3] The years up until age 21; his father's lavish spending depleted the inheritance.

[4] "Charles the Mad" or "Charles the Well Beloved" (1368–1422), king of France (1380–1422). During his minority, his uncles—chief among them Philip the Bold, duke of Burgundy—administered the crown, so depleting the treasury as to provoke popular uprisings. In 1388, Charles found a better counsel in the Duke of Orleans; but starting in 1392, bouts of mental instability weakened his ability to rule. Philip of Burgundy regained power, wresting control from the Duke of Orleans, whom he had murdered. Ensuing civil war attracted an invasion by England's King Henry V, who claimed dominion over France in 1420 (a history recounted in Shakespeare's *Henry V*).

[5] The title of the king's oldest son.

horses and their caparisons,[6] were almost unrivalled in gorgeous Paris, while the lands of my inheritance passed into possession of others.

The Duke of Orleans was waylaid and murdered by the Duke of Burgundy. Fear and terror possessed all Paris. The dauphin and the queen shut themselves up; every pleasure was suspended. I grew weary of this state of things, and my heart yearned for my boyhood's haunts. I was nearly a beggar, yet still I would go there, claim my bride, and rebuild my fortunes. A few happy ventures as a merchant would make me rich again. Nevertheless, I would not return in humble guise. My last act was to dispose of my remaining estate near Albaro for half its worth, for ready money. Then I despatched all kinds of artificers, arras,[7] furniture of regal splendour, to fit up the last relic of my inheritance, my palace in Genoa. I lingered a little longer yet, ashamed at the part of the prodigal returned,[8] which I feared I should play. I sent my horses. One matchless Spanish jennet[9] I despatched to my promised bride; its caparisons flamed with jewels and cloth of gold. In every part I caused to be entwined the initials of Juliet and her Guido. My present found favour in hers and in her father's eyes.

Still to return a proclaimed spendthrift, the mark of impertinent wonder, perhaps of scorn, and to encounter singly the reproaches or taunts of my fellow-citizens, was no alluring prospect. As a shield between me and censure, I invited some few of the most reckless of my comrades to accompany me: thus I went armed against the world, hiding a rankling feeling, half fear and half penitence, by bravado and an insolent display of satisfied vanity.

I arrived in Genoa. I trod the pavement of my ancestral palace. My proud step was no interpreter of my heart, for I deeply felt that, though surrounded by every luxury, I was a beggar. The first step I took in claiming Juliet must widely declare me such. I read contempt or pity in the looks of all. I fancied, so apt is conscience to imagine what it deserves, that rich and poor, young and old, all regarded me with derision. Torella came not near me. No wonder that my second father should expect a son's deference from me in

---

[6] Ornamental livery.

[7] Lavishly embroidered, wall-sized tapestry.

[8] In Jesus's parable (Luke 15:11–32), this seemingly lost, spendthrift (prodigal) son is reconciled with his father, and becomes his favorite.

[9] Small horse.

waiting[10] first on him. But, galled and stung by a sense of my follies and demerit, I strove to throw the blame on others. We kept nightly orgies in Palazzo Carega. To sleepless, riotous nights, followed listless, supine mornings. At the Ave Maria we showed our dainty[11] persons in the streets, scoffing at the sober citizens, casting insolent glances on the shrinking women. Juliet was not among them—no, no; if she had been there, shame would have driven me away, if love had not brought me to her feet.

I grew tired of this. Suddenly I paid the Marchese a visit. He was at his villa, one among the many which deck the suburb of San Pietro d'Arena. It was the month of May—a month of May in that garden of the world—the blossoms of the fruit trees were fading among thick, green foliage; the vines were shooting forth; the ground strewed with the fallen olive blooms; the fire-fly was in the myrtle hedge; heaven and earth wore a mantle of surpassing beauty. Torella welcomed me kindly, though seriously; and even his shade of displeasure soon wore away. Some resemblance to my father— some look and tone of youthful ingenuousness, lurking still in spite of my misdeeds, softened the good old man's heart. He sent for his daughter—he presented me to her as her betrothed. The chamber became hallowed by a holy light as she entered. Hers was that cherub look, those large, soft eyes, full dimpled cheeks, and mouth of infantine sweetness, that expresses the rare union of happiness and love. Admiration first possessed me; she is mine! was the second proud emotion, and my lips curled with haughty triumph. I had not been the *enfant gâté*[12] of the beauties of France not to have learnt the art of pleasing the soft heart of woman. If towards men I was overbearing, the deference I paid to them was the more in contrast. I commenced my courtship by the display of a thousand gallantries to Juliet, who, vowed to me from infancy, had never admitted the devotion of others; and who, though accustomed to expressions of admiration, was uninitiated in the language of lovers.

For a few days all went well. Torella never alluded to my extravagance; he treated me as a favourite son. But the time came, as we discussed the preliminaries to my union with his daughter, when

---

[10] Visiting, paying respects to.

[11] *Dainty* developed as a contraction of *dignity*. Shelley is using this nearly obsolete sense (fine, handsome; choice), but with a modern inflection of delicate, over-refined. *Ave Maria* (Hail Mary) is an evening hymn, hence a term for that time of day.

[12] "Spoiled child"; more generally, darling.

this fair face of things should be overcast. A contract had been drawn up in my father's lifetime. I had rendered this, in fact, void, by having squandered the whole of the wealth which was to have been shared by Juliet and myself. Torella, in consequence, chose to consider this bond as cancelled, and proposed another, in which, though the wealth he bestowed was immeasurably increased, there were so many restrictions as to the mode of spending it, that I, who saw independence only in free career being given to my own imperious will, taunted him as taking advantage of my situation, and refused utterly to subscribe to his conditions. The old man mildly strove to recall me to reason. Roused pride became the tyrant of my thought: I listened with indignation—I repelled him with disdain.

"Juliet, thou art mine! Did we not interchange vows in our innocent childhood? are we not one in the sight of God? and shall thy cold-hearted, cold-blooded father divide us? Be generous, my love, be just; take not away a gift, last treasure of thy Guido—retract not thy vows—let us defy the world, and setting at nought the calculations of age, find in our mutual affection a refuge from every ill."

Fiend I must have been, with such sophistry to endeavour to poison that sanctuary of holy thought and tender love. Juliet shrank from me affrighted. Her father was the best and kindest of men, and she strove to show me how, in obeying him, every good would follow. He would receive my tardy submission with warm affection; and generous pardon would follow my repentance. Profitless words for a young and gentle daughter to use to a man accustomed to make his will, law; and to feel in his own heart a despot so terrible and stern, that he could yield obedience to nought save his own imperious desires! My resentment grew with resistance; my wild companions were ready to add fuel to the flame. We laid a plan to carry off Juliet. At first it appeared to be crowned with success. Midway, on our return, we were overtaken by the agonized father and his attendants. A conflict ensued. Before the city guard came to decide the victory in favour of our antagonists, two of Torella's servitors were dangerously wounded.

This portion of my history weighs most heavily with me. Changed man as I am, I abhor myself in the recollection. May none who hear this tale ever have felt as I. A horse driven to fury by a rider armed with barbed spurs, was not more a slave than I, to the violent tyranny of my temper. A fiend possessed my soul, irritating it to madness. I felt the voice of conscience within me; but if I yielded to it for a brief interval, it was only to be a moment after torn, as by a whirlwind, away—borne along on the stream of desperate rage—the plaything of the storms engendered by pride. I was imprisoned, and, at the instance of Torella, set free. Again I returned to carry off both him and his child to France; which hapless country, then preyed on by freebooters[13] and gangs of lawless soldiery, offered a grateful refuge to a criminal like me. Our plots were discovered. I was sentenced to banishment; and, as my debts were already enormous, my remaining property was put in the hands of commissioners for their payment. Torella again offered his mediation, requiring only my promise not to renew my abortive attempts on himself and his daughter. I spurned his offers, and fancied that I triumphed when I was thrust out from Genoa, a solitary and penniless exile. My companions were gone: they had been dismissed the city some weeks before, and were already in France. I was alone—friendless; with nor sword at my side, nor ducat in my purse.

I wandered along the sea-shore, a whirlwind of passion possessing and tearing my soul. It was as if a live coal had been set burning in my breast. At first I meditated on what *I should do*. I would join a band of freebooters. Revenge!—the word seemed balm to me:— I hugged it—caressed it—till, like a serpent, it stung me. Then again I would abjure and despise Genoa, that little corner of the world. I would return to Paris, where so many of my friends swarmed; where my services would be eagerly accepted; where I would carve out fortune with my sword, and might, through success, make my paltry birth-place, and the false Torella, rue the day when they drove me, a new Coriolanus, from her walls.[14] I would return to Paris—thus, on foot—a beggar—and present myself in my poverty to those I had formerly entertained sumptuously? There was gall in the mere thought of it.

The reality of things began to dawn upon my mind, bringing despair in its train. For several months I had been a prisoner: the evils of my dungeon had whipped my soul to madness, but they had subdued my corporeal frame. I was weak and wan. Torella had used

---

[13] Pirates.

[14] The subject of another of Shakespeare's plays, general Coriolanus (5th c. BCE) was banished from Rome on the charge of tyrannical ambition. He organized a vengeful rebellion against Rome, but when he couldn't go through with it, his anti-Roman allies assassinated him.

a thousand artifices to administer to my comfort; I had detected and scorned them all—and I reaped the harvest of my obduracy. What was to be done?—Should I crouch before my foe, and sue for forgiveness?—Die rather ten thousand deaths!—Never should they obtain that victory! Hate—I swore eternal hate! Hate from whom?—to whom?—From a wandering outcast—to a mighty noble. I and my feelings were nothing to them: already had they forgotten one so unworthy. And Juliet!—her angel-face and sylph-like form gleamed among the clouds of my despair with vain beauty; for I had lost her—the glory and flower of the world! Another will call her his!—that smile of paradise will bless another!

Even now my heart fails within me when I recur to this rout of grim-visaged ideas. Now subdued almost to tears, now raving in my agony, still I wandered along the rocky shore, which grew at each step wilder and more desolate. Hanging rocks and hoar precipices overlooked the tideless ocean; black caverns yawned; and for ever, among the seaworn recesses, murmured and dashed the unfruitful waters. Now my way was almost barred by an abrupt promontory, now rendered nearly impracticable by fragments fallen from the cliff. Evening was at hand, when, seaward, arose, as if on the waving of a wizard's wand, a murky web of clouds, blotting the late azure sky, and darkening and disturbing the till now placid deep. The clouds had strange fantastic shapes; and they changed, and mingled, and seemed to be driven about by a mighty spell. The waves raised their white crests; the thunder first muttered, then roared from across the waste of waters, which took a deep purple dye, flecked with foam. The spot where I stood, looked, on one side, to the wide-spread ocean; on the other, it was barred by a rugged promontory. Round this cape suddenly came, driven by the wind, a vessel. In vain the mariners tried to force a path for her to the open sea—the gale drove her on the rocks. It will perish!—all on board will perish!—Would I were among them! And to my young heart the idea of death came for the first time blended with that of joy. It was an awful sight to behold that vessel struggling with her fate. Hardly could I discern the sailors, but I heard them. It was soon all over!—A rock, just covered by the tossing waves, and so unperceived, lay in wait for its prey. A crash of thunder broke over my head at the moment that, with a frightful shock, the skiff dashed upon her unseen enemy. In a brief space of time she went to pieces. There I stood in safety; and there were my fellow-creatures, battling, how hopelessly, with annihilation. Methought[15] I saw them struggling—too truly did I hear their shrieks, conquering the barking surges in their shrill agony. The dark breakers threw hither and thither the fragments of the wreck: soon it disappeared. I had been fascinated to gaze till the end: at last I sank on my knees—I covered my face with my hands: I again looked up; something was floating on the billows towards the shore. It neared and neared.[16] Was that a human form?—It grew more distinct; and at last a mighty wave, lifting the whole freight, lodged it upon a rock. A human being bestriding a sea-chest!—A human being!—Yet was it one? Surely never such had existed before—a misshapen dwarf, with squinting eyes, distorted features, and body deformed, till it became a horror to behold. My blood, lately warming towards a fellow-being so snatched from a watery tomb, froze in my heart. The dwarf got off his chest; he tossed his straight, straggling hair from his odious visage:

"By St. Beelzebub!"[17] he exclaimed, "I have been well bested." He looked round and saw me. "Oh, by the fiend! here is another ally of the mighty one. To what saint did you offer prayers, friend— if not to mine? Yet I remember you not on board."

I shrank from the monster and his blasphemy. Again he questioned me, and I muttered some inaudible reply. He continued:—

"Your voice is drowned by this dissonant roar. What a noise the big ocean makes! Schoolboys bursting from their prison are not louder than these waves set free to play. They disturb me. I will no more of their ill-timed brawling.—Silence, hoary One!—Winds, avaunt!—to your homes!—Clouds, fly to the antipodes,[18] and leave our heaven clear!"

As he spoke, he stretched out his two long lank arms, that looked like spider's claws, and seemed to embrace with them the expanse before him. Was it a miracle? The clouds became broken, and fled; the azure sky first peeped out, and then was spread a calm

---

[15] *Methought* is a word that typically prefaces medieval dream-allegory.

[16] Shelley echoes the advent of the ghost-ship in *Ancient Mariner*, bearing Death and the Night-Mair-Life-in-Death: "I beheld / A something . . . // And still it near'd and near'd" (147–48, 153).

[17] "Lord of the Flies," and in Milton's *Paradise Lost*, Satan's chief ally among the rebel angels.

[18] Opposite poles.

field of blue above us; the stormy gale was exchanged to the softly breathing west; the sea grew calm; the waves dwindled to riplets.[19]

"I like obedience even in these stupid elements," said the dwarf. "How much more in the tameless mind of man! It was a well got up storm, you must allow—and all of my own making."

It was tempting Providence to interchange talk with this magician. But *Power,* in all its shapes, is venerable to man. Awe, curiosity, a clinging fascination, drew me towards him.

"Come, don't be frightened, friend," said the wretch: "I am good-humoured when pleased; and something does please me in your well-proportioned body and handsome face, though you look a little woe-begone. You have suffered a land—I, a sea wreck.[20] Perhaps I can allay the tempest of your fortunes as I did my own. Shall we be friends?"—And he held out his hand; I could not touch it. "Well, then, companions—that will do as well. And now, while I rest after the buffeting I underwent just now, tell me why, young and gallant as you seem, you wander thus alone and downcast on this wild sea-shore."

The voice of the wretch was screeching and horrid, and his contortions as he spoke were frightful to behold. Yet he did gain a kind of influence over me, which I could not master, and I told him my tale. When it was ended, he laughed long and loud: the rocks echoed back the sound: hell seemed yelling around me.

"Oh, thou cousin of Lucifer!"[21] said he; "so thou too hast fallen through thy pride; and, though bright as the son of Morning, thou art ready to give up thy good looks, thy bride, and thy well-being, rather than submit thee to the tyranny of good. I honour thy choice, by my soul!—So thou hast fled, and yield the day; and mean to starve on these rocks, and to let the birds peck out thy dead eyes, while thy enemy and thy betrothed rejoice in thy ruin. Thy pride is strangely akin to humility, methinks."

As he spoke, a thousand fanged thoughts stung me to the heart.

"What would you that I should do?" I cried.

"I!—Oh, nothing, but lie down and say your prayers before you die. But, were I you, I know the deed that should be done."

---

[19] The *OED* credits Percy Shelley with coining this word: "Each riplet makes / A many-sided mirror for the sun" (*Orpheus,* 60–61).

[20] As "The Author of *Frankenstein*" would know from her multiple changes on these words, *wreck* and *wretch* (and *write*) have a common, deep etymological kinship.

[21] Satan's former name in Heaven, literally, *light-bearer* (the morning star).

I drew near him. His supernatural powers made him an oracle in my eyes; yet a strange unearthly thrill quivered through my frame as I said, "Speak!—teach me—what act do you advise?"

"Revenge thyself, man!—humble thy enemies!—set thy foot on the old man's neck, and possess thyself of his daughter!"

"To the east and west I turn," cried I, "and see no means! Had I gold, much could I achieve; but, poor and single, I am powerless."

The dwarf had been seated on his chest as he listened to my story. Now he got off; he touched a spring; it flew open!—What a mine[22] of wealth—of blazing jewels, beaming gold, and pale silver—was displayed therein. A mad desire to possess this treasure was born within me.

"Doubtless," I said, "one so powerful as you could do all things."

"Nay," said the monster, humbly, "I am less omnipotent than I seem. Some things I possess which you may covet; but I would give them all for a small share, or even for a loan of what is yours."

"My possessions are at your service," I replied, bitterly—"my poverty, my exile, my disgrace—I make a free gift of them all."

"Good! I thank you. Add one other thing to your gift, and my treasure is yours."

"As nothing is my sole inheritance, what besides nothing would you have?"

"Your comely face and well-made limbs."

I shivered. Would this all-powerful monster murder me? I had no dagger. I forgot to pray—but I grew pale.

"I ask for a loan, not a gift," said the frightful thing: "lend me your body for three days—you shall have mine to cage your soul the while, and, in payment, my chest. What say you to the bargain?—Three short days."

We are told that it is dangerous to hold unlawful talk; and well do I prove the same. Tamely written down, it may seem incredible that I should lend any ear to this proposition; but, in spite of his unnatural ugliness, there was something fascinating in a being whose voice could govern earth, air, and sea. I felt a keen desire to comply; for with that chest I could command the world. My only hesitation resulted from a fear that he would not be true to his bargain. Then, I thought, I shall soon die here on these lonely sands,

---

[22] This noun puns on all the possessive instances of the word, with the effect of linking desire to this material wealth.

and the limbs he covets will be mine no more:—it is worth the chance. And, besides, I knew that, by all the rules of art-magic, there were formula and oaths which none of its practisers dared break. I hesitated to reply; and he went on, now displaying his wealth, now speaking of the petty price he demanded, till it seemed madness to refuse. Thus is it: place our bark in the current of the stream, and down, over fall and cataract it is hurried; give up our conduct to the wild torrent of passion, and we are away, we know not whither.

He swore many an oath, and I adjured him by many a sacred name; till I saw this wonder of power, this ruler of the elements, shiver like an autumn leaf before my words; and as if the spirit spake unwillingly and per force within him, at last, he, with broken voice, revealed the spell whereby he might be obliged, did he wish to play me false, to render up the unlawful spoil. Our warm life-blood must mingle to make and to mar the charm.

Enough of this unholy theme. I was persuaded—the thing was done. The morrow dawned upon me as I lay upon the shingles,[23] and I knew not my own shadow as it fell from me. I felt myself changed to a shape of horror, and cursed my easy faith and blind credulity. The chest was there—there the gold and precious stones for which I had sold the frame of flesh which nature had given me. The sight a little stilled my emotions: three days would soon be gone.

They did pass. The dwarf had supplied me with a plenteous store of food. At first I could hardly walk, so strange and out of joint were all my limbs; and my voice—it was that of the fiend. But I kept silent, and turned my face to the sun, that I might not see my shadow, and counted the hours, and ruminated on my future conduct. To bring Torella to my feet—to possess my Juliet in spite of him—all this my wealth could easily achieve. During dark night I slept, and dreamt of the accomplishment of my desires. Two suns had set—the third dawned. I was agitated, fearful. Oh expectation, what a frightful thing art thou, when kindled more by fear than hope! How dost thou twist thyself round the heart, torturing its pulsations! How dost thou dart unknown pangs all through our feeble mechanism, now seeming to shiver us like broken glass, to nothingness—now giving us a fresh strength, which can *do* nothing, and so torments us by a sensation, such as the strong man must feel who cannot break his fetters, though they bend in his grasp. Slowly

---

[23] Flat beach-rocks.

paced the bright, bright orb up the eastern sky; long it lingered in the zenith, and still more slowly wandered down the west: it touched the horizon's verge—it was lost! Its glories were on the summits of the cliff—they grew dun and gray. The evening star shone bright. He will soon be here.

He came not!—By the living heavens, he came not!—and night dragged out its weary length, and, in its decaying age, "day began to grizzle its dark hair";[24] and the sun rose again on the most miserable wretch that ever upbraided its light. Three days thus I passed. The jewels and the gold—oh, how I abhorred them!

Well, well—I will not blacken these pages with demoniac ravings. All too terrible were the thoughts, the raging tumult of ideas that filled my soul. At the end of that time I slept; I had not before since the third sunset; and I dreamt that I was at Juliet's feet, and she smiled, and then she shrieked—for she saw my transformation—and again she smiled, for still her beautiful lover knelt before her. But it was not I—it was he, the fiend, arrayed in my limbs, speaking with my voice, winning her with my looks of love. I strove to warn her, but my tongue refused its office; I strove to tear him from her, but I was rooted to the ground—I awoke with the agony. There were the solitary hoar precipices—there the plashing sea, the quiet strand, and the blue sky over all.[25] What did it mean? was my dream but a mirror of the truth? was he wooing and winning my betrothed? I would on the instant back to Genoa—but I was banished. I laughed—the dwarf's yell burst from my lips—*I* banished! O, no! they had not exiled the foul limbs I wore; I might with these enter, without fear of incurring the threatened penalty of death, my own, my native city.

I began to walk towards Genoa. I was somewhat accustomed to my distorted limbs; none were ever so ill adapted for a straightforward movement; it was with infinite difficulty that I proceeded. Then, too, I desired to avoid all the hamlets strewed here and there on the sea-beach, for I was unwilling to make a display of my hideousness. I was not quite sure that, if seen, the mere boys would

[24] As Byron's secretary, Shelley fair-copied his drama, *Werner* (1822); she echoes Ulric's urging of his father to escape under cover of darkness: "The stars are almost faded, and the gray / Begins to grizzle the black hair of night" (3.4.152–53.)

[25] An echo of the end of the first part of *Christabel* (1816); the morning after she is seduced by mysterious, possibly fiendish Geraldine, Christabel feels a fragile hope: "saints will aid if men will call: / For the blue sky bends over all!" (318–19).

not stone me to death as I passed, for a monster: some ungentle salutations I did receive from the few peasants or fishermen I chanced to meet. But it was dark night before I approached Genoa. The weather was so balmy and sweet that it struck me that the Marchese and his daughter would very probably have quitted the city for their country retreat. It was from Villa Torella that I had attempted to carry off Juliet; I had spent many an hour reconnoitring the spot, and knew each inch of ground in its vicinity. It was beautifully situated, embosomed in trees, on the margin of a stream. As I drew near, it became evident that my conjecture was right; nay, moreover, that the hours were being then devoted to feasting and merriment. For the house was lighted up; strains of soft and gay music were wafted towards me by the breeze. My heart sank within me. Such was the generous kindness of Torella's heart that I felt sure that he would not have indulged in public manifestations of rejoicing just after my unfortunate banishment, but for a cause I dared not dwell upon.

The country people were all alive and flocking about; it became necessary that I should study to conceal myself; and yet I longed to address some one, or to hear others discourse, or in any way to gain intelligence of what was really going on. At length, entering the walks that were in immediate vicinity to the mansion, I found one dark enough to veil my excessive frightfulness; and yet others as well as I were loitering in its shade. I soon gathered all I wanted to know—all that first made my very heart die with horror, and then boil with indignation. To-morrow Juliet was to be given to the penitent, reformed, beloved Guido—to-morrow my bride was to pledge her vows to a fiend from hell! And I did this!—my accursed pride—my demoniac violence and wicked self-idolatry had caused this act. For if I had acted as the wretch who had stolen my form had acted—if, with a mien at once yielding and dignified, I had presented myself to Torella, saying, I have done wrong, forgive me; I am unworthy of your angel-child, but permit me to claim her hereafter, when my altered conduct shall manifest that I abjure my vices, and endeavour to become in some sort worthy of her. I go to serve against the infidels;[26] and when my zeal for religion and my true

---

[26] That is, join a genocidal Crusade to redeem the Christian holy-lands from its inhabitants (the "infidel" Muslims). This was a standard way to repair one's reputation. Though regarded as a noble mission in the Middle Ages, by Shelley's day, the bloody Crusades had less lustre.

penitence for the past shall appear to you to cancel my crimes, permit me again to call myself your son. Thus had he spoken; and the penitent was welcomed even as the prodigal son of scripture: the fatted calf was killed for him; and he, still pursuing the same path, displayed such open-hearted regret for his follies, so humble a concession of all his rights, and so ardent a resolve to reacquire them by a life of contrition and virtue, that he quickly conquered the kind, old man; and full pardon, and the gift of his lovely child, followed in swift succession.

O! had an angel from Paradise whispered to me to act thus![27] But now, what would be the innocent Juliet's fate? Would God permit the foul union—or, some prodigy destroying it, link the dishonoured name of Carega with the worst of crimes? To-morrow at dawn they were to be married: there was but one way to prevent this—to meet mine enemy, and to enforce the ratification of our agreement. I felt that this could only be done by a mortal struggle. I had no sword—if indeed my distorted arms could wield a soldier's weapon—but I had a dagger, and in that lay my every hope. There was no time for pondering or balancing nicely the question: I might die in the attempt; but besides the burning jealousy and despair of my own heart, honour, mere humanity, demanded that I should fall rather than not destroy the machinations of the fiend.

The guests departed—the lights began to disappear; it was evident that the inhabitants of the villa were seeking repose. I hid myself among the trees—the garden grew desert—the gates were closed—I wandered round and came under a window—ah! well did I know the same!—a soft twilight glimmered in the room—the curtains were half withdrawn. It was the temple of innocence and beauty. Its magnificence was tempered, as it were, by the slight disarrangements occasioned by its being dwelt in, and all the objects scattered around displayed the taste of her who hallowed it by her presence. I saw her enter with a quick light step—I saw her approach the window—she drew back the curtain yet further, and looked out into the night. Its breezy freshness played among her ringlets, and wafted them from the transparent marble of her brow. She clasped her hands, she raised her eyes to Heaven. I heard her voice. Guido! she softly murmured, Mine own Guido! and then, as if overcome by the fullness of her own heart, she sank on her

---

[27] In *Paradise Lost,* archangel Raphael visits Adam to warn him of Satan's temptation.

knees:—her praised[28] eyes—her negligent but graceful attitude—
the beaming thankfulness that lighted up her face—oh, these are
tame words! Heart of mine, thou imagest ever, though thou canst
not pourtray, the celestial beauty of that child of light and love.

I heard a step—a quick firm step along the shady avenue. Soon
I saw a cavalier, richly dressed, young and, methought, graceful to
look on, advance.—I hid myself yet closer.—The youth approached;
he paused beneath the window. She arose, and again looking out
she saw him, and said—I cannot, no, at this distant time I cannot
record her terms of soft silver tenderness; to me they were spoken,
but they were replied to by him.

"I will not go," he cried: "here where you have been, where
your memory glides like some Heaven-visiting ghost, I will pass the
long hours till we meet, never, my Juliet, again, day or night, to
part. But do thou, my love, retire; the cold morn and fitful breeze
will make thy cheek pale, and fill with languor thy love-lighted eyes.
Ah, sweetest! could I press one kiss upon them, I could, methinks,
repose."

And then he approached still nearer, and methought he was
about to clamber into her chamber. I had hesitated, not to terrify
her; now I was no longer master of myself. I rushed forward—
I threw myself on him—I tore him away—I cried, "O loathsome
and foul-shaped wretch!"

I need not repeat epithets, all tending, as it appeared, to rail at a
person I at present feel some partiality for. A shriek rose from
Juliet's lips. I neither heard nor saw—I *felt* only mine enemy, whose
throat I grasped, and my dagger's hilt; he struggled, but could not
escape: at length hoarsely he breathed these words: "Do!—strike
home! destroy this body—you will still live: may your life be long
and merry!"

The descending dagger was arrested at the word, and he, feeling
my hold relax, extricated himself and drew his sword, while the
uproar in the house, and flying of torches from one room to the
other, showed that soon we should be separated—and I—oh! far
better die: so that he did not survive, I cared not. In the midst of my
frenzy there was much calculation:—fall I might, and so that he did
not survive, I cared not for the death-blow I might deal against

---

[28] Referring to the illustration of Juliet gazing at the moon, and to "she raised her
eyes" (above), editor Charles Robinson emends to *upraised*; but *praised* (famously
admired) has a plausible logic.

Painted by Miss Sharpe.   Engraved by J. C. Edwards.

JULIET.

London. Thrst Chance & Cº. R. Jennings & W. Chaplin, Cheapside. & Girtaldon Bovinet & Cº Paris.

Illustration from *The Keepsake*.

myself. While still, therefore, he thought I paused, and while I saw the villanous resolve to take advantage of my hesitation, in the sudden thrust he made at me, I threw myself on his sword, and at the same moment plunged my dagger, with a true desperate aim, in his side. We fell together, rolling over each other, and the tide of blood that flowed from the gaping wound of each mingled on the grass. More I know not—I fainted.

Again I returned to life: weak almost to death, I found myself stretched upon a bed—Juliet was kneeling beside it. Strange! my first broken request was for a mirror. I was so wan and ghastly, that my poor girl hesitated, as she told me afterwards; but, by the mass! I thought myself a right proper[29] youth when I saw the dear reflection of my own well-known features. I confess it is a weakness, but I avow it, I do entertain a considerable affection for the countenance and limbs I behold, whenever I look at a glass; and have more mirrors in my house, and consult them oftener than any beauty in Venice. Before you too much condemn me, permit me to say that no one better knows than I the value of his own body; no one, probably, except myself, ever having had it stolen from him.

Incoherently I at first talked of the dwarf and his crimes, and reproached Juliet for her too easy admission of his love. She thought me raving, as well she might, and yet it was some time before I could prevail on myself to admit that the Guido whose penitence had won her back for me was myself; and while I cursed bitterly the monstrous dwarf, and blest the well-directed blow that had deprived him of life, I suddenly checked myself when I heard her say—Amen! knowing that him whom she reviled was my very self. A little reflection[30] taught me silence—a little practice enabled me to speak of that frightful night without any very excessive blunder. The wound I had given myself was no mockery of one—it was long before I recovered—and as the benevolent and generous Torella sat beside me, talking such wisdom as might win friends to repentance, and mine own dear Juliet hovered near me, administering to my wants, and cheering me by her smiles, the work of my bodily cure and mental reform went on together. I have never, indeed, wholly recovered my strength—my cheek is paler since—my person

[29] With the double meaning of socially acceptable, and self-owning (*property* is cognate).

[30] The sense of *thinking* plays double in punning on the mirror-reflection in the paragraph above.

a little bent. Juliet sometimes ventures to allude bitterly to the malice that caused this change, but I kiss her on the moment, and tell her all is for the best. I am a fonder and more faithful husband—and true is this—but for that wound, never had I called her mine.

I did not revisit the sea-shore, nor seek for the fiend's treasure; yet, while I ponder on the past, I often think, and my confessor was not backward in favouring the idea, that it might be a good rather than an evil spirit, sent by my guardian angel, to show me the folly and misery of pride. So well at least did I learn this lesson, roughly taught as I was, that I am known now by all my friends and fellow-citizens by the name of Guido il Cortese.[31]

ABSENCE

BY THE AUTHOR OF "FRANKENSTEIN"

AH! he is gone—and I alone!—
　　How dark and dreary seems the time!
'T is thus, when the glad sun is flown,
　　Night rushes o'er the Indian clime.

Is there no star to cheer this night?
　　No soothing twilight for the breast?
Yes, Memory sheds her fairy light,
　　Pleasing as sunset's golden west.

And hope of dawn—oh! brighter far
　　Than clouds that in the orient burn;
More welcome than the morning star
　　Is the dear thought—he will return!

---

[31] Guido the Courteous (a transformation, with latent suggestions of a public persona: cortex, the external shell; courtly, the public manner).

From "*Introduction*" to Frankenstein *(1831)*

This now famous novel was born of a nightmare, the atmosphere of Transformation, *of* The Strange Case of Dr. Jekyll and Mr. Hyde, *and* The Secret Sharer, *the psychic stage on which repressed doubles come to life. Just months after* Transformation *appeared, Shelley wrote a retrospective introduction to* Frankenstein *(conceived in 1816 and first published in 1818) to puff and enhance the new version in Henry Colburn and Richard Bentley's Standard Novels Series. Early in September, on the front page of the* Morning Chronicle, *the publishers advertised "Mrs. Shelley's popular Romance,* Frankenstein, *Revised by the Author, with a New Introduction explanatory of the origin of the Story," and Colburn fanned the excitement by pre-publishing the "Introduction" in his* Court Journal *(October 22, p. 724). The selection here is from the novel, which hit the bookstores on Halloween. (For the full text, see the Longman Cultural Edition of* Frankenstein.*)*

The Publishers of the Standard Novels, in selecting "Frankenstein" for one of their series, expressed a wish that I should furnish them with some account of the origin of the story. I am the more willing to comply, because I shall thus give a general answer to the question, so very frequently asked me—"How I, then a young girl, came to think of, and to dilate upon, so very hideous an idea?" It is true that I am very averse to bringing myself forward in print; but as my account will only appear as an appendage to a former production, and as it will be confined to such topics as have connection with my authorship alone, I can scarcely accuse myself of a personal intrusion.

It is not singular that, as the daughter of two persons of distinguished literary celebrity, I should very early in life have thought of writing. As a child I scribbled; and my favourite pastime, during the hours given me for recreation, was to "write stories." Still I had a dearer pleasure than this, which was the formation of castles in the air—the indulging in waking dreams—the following up trains of thought, which had for their subject the formation of a succession of imaginary incidents. My dreams were at once more fantastic and agreeable than my writings. In the latter I was a close imitator—rather doing as others had done, than putting down the suggestions of my own mind. What I wrote was intended at least for one other eye—my childhood's companion and friend; but my dreams were all my own; I accounted for them to nobody; they were my refuge when annoyed—my dearest pleasure when free. [. . .]

In the summer of 1816, we[1] visited Switzerland, and became the neighbours of Lord Byron. [. . .] it proved a wet, ungenial summer, and incessant rain often confined us for days to the house. Some volumes of ghost stories, translated from the German into French, fell into our hands.[2] There was the History of the Inconstant Lover, who, when he thought to clasp the bride to whom he had pledged his vows, found himself in the arms of the pale ghost of her whom he had deserted. There was the tale of the sinful founder of his race, whose miserable doom it was to bestow the kiss of death on all the younger sons of his fated house, just when they reached the age of promise. His gigantic, shadowy form, clothed like the ghost in Hamlet, in complete armour, but with the beaver[3] up, was seen at midnight, by the moon's fitful beams, to advance slowly along the gloomy avenue. The shape was lost beneath the shadow of the castle walls; but soon a gate swung back, a step was heard, the door of the chamber opened, and he advanced to the couch of the blooming youths, cradled in healthy sleep. Eternal sorrow sat upon his face as he bent down and kissed the forehead of the boys, who from that hour withered like flowers snapt upon the stalk. I have not seen these stories since then; but their incidents are as fresh in my mind as if I had read them yesterday.

"We will each write a ghost story," said Lord Byron; and his proposition was acceded to. . . . I busied myself *to think of a story*,—a story to rival those which had excited us to this task. One which would speak to the mysterious fears of our nature, and awaken thrilling horror—one to make the reader dread to look round, to curdle the blood, and quicken the beatings of the heart. If I did not accomplish these things, my ghost story would be unworthy of its name. I thought and pondered—vainly. I felt that blank incapability of invention which is the greatest misery of authorship, when dull Nothing replies to our anxious invocations. *Have you thought of a story?* I was asked each morning, and each morning I was forced to reply with a mortifying negative. . . .

---

[1] Mary Godwin and Percy Shelley, whom she would marry at the end of 1816.

[2] Originally a collection in German, *Fantasmagoriana; or Collected Stories of Apparitions of Specters, Ghosts, Phantoms, etc.* was translated into French in 1812.

[3] Visor. The ghost of Hamlet's murdered, vengeance-seeking father appears to Hamlet in this form, on the nighttime ramparts of the castle (1.2.226–30).

Many and long were the conversations between Lord Byron and Shelley, to which I was a devout but nearly silent listener. During one of these, various philosophical doctrines were discussed, and among others the nature of the principle of life, and whether there was any probability of its ever being discovered and communicated. They talked of the experiments of Dr. Darwin, (I speak not of what the Doctor really did, or said that he did, but, as more to my purpose, of what was then spoken of as having been done by him,) who preserved a piece of vermicelli in a glass case, till by some extraordinary means it began to move with voluntary motion. Not thus, after all, would life be given. Perhaps a corpse would be reanimated; galvanism had given token of such things: perhaps the component parts of a creature might be manufactured, brought together, and endued with vital warmth.[4]

Night waned upon this talk, and even the witching hour had gone by,[5] before we retired to rest. When I placed my head on my pillow, I did not sleep, nor could I be said to think. My imagination, unbidden, possessed and guided me, gifting the successive images that arose in my mind with a vividness far beyond the usual bounds of reverie. I saw—with shut eyes, but acute mental vision,—I saw the pale student of unhallowed arts kneeling beside the thing he had put together. I saw the hideous phantasm of a man stretched out, and then, on the working of some powerful engine, show signs of life, and stir with an uneasy, half vital motion. Frightful must it be; for supremely frightful would be the effect of any human endeavour to mock the stupendous mechanism of the Creator of the world. His success would terrify the artist; he would rush away from his odious handywork, horror-stricken. He would hope that, left to itself, the slight spark of life which he had communicated would fade; that this thing, which had received such imperfect animation, would subside into dead matter; and he might sleep in the belief that the silence of the grave would quench for ever the transient

---

[4] Erasmus Darwin (Charles Darwin's grandfather) refers to this pasta-experiment (*vermicelli* means *little worms* in Italian) in *The Temple of Nature, or, The Origin of Society: A Poem* (1803). Galvanism, the inducement of spasms in dead tissue by means of electric current, was given a sensational, widely reported demonstration when Giovanni Aldini (physiologist Luigi Galvani's nephew) "animated" the corpse of an executed convict, causing it to sit upright.

[5] Another reference to *Hamlet*: "'Tis now the very witching time of night, / When churchyards yawn, and Hell itself breathes out / Contagion to this world," says Hamlet as he prepares to murder his uncle and, perhaps, his mother (3.2.396–98).

existence of the hideous corpse which he had looked upon as the cradle of life. He sleeps; but he is awakened; he opens his eyes; behold the horrid thing stands at his bedside, opening his curtains, and looking on him with yellow, watery, but speculative eyes.

I opened mine in terror. The idea so possessed my mind, that a thrill of fear ran through me, and I wished to exchange the ghastly image of my fancy for the realities around. I see them still; the very room, the dark *parquet,* the closed shutters, with the moonlight struggling through, and the sense I had that the glassy lake and white high Alps were beyond. I could not so easily get rid of my hideous phantom; still it haunted me. I must try to think of something else. I recurred to my ghost story,—my tiresome unlucky ghost story! O! if I could only contrive one which would frighten my reader as I myself had been frightened that night!

Swift as light and as cheering was the idea that broke in upon me. "I have found it! What terrified me will terrify others; and I need only describe the spectre which had haunted my midnight pillow." On the morrow I announced that I had *thought of a story.* I began that day with the words, *It was on a dreary night of November,* making only a transcript of the grim terrors of my waking dream.[6] . . .

London, October 15, 1831

M.W.S.

---

[6] This is the creation scene in *Frankenstein,* vol. 1, chapter 4.

Charles Darwin
1809–1882

Although he knew the speculations on evolution by his grandfather, Erasmus Darwin, Charles Darwin did not doubt the Biblical account of creation until he began organizing the notes he took as ship-naturalist (scientist) on the voyage of the H.M.S. Beagle, 1831–1836. *His attention was arrested both by the stupendous variety of flora and fauna, and by relays of affinity and repulsion in his encounters with indigenous tribes. He published his chronicle of the* Beagle *in 1839, but it wasn't until 1859 that* On the Origin of Species by Means of Natural Selection *appeared. It was a sensational best-seller, at once fascinating and deeply disturbing in its proposal of a "natural" alternative to the Biblical account of creation. While the "Species" surveyed did not yet include humankind, some of the tribes of Tierra del Fuego evoked a sense of brute animal creation. In 1871,* The Descent of Man *finally stated the thesis: man is an animal, not just "descended from some less highly organized form" but similar to "the lower animals in embryonic development." Moreover, anyone who doubted this was equivalent to a savage in intellection: "He who is not content to look, like a savage, at the phenomena of nature as disconnected, cannot any longer believe that man is the work of a separate act of creation." The dwarf in* Transformation *and Mr. Hyde embody this heterodoxy, and more: an apprehension that not only may rational, civilized human beings degenerate, but that this potential is almost genetically embedded, repressed only by a veneer of social and moral discipline. In* The Secret Sharer *Conrad suggests something even more urgent in Mr. Leggatt: that this primitive, violent self can be released in a moment's anger. Yet if this is the darkest suggestion of Darwinian science, Darwin also theorized the antidote: natural selection favors the "intellectual power" and "moral sense," the "greatest of all distinctions" between human beings and "the lower animals."*

From *The Voyage of the Beagle* (1839):
"Tierra del Fuego" (chapter 10)

> This *"Land of Fire,"* named for the fire-signal towers used by the
> tribes, is the southern tip of South America. Darwin's reports alternate
> between describing some Fuegians as if they were a different species,
> exotic, alien, scarcely human, and others as if they were recognizably
> human, though culturally different, more primitive, more childlike.
> Jemmy Button (purchased for a button on a previous trip and taken
> to England for "civilizing") enters Darwin's narrative as figure of
> poignant, arresting sympathy.

December 17th, 1832. . . . our first arrival. . . . A group of Fuegians
partly concealed by the entangled forest, were perched on a wild
point overhanging the sea; and as we passed by, they sprang up and
waving their tattered cloaks sent forth a loud and sonorous shout.
The savages followed the ship, and just before dark we saw their
fire, and again heard their wild cry. The harbour consists of a fine
piece of water half surrounded by low rounded mountains of clay-
slate, which are covered to the water's edge by one dense gloomy
forest. A single glance at the landscape was sufficient to show me
how widely different it was from anything I had ever beheld. . . . In
the morning the Captain sent a party to communicate with the
Fuegians. When we came within hail, one of the four natives who
were present advanced to receive us, and began to shout most vehe-
mently, wishing to direct us where to land. When we were on shore
the party looked rather alarmed, but continued talking and making
gestures with great rapidity. It was without exception the most curious and interesting spectacle I ever beheld: I could not have believed
how wide was the difference between savage and civilized man: it is
greater than between a wild and domesticated animal, inasmuch as
in man there is a greater power of improvement. . . .

They are excellent mimics: as often as we coughed or yawned, or
made any odd motion, they immediately imitated us. Some of our
party began to squint and look awry; but one of the young Fuegians
(whose whole face was painted black, excepting a white band
across his eyes) succeeded in making far more hideous grimaces.
They could repeat with perfect correctness each word in any sentence
we addressed them, and they remembered such words for some time.
Yet we Europeans all know how difficult it is to distinguish apart the

sounds in a foreign language. Which of us, for instance, could follow an American Indian through a sentence of more than three words? All savages appear to possess, to an uncommon degree, this power of mimicry. I was told, almost in the same words, of the same ludicrous habit among the Caffres;[1] the Australians, likewise, have long been notorious for being able to imitate and describe the gait of any man, so that he may be recognized. How can this faculty be explained? is it a consequence of the more practised habits of perception and keener senses, common to all men in a savage state, as compared with those long civilized? . . .

I have not as yet noticed the Fuegians whom we had on board. During the former voyage of the *Adventure* and *Beagle* in 1826 to 1830, Captain Fitz Roy seized on a party of natives, as hostages for the loss of a boat, which had been stolen, to the great jeopardy of a party employed on the survey; and some of these natives, as well as a child whom he bought for a pearl-button, he took with him to England, determining to educate them and instruct them in religion at his own expense. To settle these natives in their own country, was one chief inducement to Captain Fitz Roy[2] to undertake our present voyage. . . . Two men, one of whom died in England of the smallpox, a boy and a little girl, were originally taken; and we had now on board, York Minster, Jemmy Button (whose name expresses his purchase-money), and Fuegia Basket. York Minster was a full-grown, short, thick, powerful man: his disposition was reserved, taciturn, morose, and when excited violently passionate; his affections were very strong towards a few friends on board; his intellect good. Jemmy Button was a universal favourite, but likewise passionate; the expression of his face at once showed his nice disposition. He was merry and often laughed, and was remarkably sympathetic with any one in pain: when the water was rough, I was often a little seasick, and he used to come to me and say in a plaintive voice, "Poor, poor fellow!" but the notion, after his aquatic life, of a man being sea-sick, was too ludicrous, and he was generally obliged to turn on one side to hide a smile or laugh, and then he would repeat his

---

[1] Kaffirs; then a common term for Bantu-speaking Africans, now considered derogatory.

[2] Darwin had a sometimes contentious relationship with the *Beagle*'s captain, Robert Fitz-Roy, 4 years his senior.

"Poor, poor fellow!" He was of a patriotic disposition; and he liked to praise his own tribe and country, in which he truly said there were "plenty of trees," and he abused all the other tribes: he stoutly declared that there was no Devil in his land. Jemmy was short, thick, and fat, but vain of his personal appearance; he used always to wear gloves, his hair was neatly cut, and he was distressed if his well-polished shoes were dirtied. He was fond of admiring himself in a looking glass; and a merry-faced little Indian boy from the Rio Negro, whom we had for some months on board, soon perceived this, and used to mock him: Jemmy, who was always rather jealous of the attention paid to this little boy, did not at all like this, and used to say, with rather a contemptuous twist of his head, "Too much skylark." It seems yet wonderful to me, when I think over all his many good qualities that he should have been of the same race, and doubtless partaken of the same character, with the miserable, degraded savages whom we first met here. . . . both York and Jemmy were much superior to any sailor on board: several times they have declared what some distant object has been, and though doubted by every one, they have proved right, when it has been examined through a telescope. They were quite conscious of this power; and Jemmy, when he had any little quarrel with the officer on watch, would say, "Me see ship, me no tell."

It was interesting to watch the conduct of the savages, when we landed, towards Jemmy Button: they immediately perceived the difference between him and ourselves, and held much conversation one with another on the subject. . . . But Jemmy understood very little of their language, and was, moreover, thoroughly ashamed of his countrymen. . . . One of our arms being bared, they expressed the liveliest surprise and admiration at its whiteness, just in the same way in which I have seen the ourangoutang do at the Zoological Gardens. We thought that they mistook two or three of the officers, who were rather shorter and fairer, though adorned with large beards, for the ladies of our party. The tallest amongst the Fuegians was evidently much pleased at his height being noticed. When placed back to back with the tallest of the boat's crew, he tried his best to edge on higher ground, and to stand on tiptoe. . . .

December 25th. 1832 . . . we pulled alongside a canoe with six Fuegians. These were the most abject and miserable creatures I anywhere beheld. On the east coast the natives, as we have seen, have guanaco cloaks, and on the west they possess seal-skins. Amongst these central tribes the men generally have an otter-skin, or some small scrap about as large as a pocket-handkerchief, which is barely sufficient to cover their backs as low down as their loins. It is laced across the breast by strings, and according as the wind blows, it is shifted from side to side. But these Fuegians in the canoe were quite naked, and even one full-grown woman was absolutely so. It was raining heavily, and the fresh water, together with the spray, trickled down her body. In another harbour not far distant, a woman, who was suckling a recently-born child, came one day alongside the vessel, and remained there out of mere curiosity, whilst the sleet fell and thawed on her naked bosom, and on the skin of her naked baby! These poor wretches were stunted in their growth, their hideous faces bedaubed with white paint, their skins filthy and greasy, their hair entangled, their voices discordant, and their gestures violent. Viewing such men, one can hardly make one's self believe that they are fellow-creatures, and inhabitants of the same world. It is a common subject of conjecture what pleasure in life some of the lower animals can enjoy: how much more reasonably the same question may be asked with respect to these barbarians! At night, five or six human beings, naked and scarcely protected from the wind and rain of this tempestuous climate, sleep on the wet ground coiled up like animals. Whenever it is low water, winter or summer, night or day, they must rise to pick shellfish from the rocks; and the women either dive to collect sea-eggs, or sit patiently in their canoes, and with a baited hair-line without any hook, jerk out little fish. If a seal is killed, or the floating carcass of a putrid whale is discovered, it is a feast; and such miserable food is assisted by a few tasteless berries and fungi. . . . From the concurrent, but quite independent evidence of the boy taken by Mr. Low, and of Jemmy Button, it is certainly true, that when pressed in winter by hunger, they kill and devour their old women before they kill their dogs: the boy, being asked by Mr. Low why they did this, answered, "Doggies catch otters, old women no." This boy described the manner in which they are killed by being held over smoke and thus choked; he imitated their screams as a joke, and described the parts of their bodies which are considered best to eat. Horrid as such a death by the hands of their friends and relatives must be, the fears of the old women, when hunger begins to press, are more painful to think of; we are told that they then often run away into the mountains, but that they are pursued by the men and brought back to the slaughter-house at their own firesides! . . .

Their country is a broken mass of wild rocks, lofty hills, and useless forests: and these are viewed through mists and endless storms. The habitable land is reduced to the stones on the beach; in search of food they are compelled unceasingly to wander from spot to spot, and so steep is the coast, that they can only move about in their wretched canoes. They cannot know the feeling of having a home, and still less that of domestic affection; for the husband is to the wife a brutal master to a laborious slave. Was a more horrid deed ever perpetrated, than that witnessed on the west coast by Byron,[3] who saw a wretched mother pick up her bleeding dying infant-boy, whom her husband had mercilessly dashed on the stones for dropping a basket of sea-eggs! How little can the higher powers of the mind be brought into play: what is there for imagination to picture, for reason to compare, or judgment to decide upon? to knock a limpet from the rock does not require even cunning, that lowest power of the mind. Their skill in some respects may be compared to the instinct of animals; for it is not improved by experience: the canoe, their most ingenious work, poor as it is, has remained the same, as we know from Drake,[4] for the last two hundred and fifty years. . . .

[January] *22nd.* [1833] . . . During the night the news had spread, and early in the morning (23rd) a fresh party arrived, belonging to the Tekenika, or Jemmy's tribe. Several of them had run so fast that their noses were bleeding, and their mouths frothed from the rapidity with which they talked; and with their naked bodies all bedaubed with black, white, and red, they looked like so many demoniacs who had been fighting. We then proceeded (accompanied by twelve canoes, each holding four or five people) down Ponsonby Sound to the spot where poor Jemmy expected to find his mother and relatives. He had already heard that his father was dead; but as he had had a "dream in his head" to that effect, he did not seem to care much about it, and repeatedly comforted himself with the very natural reflection—"Me no help it." He was not able to learn any particulars regarding his father's death, as his relations would not speak about it. . . . The next morning after our arrival (the 24th) the

---

[3] *Narrative of Great Distresses on the Shores of Patagonia,* by John Byron (1723–1786), was published in 1768; he is the grandfather of famous poet Lord Byron, friend of the Shelleys.

[4] The adventures of English explorer Sir Francis Drake took him past Tierra del Fuego in 1577.

Fuegians began to pour in, and Jemmy's mother and brothers arrived. Jemmy recognised the stentorian voice of one of his brothers at a prodigious distance. The meeting was less interesting than that between a horse, turned out into a field, when he joins an old companion. There was no demonstration of affection; they simply stared for a short time at each other; and the mother immediately went to look after her canoe. We heard, however, through York that the mother has been inconsolable for the loss of Jemmy and had searched everywhere for him, thinking that he might have been left after having been taken in the boat. The women took much notice of and were very kind to Fuegia. We had already perceived that Jemmy had almost forgotten his own language. I should think there was scarcely another human being with so small a stock of language, for his English was very imperfect. It was laughable, but almost pitiable, to hear him speak to his wild brother in English, and then ask him in Spanish ("no sabe?") whether he did not understand him. . . .

February 6th. . . . It was quite melancholy leaving the three Fuegians with their savage countrymen; but it was a great comfort that they had no personal fears. York, being a powerful resolute man, was pretty sure to get on well, together with his wife Fuegia. Poor Jemmy looked rather disconsolate, and would then, I have little doubt, have been glad to have returned with us. His own brother had stolen many things from him; and as he remarked, "What fashion call that?" he abused his countrymen, "all bad men, no sabe (know) nothing" and, though I never heard him swear before, "damned fools." Our three Fuegians, though they had been only three years with civilized men, would, I am sure, have been glad to have retained their new habits; but this was obviously impossible. I fear it is more than doubtful, whether their visit will have been of any use to them. . . .

On the 5th of March, we anchored in a cove at Woollya, but we saw not a soul there. We were alarmed at this, for the natives in Ponsonby Sound showed by gestures, that there had been fighting; and we afterwards heard that the dreaded Oens men had made a descent. Soon a canoe, with a little flag flying, was seen approaching, with one of the men in it washing the paint off his face. This man was poor Jemmy,—now a thin, haggard savage, with long disordered hair, and naked, except a bit of blanket round his waist. We did not recognize him till he was close to us, for he was ashamed of himself, and turned his back to the ship. We had left him plump, fat, clean, and well-dressed;—I never saw so complete and grievous a change. As soon, however, as he was clothed, and the first flurry was over, things wore a good appearance. He dined with Captain Fitz Roy, and ate his dinner as tidily as formerly. He told us that he had "too much" (meaning enough) to eat, that he was not cold, that his relations were very good people, and that he did not wish to go back to England: in the evening we found out the cause of this great change in Jemmy's feelings, in the arrival of his young and nice-looking wife. With his usual good feeling he brought two beautiful otter-skins for two of his best friends, and some spear-heads and arrows made with his own hands for the Captain. He said he had built a canoe for himself, and he boasted that he could talk a little of his own language! But it is a most singular fact, that he appears to have taught all his tribe some English: an old man spontaneously announced "Jemmy Button's wife." Jemmy had lost all his property. He told us that York Minster had built a large canoe, and with his wife Fuegia, had several months since gone to his own country, and had taken farewell by an act of consummate villainy; he persuaded Jemmy and his mother to come with him, and then on the way deserted them by night, stealing every article of their property.

Jemmy went to sleep on shore, and in the morning returned, and remained on board till the ship got under way, which frightened his wife, who continued crying violently till he got into his canoe. He returned loaded with valuable property. Every soul on board was heartily sorry to shake hands with him for the last time. I do not now doubt that he will be as happy as, perhaps happier than, if he had never left his own country. Every one must sincerely hope that Captain Fitz Roy's noble hope may be fulfilled, of being rewarded for the many generous sacrifices which he made for these Fuegians, by some shipwrecked sailor being protected by the descendants of Jemmy Button and his tribe! When Jemmy reached the shore, he lighted a signal fire, and the smoke curled up, bidding us a last and long farewell, as the ship stood on her course into the open sea.

From *The Descent of Man* (1871), "General Summary and Conclusion"

. . . The main conclusion here arrived at, and now held by many naturalists who are well competent to form a sound judgment is that man is descended from some less highly organised form. The grounds upon which this conclusion rests will never be shaken, for the close similarity between man and the lower animals in embryonic development, as well as in innumerable points of structure and constitution, both of high and of the most trifling importance,—the rudiments which he retains, and the abnormal reversions to which he is occasionally liable,—are facts which cannot be disputed. They have long been known, but until recently they told us nothing with respect to the origin of man. Now when viewed by the light of our knowledge of the whole organic world, their meaning is unmistakable. The great principle of evolution stands up clear and firm, when these groups or facts are considered in connection with others, such as the mutual affinities of the members of the same group, their geographical distribution in past and present times, and their geological succession. It is incredible that all these facts should speak falsely. He who is not content to look, like a savage, at the phenomena of nature as disconnected, cannot any longer believe that man is the work of a separate act of creation. He will be forced to admit that the close resemblance of the embryo of man to that, for instance, of a dog—the construction of his skull, limbs and whole frame on the same plan with that of other mammals, independently of the uses to which the parts may be put—the occasional re-appearance of various structures, for instance of several muscles, which man does not normally possess, but which are common to the Quadrumana[1]—and a crowd of analogous facts—all point in the plainest manner to the conclusion that man is the co-descendant with other mammals of a common progenitor. . . .

The higher intellectual powers of man, such as those of ratiocination, abstraction, self-consciousness, &c., probably follow from the continued improvement and exercise of the other mental faculties.

The development of the moral qualities is a more interesting problem. The foundation lies in the social instincts, including under this term the family ties. These instincts are highly complex, and in the case of the lower animals give special tendencies towards

---

[1] "Four-handed" primates, in which the feet, too, have opposable digits.

certain definite actions; but the more important elements are love, and the distinct emotion of sympathy. Animals endowed with the social instincts take pleasure in one another's company, warn one another of danger, defend and aid one another in many ways. These instincts do not extend to all the individuals of the species, but only to those of the same community. As they are highly beneficial to the species, they have in all probability been acquired through natural selection.

A moral being is one who is capable of reflecting on his past actions and their motives—of approving of some and disapproving of others; and the fact that man is the one being who certainly deserves this designation, is the greatest of all distinctions between him and the lower animals. But in the fourth chapter I have endeavoured to shew that the moral sense follows, firstly, from the enduring and ever-present nature of the social instincts; secondly, from man's appreciation of the approbation and disapprobation of his fellows; and thirdly, from the high activity of his mental faculties, with past impressions extremely vivid; and in these latter respects he differs from the lower animals. Owing to this condition of mind, man cannot avoid looking both backwards and forwards, and comparing past impressions. Hence after some temporary desire or passion has mastered his social instincts, he reflects and compares the now weakened impression of such past impulses with the ever-present social instincts; and he then feels that sense of dissatisfaction which all unsatisfied instincts leave behind them, he therefore resolves to act differently for the future,—and this is conscience. Any instinct, permanently stronger or more enduring than another, gives rise to a feeling which we express by saying that it ought to be obeyed. A pointer dog, if able to reflect on his past conduct, would say to himself, I ought (as indeed we say of him) to have pointed at that hare and not have yielded to the passing temptation of hunting it. . . .

Social animals are impelled partly by a wish to aid the members of their community in a general manner, but more commonly to perform certain definite actions. Man is impelled by the same general wish to aid his fellows; but has few or no special instincts. He differs also from the lower animals in the power of expressing his desires by words, which thus become a guide to the aid required and bestowed. The motive to give aid is likewise much modified in man: it no longer consists solely of a blind instinctive impulse, but is much influenced by the praise or blame of his fellows. The appreciation and the bestowal of praise and blame both rest on sympathy; and this emotion, as we have seen, is one of the most important elements of the social instincts. Sympathy, though gained as an instinct, is also much strengthened by exercise or habit. As all men desire their own happiness, praise or blame is bestowed on actions and motives, according as they lead to this end; and as happiness is an essential part of the general good, the greatest-happiness principle indirectly serves as a nearly safe standard of right and wrong. As the reasoning powers advance and experience is gained, the remoter effects of certain lines of conduct on the character of the individual, and on the general good, are perceived; and then the self-regarding virtues come within the scope of public opinion, and receive praise, and their opposites blame. But with the less civilised nations reason often errs, and many bad customs and base superstitions come within the same scope, and are then esteemed as high virtues, and their breach as heavy crimes.

The moral faculties are generally and justly esteemed as of higher value than the intellectual powers. But we should bear in mind that the activity of the mind in vividly recalling past impressions is one of the fundamental though secondary bases of conscience. This affords the strongest argument for educating and stimulating in all possible ways the intellectual faculties of every human being. No doubt a man with a torpid mind, if his social affections and sympathies are well developed, will be led to good actions, and may have a fairly sensitive conscience. But whatever renders the imagination more vivid and strengthens the habit of recalling and comparing past impressions, will make the conscience more sensitive, and may even somewhat compensate for weak social affections and sympathies.

The main conclusion arrived at in this work, namely, that man is descended from some lowly organised form, will, I regret to think, be highly distasteful to many. But there can hardly be a doubt that we are descended from barbarians. The astonishment which I felt on first seeing a party of Fuegians on a wild and broken shore will never be forgotten by me, for the reflection at once rushed into my mind—such were our ancestors. These men were absolutely naked and bedaubed with paint, their long hair was tangled, their mouths frothed with excitement, and their expression was wild, startled, and distrustful. They possessed hardly any arts, and like wild animals lived on what they could catch; they had no government, and were merciless to every one not of their own small tribe. He who has seen a savage in his native land will not feel much shame, if forced to

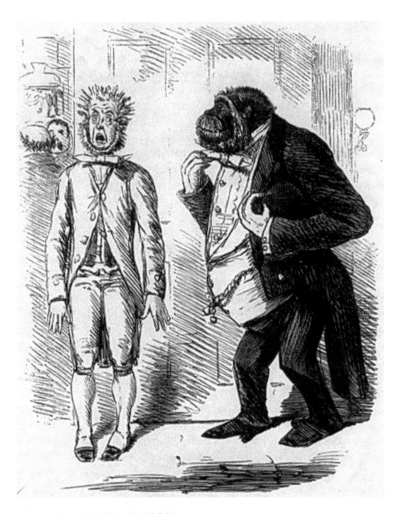

THE LION OF THE SEASON
Alarmed Flunky, "Mr. G-G-G-O-O-O-RILLA!"
The multiple anxieties posed by evolutionary theory are spoofed in this
famous cartoon from the British magazine, *Punch* (1861), titled *THE LION
OF THE SEASON,* with a caption that has an "Alarmed Flunky" sputter,
"Mr. G-G-G-O-O-O-RILLA!" (A "Lion" is a celebrity; the beast is punned
in the flunky's alarmed, mane-like hair.) This fashionable gentleman is
alarmed not only at this spectacle of man's animal origins, but also at the
freedom with which this primate can don gentleman's attire and enter
cultured society. In his horror (literally with hair standing on end), the
gentleman seems less humanly composed than the serene and courtly gorilla,
who looks at him with a certain amount of curiosity and equanimity.

acknowledge that the blood of some more humble creature flows in his veins. For my own part I would as soon be descended from that heroic little monkey, who braved his dreaded enemy in order to save the life of his keeper, or from that old baboon, who descending from the mountains, carried away in triumph his young comrade from a crowd of astonished dogs—as from a savage who delights to torture his enemies, offers up bloody sacrifices, practices infanticide without remorse, treats his wives like slaves, knows no decency, and is haunted by the grossest superstitions.

Man may be excused for feeling some pride at having risen, though not through his own exertions, to the very summit of the organic scale; and the fact of his having thus risen, instead of having been aboriginally placed there, may give him hope for a still higher destiny in the distant future. But we are not here concerned with hopes or fears, only with the truth as far as our reason permits us to discover it; and I have given the evidence to the best of my ability. We must, however, acknowledge, as it seems to me, that man with all his noble qualities, with sympathy which feels for the most debased, with benevolence which extends not only to other men but to the humblest living creature, with his god-like intellect which has penetrated into the movements and constitution of the solar system—with all these exalted powers—Man still bears in his bodily frame the indelible stamp of his lowly origin.

Mr. Mansfield. An albumen print cabinet card, circa 1895, by Henry Van der Weyde, London. The year following the publication of R. L. Stevenson's *Dr. Jekyll and Mr. Hyde,* renowned American actor Richard Mansfield (1857–1907) appeared on stage in the dual role, a theatrical sensation, first in Boston in May 1887, then in New York, in December. Across the decade, Mansfield continued in the roles in these cities as well as in London, including a tenth anniversary celebration (and 1000th performance) in March 1906. The photographer, Henry Van der Weyde (1838–1924), began as a painter and turned to professional portrait photography, and was the first, in 1877, to take portraits by electric light.

Robert Louis Stevenson
1850–1894

The opening of MGM's *Dr. Jekyll and Mr. Hyde* (1941) does nearly everything Robert Louis Stevenson set his writing not to do. Whether in boys' stories or in the adult terrain of *Dr. Jekyll and Mr. Hyde,* he rejected Victorian domesticity, along with the domestic realism that had become the mainstream of nineteenth-century British fiction. "This is a poison bad world for the romancer, this Anglo-Saxon world," Stevenson sighed in 1892, confessing, "I usually get out of it by not having any women in it at all." No angels in the house; only bachelors. In *Dr. Jekyll and Mr. Hyde,* no man has a love-interest, a family, or even a pet; moments of intimacy are rare, cautious, or nonexistent. With Hollywood intelligence, MGM thought to introduce women, to (hetero)sexualize the crisis. The film opens on an image of a church steeple, a choir singing "The Lord is My Shepherd," and a rector extolling Victoria's Golden Jubilee of 1887 as a sign of the continued triumph of English "virtue and moral blessings" over "the forces of evil" ("the world moves forward"). Just as he is indexing "family hearths" and "shops of industry" to celebrate England's preeminence, he is interrupted by a lower-class man ranting about "taking all the fun out of life." Dr. Jekyll (Spencer Tracy) goes to assist him (his wife reports that she hoped church would help), and finds a case of a soul in conflict. Not long after, Dr. Jekyll experiences such agitation when he meets a streetwalker (Ingrid Bergman), a foil to his blonde fiancée (Lana Turner). It is this conflict that drives him, once back in his lab, to down a potion and become Mr. Hyde, a transformation laced with Freudian dream imagery.

Stevenson seems destined for the divisions of *The Strange Case of Dr. Jekyll and Mr. Hyde.* In his prosperous Edinburgh family, his father was an embodiment of law and order: a political conservative (High Tory); a stern Calvinist (the war of body and soul; eternal damnation for sin); and by profession, a lighthouse builder and civil engineer. His mother's family was populated by lawyers and ministers. When Robert was seven, the Stevensons moved from the crowded slums of old Edinburgh, a gothic maze of ruins, alleyways, bars, and brothels, to the new town across the river, a district of tree-lined streets and graceful neoclassic townhouses. It was his first experience of two worlds in one domain, close neighbors but categorically different. Even so, the new town was a fragile escape: his mother suffered from ill health, and Robert was sickly from birth with the bronchial problems that would shadow his entire life. Prone to nightmares, he was beguiled by fantastic stories told to him by his father and his nurse, Alison Cunningham ("my second mother and my first wife," he said later). The deeply devout "Cummy" seems also divided: her favorite genre, contained in a Calvinist frame, was the horror story. The very furniture of the household (remarks critic William Sharpe) "served as a reminder of the battle between flesh and spirit," a prized piece "a cabinet that had been made by a double personality, Deacon Brodie—upstanding citizen by day, infamous serial killer by night,"[1] and a habitué of old Edinburgh. No wonder that at age three, while drawing and playing games, young Robert put these twinned queries to his mother, "I have drawed a man's body, shall I do his soul now?" and "Why has God got a Hell?" "I would fear to trust myself to slumber," he recalled, "lest I was not accepted and should slip, ere I awoke, into eternal ruin. I remember repeatedly . . . waking from a dream of Hell, clinging to the horizontal bar of the bed, with my knees and chin together, my soul shaken, my body convulsed with agony." This fear possessed him: "A fierce underlying pessimism appears . . . to be the last word of the Stevensons; their sense of the tragedy of life is acute and unbroken."

Such pessimism was not strange to a Victorian world in which ideals of progress fell athwart dark terrains disclosed by new sciences of human nature. Prosperity, power, and the "march of mind" almost daily produced new ideas and challenges to tradition. "Since yesterday, a century has passed away," says a character in George Eliot's *Middlemarch*. By 1850 Britain was in the "age of steam" and, fueled by its Industrial Revolution, the premier international power. By 1860, it was also embroiled in debate over Charles Darwin's

---

[1] *Longman Anthology of British Literature* (3d edition, 2006) vol. 2, p. 1937.

Origin of Species. Arguing that the origin of humanity was natural and not divine, Darwin challenged ideas of religious and social stability. During the same years, Thomas Carlyle, John Ruskin, and Karl Marx described the endless fissures in the social foundation of modern life. The nexus of capitalist industrial society, they argued, was not fellow-feeling but competition, "naked self-interest and callous cash-payment," as Carlyle put it in *Past and Present* (1843). By 1860, John Stuart Mill and Matthew Arnold were extending such views to civilization at large, tracing the tension of liberty and constraints, of culture and anarchy. And by 1859 a "Godless"—that is, secular—novelist emerged. George Eliot is "the first legitimate fruit of our modern atheistic pietism," said critic W. H. Mallock in 1879: "in her writings we have some sort of presentation of a world of high endeavour, pure morality, and strong enthusiasm, existing and in full work, without any reference to, or help from, the thought of God. Godless in its literal sense, and divested of all vindictive meaning, exactly describes her writings. They are without God, not against Him." Eliot wasn't immoral (far from it); but she was willing to imagine social ties and duties not grounded in theology and chastened by divine judgment. Authority was open to negotiation. Even the Bible was challenged by theories about its origins and meanings, while long-standing political and social systems were rattled by revolutions in Europe and workers' protests at home. To Carlyle, the "old spiritual highways and recognized paths" were obliterated. There was "no assurance of the truth of anything," said Mill.

Within this ferment, and restless under his family's religious traditions, Stevenson tested life in what he called "the pattern of an idler." At seventeen, he entered Edinburgh University to study engineering and follow the family enterprise of lighthouse design, but his attention was sporadic; he really wanted to be a writer. All his father would allow was a switch of study to law, and Stevenson rebelled by becoming a "dandy," sporting a velvet coat and long hair, and exploring the lowlife streets of old Edinburgh, its pubs and demimonde haunts. Another escape was travel—to Italy, Germany, and France, where he spent summers, not only for his health but also for the society of writers and artists. He was an avid reader—of Sir Walter Scott and Alexander Dumas, Dickens and Thackeray, Poe, Hawthorne, and Whitman—and soon met the writers and critics who would provide a new community, particularly Sidney Colvin, Professor of Art at Cambridge, an enduring support as critic and friend. He was also becoming a skeptic, precipitating the first great crisis of his life when, in 1873, he confessed his agnosticism to his father (who also discovered that his son had joined a socialist club at the university).

In France in 1876, Stevenson met Fanny Osbourne, an American ten years his senior and mother of two, estranged from her husband in San Francisco. When this husband threatened to terminate financial support if she stayed abroad, she returned to him in 1878, and Stevenson went to London. The Osbourne marriage was beyond repair, however, and when in the summer of 1879 Fanny told Stevenson that her husband had left her, he took a steamship to New York and then a railroad across a still dangerous continent to reunite with her. They married in 1880. Yet marriage was not nearly as exciting as the courtship, and Stevenson found himself (he commented later) "as limp as a lady's novel," "the embers of the once gay R.L.S."—the very initials seeming epitaphic.

What kept him vital was writing—essays, travel stories, poetry, adventures, and vast numbers of letters. In 1883 he published a "boy's story," *Treasure Island.* Chronic bronchial problems soon sent him in search of health to Switzerland, France, and the resort town of Bournemouth, on England's west coast. It was here that he wrote *Dr. Jekyll and Mr. Hyde* and *Kidnapped* (both 1886). *Dr. Jekyll and Mr. Hyde* secured his fame, and when his father died in May 1887, Stevenson became heir to a decent fortune, the resource to travel at will. The family left for New York in August, thence upstate to a health resort on Saranac Lake; when that didn't improve things, they hired a yacht to Hawaii and then to the South Seas in 1888, settling in Samoa in 1889. In love with the tropical warmth and beauty, Stevenson found his new life "far better fun than people dream who fall asleep among the chimney stacks and telegraph wires." To the Samoans, he was "Tusitala" ("teller of tales"); in gratitude for his defense of them against exploitation by European and American colonists, they built a road to his estate, Vailima: "The Road of Loving Hearts." Just weeks after his forty-fourth birthday in 1894, Stevenson died suddenly of a cerebral hemorrhage while at work on *Weir of Hermiston.* The Samoans buried him at the summit of Mount Vaea.

THE STRANGE CASE OF DR. JEKYLL AND MR. HYDE

A "Jekyll-and-Hyde" character is the bequest of this tale for naming unhomogenized polar personalities. Although Stevenson could not have known that his "strange case" would enter our language this way, it is clear that he grasped the cultural determinant. Mr. Hyde's name, involved in a recurrent vocabulary of "hid," "hidden," "secret," and "concealed," is almost too obviously punning: "You have not been mad enough to hide this fellow?" cries Mr. Utterson to Dr. Jekyll. Stevenson's tale works a method in such madness, from its title figures, to its social relays, to the urban architecture itself. All configure not just one strange case, but a text of human psychology and social alienation. In *A Chapter on Dreams* (pp. 133–44), Stevenson renders a student (part autobiographical, part representative) dreaming of being able to lead "a double life—one of the day, one of the night," and he says that he found this dream in *The Strange Case of Dr. Jekyll and Mr. Hyde:* "I had long been trying to write a story on this subject, to find a body, a vehicle, for that strong sense of man's double being which must at times come in upon and overwhelm the mind of every thinking creature." The elements of *The Strange Case* came to him in a dream, and he wrote this "fine bogy tale" in three feverish days. Fanny felt that he had "missed the allegory"; it was "merely a story—a magnificent bit of sensationalism—when it should have been a masterpiece." So he fed his pages to the flames and began again, and in three more days produced *The Strange Case* as we have it. Victorian novels typically plumped to three massive volumes, an entertainment for weeks, or months, on end. Stevenson's tale was printed up in the mode of "sensation" novels and other "trash" books, and put for sale in railway bookstalls to readers on the run looking for entertainment rather than "literature."

Its immediate success in England and America made Stevenson a celebrity. *Dr. Jekyll and Mr. Hyde* struck this vast chord in no small part because its anti-realism bristled with uncannily familiar sensations—this, despite Stevenson's aversion to the fiction of "resemblances to life" and preference, in "both the method and meaning of the work," for an "immeasurable difference from life" (*A Humble Remonstrance*, 1884). The paradox of *Dr. Jekyll and Mr. Hyde* is that its very difference from life is the medium of a startling resemblance to life, in its deepest registers. "It is proof of Mr. Stevenson's skill," said Andrew Lang, "that he has chosen the scene for his wild 'Tragedy of a Body and a Soul,' as it might have been called, in the most ordinary and respectable quarters of London" (*Saturday Review*, 9 January, 1886). So mundane are these men that we almost do not notice that Stevenson, as James said, always tells us less so that we may believe more. Far more than a "shilling shocker," *Dr. Jekyll and Mr. Hyde*, like Mary Braddon's *Lady Audley's Secret* or Wilkie Collins's *The Woman in White,* resonates with the strangeness of ordinary lives. Collins, noted Henry James in 1865, "introduced into fiction those most mysterious of mysteries, the mysteries which are at our own doors." To Henry Mansel the genre of "sensation" was "a tale of our own times":

> Proximity is, indeed, one great element of sensation. . . . The man who shook our hand with a hearty English grasp half an hour ago—the woman whose beauty and grace were the charm of last night, and whose gentle words sent us home better pleased with the world and with ourselves—how exciting to think that under these pleasing outsides may be concealed some demon in human shape.

Stevenson's conception persists in countless stage versions, from his day to ours. There are three famous films, as well as comic refractions in the performances of Stan Laurel, Abbott and Costello, Mighty Mouse and Bugs Bunny, Jerry Lewis and Eddie Murphy (both in *The Nutty Professor*). There are musicals, and prose retellings by Susan Sontag and Thomas Berger. Female formations have been proposed by Emma Tennant, in *Two Women of London: The Strange Case of Ms. Jekyll and Mrs. Hyde* (1989), and the film, *Dr. Jekyll and Ms. Hyde.* In 1990, Valerie Martin wrote *Mary Reilly: The Untold Story of Dr. Jekyll and Mr. Hyde,* the "diary" of Dr. Jekyll's maid (a fiction), which also became a movie, starring John Malkovich and Julia Roberts.

This endurance draws on a long tradition of dark doubles in literary imagination. Magician Prospero's words about the monster Caliban in Shakespeare's *Tempest,* "This thing of darkness I / Acknowledge mine," set the stage for the Doppelgänger (double). The dark partner has ancestors too in Faust and Macbeth, in Scots writer James Hogg's *Confessions of a Justified Sinner* (1824), Edgar Allen Poe's *William Wilson,* Nathaniel Hawthorne's *The Scarlet Letter,* and Diogenes Teufelsdröckh ("God-born devil's dung") in Carlyle's *Sartor Resartus* (1834): "In every the wisest Soul lies a whole world of internal Madness, an authentic Demon-Empire out of which, indeed, his world of Wisdom has been creatively built together, and now rests there, as on its dark foundations does a habitable flowery Earth-rind."

Shelley's *Frankenstein* (1818 and 1831) is the most apparent progenitor, as reviewers noted. Though its Creature (usually called

"Monster") is cast as separate being, in the novel's symbolic structure he shimmers as Frankenstein's double, the bearer of repressed, transgressive, violent, antisocial energies, energies that finally alienate him from human community and life itself. Popular culture reflects this status in its habit of calling the Creature "Frankenstein." Like *Frankenstein, Dr. Jekyll and Mr. Hyde* deals in heterodox scientific experimentation, man's double nature, and flight from women and domesticity. Like *Frankenstein,* Stevenson's novel is a hybrid: Gothic sensation and advanced science fiction, a child's nightmare and a reverse Pilgrim's Progress, a romance of dark rather daylight intimacies. Stevenson's novel is distinctly Victorian, however, in its psychological self-consciousness. Shelley's Frankenstein is a student enchanted by the intellectual ferment of late eighteenth-century Germany. Impelled by scientific idealism and traumatized by his mother's death, young Frankenstein means to create a being immune to destruction by disease or ordinary physical afflictions. Shocked by his handiwork, he flees in horror. In Stevenson's tale, the impulse is quite otherwise: middle-aged Dr. Jekyll sets out to create and revel in a youthful self liberated from social surveillance.

In this canny deliberation, Stevenson lays claim to the title of "the fin-de-siècle laureate of the double life," so critic Elaine Showalter dubs him. He earned his laurels on the pulse of his own experience. "If you want to realize the kind of effect he made," said Sidney Colvin,

> imagine this attenuated but extraordinarily vivid and vital presence, with something about it that at first struck you as freakish, rare, fantastic, a touch of the elfin and unearthly, a sprite, an Ariel. . . . He was a fellow of infinite and unrestrained jest and yet of infinite earnest, the one very often a mask for the other; a poet, an artist, an adventurer; a man beset with fleshly frailties, and despite his infirm health of strong appetites and unchecked curiosities; and yet a profoundly sincere moralist and preacher and son of the Covenanters after his fashion, deeply conscious of the war within his members, and deeply bent on acting up to the best he knew.

Colvin's "Stevenson" is a bit of an actor in his mask-adventures, now the sprite from *The Tempest,* now Hamlet's childhood jester Yorick. Yet the acting up was just as earnest. "The war within his members" is taken from Dr. Jekyll's lament about "the perennial war among my members." Stevenson relayed the same phrase to John Addington Symonds, as one chapter in "that damned old business of the war in the members"—not a war between social factions or even individuals, but in one body.

Symonds was an apt interlocutor, in struggle with his own, socially forbidden, homosexuality. Stevenson gave a language for this and other hidden agons, wrought of self-reflection. "From his early days in Scotland till the last chapter of his life as enacted in Samoa," writes Karl Miller (*New York Review,* 29 May 1975), "there were at least two Stevensons: the respectable and the bohemian, the successful and the delinquent." Like his author, Dr. Jekyll reports a childhood disciplined and constrained by paternal strictures: "the days of my childhood when I walked with my father's hand." Here is a social existence whose dominant syntax is conformity, duty, and propriety, whose economy is thus one of repression, of denying all but the most curtailed and meager indulgences of pleasure. And yet, the pull is of "two natures" or "polar twins" contending in consciousness: one desires and labors for social approval; the other rebels and labors to avoid social apprehension.

It's not just Jekyll's malady, and the sensation of "man's dual nature" is not just metaphysical and psychological, as Dr. Jekyll's summary "Statement of the Case" proposes. The terrain of Stevenson's novel projects "Jekyll & Hyde" less as a strange case than an uncannily familiar one, representative of society itself: the social contradictions and conditions that, as Jekyll puts it, "committed [him] to a profound duplicity of life" well before the idea of Mr. Hyde emerged. All the tensions that Stevenson traces in the world of grim, gray, proper Victorian London—between the regime of law and order and the energies of spontaneity and violence, between the devotion to work and discipline and the desire for liberty and vitality, between the code of respectability and the appetite for sensation—all these remain insoluble in daylight social existence, where they define and permeate a culture of propriety. To speculate, as Dr. Jekyll has, about sorting these enmities into discrete entities— one proper and respectable, the other wayward and hidden from exposure—is to take the measure of how fully cultural values, practices, and beliefs regulate and inhibit certain kinds of human experience, driving it underground or into alienated forms such as "Mr. Hyde." The conflict that issues into alter egos is also mapped onto the larger, encompassing social world of Victorian London, where respectable daylight streets, well-polished brasses, general cleanliness, and dull Sunday walks are closely shadowed by a nether world of back alleys, secret entrances, and cellar doorways and rumors of "Blackmail House" and "Queer Street."

In this dual geography, *The Strange Case of Dr. Jekyll and Mr. Hyde* seems not so strange after all. It is only the extremity of Dr. Jekyll's case that is so, not its contours. On the first page, we meet "Mr. Utterson the lawyer." A lawyer upholds social order and its legislations of right and wrong, crime and punishment; the biblical force of this lawyer's full name, "Gabriel John Utterson," evokes highest authority. Yet here is how the opening sentence unfolds:

> Mr. Utterson the lawyer was a man of a rugged countenance, that was never lighted by a smile; cold, scanty and embarrassed in discourse; backward in sentiment; lean, long, dusty, dreary, and yet somehow lovable. At friendly meetings, and when the wine was to his taste, something eminently human beaconed from his eye.

In this anatomy, Mr. Utterson (of "Gaunt Street," we later find out) seems a figure more of death than life, with one striking exception: the "rugged countenance, that was never lighted by a smile" can be lit by means of a drug, wine. With this drug, Mr. Utterson shows another self—indeed, a strangely "human" one.

Wine is a pervasive drug in the world of this novel, the common agent of access to humanness, sentiment, and light. Mr. Utterson pours wine for Dr. Jekyll's rattled housekeeper Mr. Poole; Dr. Lanyon is discovered sitting "alone over his wine." Utterson cherishes "a bottle of a particular old wine that had long dwelt unsunned in the foundations of the house." Exhuming it to share with his clerk (appropriately, a Mr. Guest), Utterson is inspired to utter a lyric ode to what wine releases into mellow being, amid the gray city-fogs:

> the room was gay with firelight. In the bottle the acids were long ago resolved; the imperial dye had softened with time, as the colour grows richer in stained windows; and the glow of hot autumn afternoons on hillside vineyards was ready to be set free and to disperse the fogs of London. Insensibly the lawyer melted.

Circumventing ordinary good sense, wine warms, melts, and sets free another reality.

Dr. Jekyll's drug, that transformative chemical potion, is not very different in appearance and effect: "The mixture, which was at first of a reddish hue, began, in proportion as the crystals melted, to brighten in colour, to effervesce." The "blood-red liquor," Dr. Jekyll recalls of his first ingestion, "braced and delighted me like wine"—a giddier version of the melting warmth, the release of "something human" that Utterson experiences:

> There was something strange in my sensations, something inde-scribably new and, from its very novelty, incredibly sweet. I felt younger, lighter, happier in body; within I was conscious of a heady recklessness, a current of disordered sensual images run-ning like a mill race in my fancy, a solution of the bonds of obli-gation, an unknown but not an innocent freedom of the soul.

That these effects seem strange, indescribably new, and unknown reflects the denials that constitute normal life, not just for Jekyll but for all of London's drab professional men.

Yet there is a difference between Dr. Jekyll's potion and everyone else's wine. Wine is a limited, measured indulgence (no lost week-ends in this novel). It opens islands of warmth in after-dinner hours by the fireside, but does not demand an ultimate "solution of the bonds of obligation." Mr. Utterson knows that for him, more than a little wine is a dangerous thing. The very next detail we hear of him in that opening paragraph is that "He was austere with himself; drank gin when he was alone, to mortify a taste for vintages" (wine). Utterson won't indulge his real pleasure, just a compromise that will "mortify" (deaden) desire. We get the significance of Mr. Hyde's having a "closet" (private room) "filled with wine." Utterson is a closet drinker of gin, allowing himself wine only in convivial society. Stevenson repeats the dynamic of mortifying to describe Utterson's fascination with Jekyll's activities. "It is one thing to mortify curios-ity, another to conquer it," we hear of Utterson after he receives a strange packet signed by the late Dr. Lanyon. Mortifying an insistent appetite is the pulse and flow of his existence. Continuing the sen-tence about his drinking gin instead of wine, Stevenson writes, "and though he enjoyed the theatre, had not crossed the doors of one for twenty years." Temperance is Utterson's spiritual regimen. "It was his custom" on Sunday evenings to sit with "a volume of some dry divinity" until midnight, "when he would go soberly" to bed. Recalling some past conduct, he is "raised up again into a sober and fearful gratitude by the many that he had come so near to doing, yet avoided."

Denial is vulnerable discipline, however, and compels repeated trials.

> I was born in the year 18— to a large fortune, endowed besides with excellent parts, inclined by nature to industry, fond of the respect of the wise and good among my fellow-men, and thus, as might have been supposed, with every guarantee of an honourable and distinguished future. And indeed, the worst of my faults was a certain impatient gaiety of disposition, such as has made the happiness of many, but such as I found it hard to reconcile with my imperious desire to carry my head high, and wear a more than commonly grave countenance before the public. Hence it came about that I concealed my pleasures; and that when I reached years of reflection, and began to look round me and take stock of my progress and position in the world, I stood already committed to a profound duplicity of life.

This is not Mr. Utterson's story but the opening of "Henry Jekyll's Full Statement of the Case," the novel's last chapter. By this point, such autobiography sounds more familiar than strange. Here is another inventory of proper Victorian manhood: "large fortune," "excellent parts," a character of "industry," an ethos of "respect" and social reputation. Here, too, are admissions to "concealed pleasures," censurable from the perspective of respectability, not trusted, but evoking "a morbid sense of shame." Here, too, is a self whose "impatient gaiety" is judged a fault by a more "imperious" self, the disciplinarian of an "uncommonly grave," anti-vital social persona. No wonder puns and figures of doubleness pervade Dr. Jekyll's statement, even before its confession of a manufactured second self: a "profound duplicity of life" is a life in two forms, each belying and refusing the other; "reflection" (of mind) also names self-mirroring, a sense brought into focus when Dr. Jekyll says that when he saw Mr. Hyde "in the glass, I was conscious of no repugnance, rather of a leap of welcome. This, too, was myself. In my eyes it bore a livelier image of the spirit."

This, too, is Utterson's fascination with Hyde, who evokes his own dual nature. Aware of his poise on the threshold between blameless and ill conduct, Utterson sometimes wonders, "almost with envy, at the high pressure of spirits" in the misdeeds of his friends. As if these were expression of his own inner "Mr. Hyde," he takes vicarious pleasure in their forbidden life. He does not censure them, but develops a compromise "character" to entertain them: "In this character it was frequently his fortune to be the last reputable acquaintance and the last good influence in the lives of down-going men." Utterson is the one man whose imagination is more intrigued than revolted by Mr. Hyde. More than intrigued, he is "enslaved" and "haunted" by this figure, as if he were doubling Jekyll's "strange preference or bondage." Utterson finds himself shaping a private identity—a more extreme and proactive form of the "character" in which he maintains his acquaintance with down-going men—to accommodate his haunting: "'If he be Mr. Hyde,' he had thought, 'I shall be Mr. Seek.'" What is Mr. Seek seeking? The encounter with Hyde calls up ghosts from "the corners of memory." Though "fairly blameless," these memories are blameworthy enough for Utterson to hope that his overall record of sobriety might balance "the many ill things he had done." And yet, he can't stop seeking.

Like *Frankenstein,* Stevenson's narrative does not just move us forward on the stretch of suspense (indeed, most readers now, unlike the first readers, know the secret of Mr. Hyde). The patterning is recursive as well as linear, moving our attention back and forth—from Mr. Utterson, to Mr. Hyde, to Dr. Jekyll, to Dr. Lanyon, and always to the city itself—as we hear echoes, and discern parallels and repetitions. In these relays across a world of stolid, professional, bachelor gentlemen, Dr. Jekyll's experiment comes to seem less a "strange case" than a mirror of social pathology, reported in vivid fragments from several perspectives, and drawing power from an intensifying, expanding panorama of social and psychological contradictions. London seems both the cause of Jekyll's double life and an extended figure of it. The worst fate is not unhappiness but "scandal," the death of a socially viable self: name, reputation, and public credit. This is what Mr. Hyde is threatened with, after trampling a little girl: "We told the man we could and would make such a scandal out of this, as should make his name stink from one end of London to the other. If he had any friends or any credit, we undertook that he should lose them." Just as a "name" is a social exterior, and a good name the badge of respectability and credit, so all the townhouses inhabited by these respectable men have proper front-door appearances. It is on this symbolic grammar that we "read" the syntax of Mr. Hyde's residence, where every mark spells a hiddenness, social unacceptability. Without windows and repelling all invitation (the door has neither bell nor knocker), Hyde's house bears "in every feature the marks of prolonged and sordid negligence." Its doorway hosts figures outside the patriarchal social order: "Tramps slouched into the recess"; children play on its steps, and schoolboys commit minor vandalism on the moldings; his street is a place of ragged children and foreign domestics seeking a morning glass of gin.

Just as these details name what is rejected (or kept in the back streets) by official proprieties, so Mr. Hyde's actions suggest repressed and alienated energies in the comprehensive duplicity of Victorian London. His victims are cultural icons—an angelic girl, a benign patriarch of Parliament. The fate of this last victim, moreover, suggests another world in hiding in Victorian London, a homoerotic subculture: the scene faintly suggests a horrible turn of events in a respectable MP's concealed nightlife, a miscalculated proposition turned violent, from which Utterson is quick to sense "the eddy of a scandal." When Mr. Enfield first reports to him the strange affiliation of Mr. Hyde and Dr. Jekyll, whereby Hyde is able to buy his way out of a crime, he uses dark terms to describe Hyde's hold: "Blackmail, I suppose; an honest man paying through the nose for some of the capers of his youth. Blackmail House . . . the more it looks like Queer Street, the less I ask." *Queer* was a new word in English slang for homosexual, and blackmail was a frequent peril of discovery (the word *blackmail* first arose in Scotland in the sixteenth century, linked to such accusations). Stevenson doesn't settle the case this way; but this is an intensely homosocial world. The "heroes (surely this is original) are all middle-aged professional men. No woman appears," said Andrew Lang in the *Saturday Review* (9 January 1886). Julia Wedgwood was similarly struck: "Whereas most fiction deals with the relation between man and woman, . . . no woman's name occurs in the book" (*Contemporary Review,* April 1886). In this society, Hyde produces panic, "loathing" and "repulsion," a sense of scandal, of unnamable sins. All agree on "the haunting sense of unexpressed deformity with which the fugitive impressed his beholders," and Dr. Jekyll, like Victor Frankenstein, finds himself in a demonic marriage: Hyde was an "insurgent horror . . . knit to him closer than a wife, . . . caged in his flesh." This panic is cast into relief by overt aggression against the signs of patriarchal social order. Mr. Hyde burns the letters and destroys the portrait of Dr. Jekyll's father and writes "startling blasphemies" on "a copy of pious work for which Jekyll had several times expressed a great esteem." The hostility seems to boil from the simmerings of Jekyll's "days of childhood, when I had walked with my father's hand" and "the self-denying toils of my professional life." *Kill* and *ill* are syllables hiding in *Jekyll*—as if this name were designed to suggest that Hyde's killings, real and symbolic, were aimed to do ill to the patronym. "I was conscious, even when I took the draught, of a more unbridled, a more furious propensity to ill," writes Jekyll, whose father is also a Jekyll. Is Hyde's rebellion against Dr. Jekyll also Jekyll's rebellion against his Jekyll? The alter egos are a father and a son with a difference: "Jekyll had more than a father's interest" in the "pleasures and adventures of Hyde," and "Hyde had more than a son's indifference" to Jekyll's qualms and misgivings.

In the horrors of Hyde, Stevenson may be sounding a Calvinist caution: "Hyde" is always "evil," "wicked," violent, requiring stern suppression by social stricture and individual conscience and liberated only at peril. Thus Jekyll feels an "ape-like fury" in Hyde's rages, and even when Hyde is repressed, he stirs as a caged devil or an animal licking his chops. Hyde is a Satanic enemy of reason, morality, and "the spiritual side"; he is the worst nightmare of Darwinian theory, the beast lurking within the most cultured, civilized, and rational of consciousnesses. As Jekyll puts it in his "Statement," with his identity on the verge of extinction, "I was slowly losing hold of my original and better self, and becoming slowly incorporated with my second and worse." This paradigm of better and worse is emphatic. Whatever the initial thrills, Jekyll will find no self-completion in Mr. Hyde, only the erosion of self-possession and "original" self. "Here, then, as I lay down the pen and proceed to seal up my confession, I bring the life of that unhappy Henry Jekyll to an end" are Jekyll's last words, with "seal up" suggesting self-interment, and the slip from first person ("I") to third person ("that unhappy Henry Jekyll") conveying a Jekyll that now exists only in the "statement" of writing. Heralding this loss, Dr. Jekyll laments that the terrors of Mr. Hyde are "unmanning" him, and butler Poole reports to Utterson that he once heard sounds from Jekyll's laboratory that seemed to be the weeping of a woman or a lost soul. Dr. Lanyon describes Jekyll "wrestling against the approaches of the hysteria," a "female" malady (a disease of the wandering womb, or *hyster*). Male hysterics imperil a claim to manliness. The peril is not only personal but also social: if those who meet Mr. Hyde manage to survive the encounter, it is usually to confront their own worst selves.

This is the bill of indictment. Yet the structure of repression that haunts all reactions to Mr. Hyde suggests that he is not reducible to this. He is also the agent of nostalgic fantasy: access to youth, health, natural enthusiasm, and adolescent rebelliousness. The mortifying of these energies, not only in Dr. Jekyll but in just about everybody, defines mature social rectitude, but it also seems the symptom of emotional and spiritual pathology. "Smaller, slighter, and younger" than Dr. Jekyll, Mr. Hyde reanimates Jekyll's lost youth; "He was wild when he was young; a long while ago, to be sure," Utterson remembers. Jekyll's regime of respectability has necessarily kept under wraps everything released "in the disguise of Hyde"—"the liberty, the comparative youth, the light step, leaping pulses and secret pleasures." In this perspective, Hyde seems less a demon than a more human, more lively self: "I was the first that could thus plod in the public eye with a load of genial respectability, and in a moment, like a schoolboy, strip off these lendings and spring headlong into the sea of liberty." Life in the public eye is a life of surveillance and supervision, with its boon of respectability feeling like a slow-killing burden, one that turns the pace to dull plodding under a crushing load. Jekyll's life as Hyde is a liberation from what had come to seem a false existence, composed only of artificial lendings. With a pointed pun, he sneers at Dr. Lanyon's fastidious disapproval of his "scientific heresies" as the reaction of a "hide-bound pedant," as if to say that men such as the good doctor were too unimaginative to sense, let alone liberate, their own Mr. Hydes. When Dr. Lanyon finally witnesses Jekyll's transformation into Hyde, it is too much for him; it is truly mortifying. Lanyon's fatal hysteria, and not Jekyll's impulse for finding Mr. Hyde, may be the real disease.

Although Dr. Jekyll's "Full Statement of the Case" renders a moral caution, *Dr. Jekyll and Mr. Hyde* issues more than this final judgment. Stevenson presents four different points of view: Mr. Utterson's fascination with Hyde; Mr. Enfield's fear of probing (his discomfort at being "surprised out of himself"—a telling phrase);

Dr. Lanyon's moral disapproval and collapse at the revelation of Mr. Hyde; and finally, Dr. Jekyll's own statement. While Dr. Jekyll has the last word, the novel's trajectory leaves Mr. Utterson, like Shelley's frame-narrator Robert Walton, in possession of the case and its several textual materials. Jekyll can refer only to a "nameless situation" and urge Utterson, the vehicle of future utterance, to "read the narrative" that Lanyon has written, and then to read his own "confession." As privy to this hidden history, Utterson becomes a second Hyde, a doubling suggested by Jekyll's rewriting of his will to name Utterson his heir rather than Hyde: "in the place of the name of Edward Hyde, the lawyer, with indescribable amazement, read the name of Gabriel John Utterson." The word order, Garrett Stewart observes, briefly allows "Edward Hyde, the lawyer" to seem appositive, a false syntactic cue that nonetheless yields a truth about the linking of the two in Dr. Jekyll's willful secret.

As a reader of Hyde through these several narratives, Utterson is our double. He is the investigator of this strange case, and as his name suggests, its ultimate repository, its "utterer" and heir ("son"). Like Utterson, we're left with several texts to peruse and assemble in our own self-reflection. Like Utterson, we may read ourselves in Dr. Jekyll's strange case. "Viewed as allegory, it touches one too closely," Stevenson's friend Symonds wrote to him in March 1886; "Most of us at some epoch of our lives have been upon the verge of developing a Mr. Hyde." Symonds may have been thinking of his own homosexuality, but the sense of a hidden, forbidden self is not limited to this. Tortured by theological doubts, an irrepressibly sensuous imagination, and his own unresolved sexuality, Jesuit priest and poet Gerard Manley Hopkins told his friend Robert Bridges (England's poet laureate), "You are certainly wrong about Hyde being overdrawn; my Hyde is worse." Stevenson drew the connection between the textual stimulation to these self-recognitions and the chemistry that releases Mr. Hyde when he described his appetite for popular fictions: "I take them like opium . . . a drug" (letter, February 1880). The Doctors Jekyll and Lanyon mark extremes of indulgence and inhibition, within which Utterson must figure out how to judge "Henry Jekyll's Full Statement of the Case"—not as a lawyer, but as a fellow human being, even an alter ego. "Judge for yourself" is Dr. Jekyll's plea to Dr. Lanyon. Utterson inherits this challenge, and so do we.

The Strange Case
of
Dr. Jekyll and Mr. Hyde

ॐ ॐ ॐ ॐ ॐ ॐ ॐ

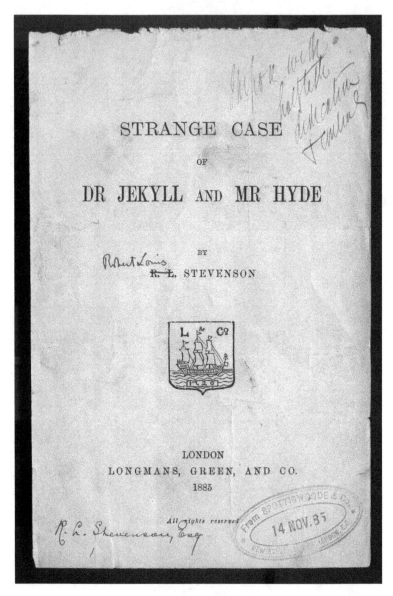

STRANGE CASE

OF

DR JEKYLL AND MR HYDE

BY

Robert Louis
~~R. L.~~ STEVENSON

LONDON
LONGMANS, GREEN, AND CO.
1885

All rights reserved

Courtesy of Rare Books and Special Collections, Princeton University Library. On Stevenson's marked page-proof, notice his changing initials to full name, and the first title: *Strange Case*. In 1886, the novel (now *The Strange Case*) was published by Charles Scribner's Sons in New York (our text) and by Longmans, Green & Co. in London. It was issued in alter-ego forms: a handsome clothbound for polite society, and an inexpensive paperback for the "shilling-shocker" market.

To
Katharine de Mattos[1]

It's ill to loose the bands that God decreed to bind;
Still will we be the children of the heather and the wind;
Far away from home, O it's still for you and me
That the broom is blowing bonnie in the north countrie.

Story of the Door[1]

MR. UTTERSON the lawyer was a man of a rugged countenance, that was never lighted by a smile; cold, scanty and embarrassed in discourse; backward in sentiment; lean, long, dusty, dreary, and yet somehow lovable. At friendly meetings, and when the wine was to his taste, something eminently human beaconed from his eye; something indeed which never found its way into his talk, but which spoke not only in these silent symbols of the after-dinner face, but more often and loudly in the acts of his life. He was austere with himself; drank gin when he was alone, to mortify a taste for vintages;[2] and though he enjoyed the theatre, had not crossed the doors of one for twenty years. But he had an approved tolerance for others; sometimes wondering, almost with envy, at the high pressure of spirits involved in their misdeeds; and in any extremity inclined to help rather than to reprove. "I incline to Cain's heresy,"[3] he used to say quaintly: "I let my brother go to the devil in his own way." In this character, it was

---

[1] Mrs. Katharine de Mattos (sister of Robert A. M. Stevenson) was a favorite cousin. Stevenson dedicated two other poems to her in *Underwoods,* and he wrote this verse for this dedication.

---

[1] In this tale of double-selves, even the words double into puns or double-meaning. The opening chapter title sets *Story* not only as a tale (an anecdote, or perhaps a calculated narrative), but also as a level of a building, here a lower storey with a door (see this use in paragraph 4).

[2] That is, he preferred wine (vintages), but killed this appetite with another kind of alcohol.

[3] Cain's retort to the Lord's question about the whereabouts of his brother Abel, whom he has murdered in a jealous rage over the preference for Abel's sacrifice (Genesis 4.8–15): "And the Lord said unto Cain, Where is Abel thy brother? And he said, I know not: Am I my brother's keeper?"

frequently his fortune to be the last reputable acquaintance and the last good influence in the lives of down-going men. And to such as these, so long as they came about his chambers, he never marked a shade of change in his demeanour.

No doubt[4] the feat was easy to Mr. Utterson; for he was undemonstrative at the best, and even his friendship seemed to be founded in a similar catholicity[5] of good-nature. It is the mark of a modest man to accept his friendly circle ready-made from the hands of opportunity; and that was the lawyer's way. His friends were those of his own blood, or those whom he had known the longest; his affections, like ivy, were the growth of time, they implied no aptness in the object. Hence, no doubt, the bond that united him to Mr. Richard Enfield, his distant kinsman, the well-known man about town. It was a nut to crack for many, what these two could see in each other, or what subject they could find in common. It was reported by those who encountered them in their Sunday walks, that they said nothing, looked singularly dull, and would hail with obvious relief the appearance of a friend. For all that, the two men put the greatest store by these excursions, counted them the chief jewel of each week, and not only set aside occasions of pleasure, but even resisted the calls of business, that they might enjoy them uninterrupted.

It chanced on one of these rambles that their way led them down a by-street in a busy quarter of London. The street was small and what is called quiet, but it drove a thriving trade on the week-days. The inhabitants were all doing well, it seemed, and all emulously hoping to do better still, and laying out the surplus of their gains in coquetry; so that the shop fronts stood along that thoroughfare with an air of invitation, like rows of smiling saleswomen. Even on Sunday, when it veiled its more florid charms and lay comparatively empty of passage, the street shone out in contrast to its dingy neighbourhood, like a fire in a forest; and with its freshly painted shutters, well-polished brasses, and general cleanliness and gaiety of note, instantly caught and pleased the eye of the passenger.

Two doors from one corner, on the left hand[6] going east, the line was broken by the entry of a court; and just at that point, a certain sinister block of building thrust forward its gable on the street.

---

[4] *Doubt* (to be of two minds) shares word-origin with *double* (both involving *duo,* Latin for *two*).

[5] Liberal inclusiveness.

[6] The Latin for *left* is *sinister* (a translingual pun soon called into play).

It was two storeys high; showed no window, nothing but a door on the lower storey and a blind forehead of discoloured wall on the upper; and bore in every feature, the marks of prolonged and sordid negligence. The door, which was equipped with neither bell nor knocker, was blistered and distained.[7] Tramps slouched into the recess and struck matches on the panels; children kept shop upon the steps; the schoolboy had tried his knife on the mouldings; and for close on a generation, no one had appeared to drive away these random visitors or to repair their ravages.

Mr. Enfield and the lawyer were on the other side of the by-street; but when they came abreast of the entry, the former lifted up his cane and pointed.

"Did you ever remark that door?" he asked; and when his companion had replied in the affirmative, "It is connected in my mind," added he, "with a very odd story."

"Indeed?" said Mr. Utterson, with a slight change of voice, "and what was that?"

"Well, it was this way," returned Mr. Enfield: "I was coming home from some place at the end of the world, about three o'clock of a black winter morning, and my way lay through a part of town where there was literally nothing to be seen but lamps. Street after street, and all the folks asleep—street after street, all lighted up as if for a procession, and all as empty as a church—till at last I got into that state of mind when a man listens and listens and begins to long for the sight of a policeman. All at once, I saw two figures: one a little man who was stumping along eastward at a good walk, and the other a girl of maybe eight or ten who was running as hard as she was able down a cross-street. Well, sir, the two ran into one another naturally enough at the corner; and then came the horrible part of the thing; for the man trampled calmly over the child's body and left her screaming on the ground. It sounds nothing to hear, but it was hellish to see. It wasn't like a man; it was like some damned Juggernaut.[8] I gave a few halloa,[9] took to my heels, collared my

---

[7] Stained, discolored; with a pun on disdained, treated with scorn.

[8] From *Jagannath*, the Hindi title of the eighth avatar of the god Vishnu; literally *Lord of the world* (*Jaga*: world + *natha*: protector), an all-destroying, inexorable force. In India, an idol of this deity was dragged annually in procession on a huge chariot, in front of which frantic devotees threw themselves, to be crushed to death. Reports of this ritual entered England in the late 1300s and circulated into the 19th century.

[9] On a foxhunt, the cry on sighting a fox.

gentleman, and brought him back to where there was already quite a group about the screaming child. He was perfectly cool and made no resistance, but gave me one look, so ugly that it brought out the sweat on me like running. The people who had turned out were the girl's own family; and pretty soon, the doctor, for whom she had been sent put in his appearance. Well, the child was not much the worse, more frightened, according to the Sawbones;[10] and there you might have supposed would be an end to it. But there was one curious circumstance. I had taken a loathing to my gentleman at first sight. So had the child's family, which was only natural. But the doctor's case was what struck me. He was the usual cut and dry apothecary, of no particular age and colour, with a strong Edinburgh accent and about as emotional as a bagpipe. Well, sir, he was like the rest of us; every time he looked at my prisoner, I saw that Sawbones turn sick and white with desire to kill him. I knew what was in his mind, just as he knew what was in mine; and killing being out of the question, we did the next best. We told the man we could and would make such a scandal out of this, as should make his name stink from one end of London to the other. If he had any friends or any credit, we undertook that he should lose them. And all the time, as we were pitching it in red hot, we were keeping the women off him as best we could for they were as wild as harpies.[11] I never saw a circle of such hateful faces; and there was the man in the middle, with a kind of black sneering coolness—frightened too, I could see that—but carrying it off, sir, really like Satan. 'If you choose to make capital out of this accident,' said he, 'I am naturally helpless. No gentleman but wishes to avoid a scene,' says he. 'Name your figure.' Well, we screwed him up to a hundred pounds for the child's family; he would have clearly liked to stick out; but there was something about the lot of us that meant mischief, and at last he struck. The next thing was to get the money; and where do you think he carried us but to that place with the door?—whipped out a key, went in, and presently came back with the matter of ten pounds in gold and a cheque for the balance on Coutts's,[12] drawn

[10] Slang: doctor (surgeon).

[11] In Greek mythology, agents of divine vengeance, with wings, claws, and a woman's face and body.

[12] A major English bank. One hundred pounds is a considerable sum.

payable to bearer and signed with a name that I can't mention, though it's one of the points of my story, but it was a name at least very well known and often printed. The figure was stiff; but the signature was good for more than that if it was only genuine. I took the liberty of pointing out to my gentleman that the whole business looked apocryphal, and that a man does not, in real life, walk into a cellar door at four in the morning and come out with another man's cheque for close upon a hundred pounds. But he was quite easy and sneering. 'Set your mind at rest,' says he, 'I will stay with you till the banks open and cash the cheque myself.' So we all set off, the doctor, and the child's father, and our friend and myself, and passed the rest of the night in my chambers; and next day, when we had breakfasted, went in a body to the bank. I gave in the cheque myself, and said I had every reason to believe it was a forgery. Not a bit of it. The cheque was genuine."

"Tut-tut," said Mr. Utterson.

"I see you feel as I do," said Mr. Enfield. "Yes, it's a bad story. For my man was a fellow that nobody could have to do with, a really damnable man; and the person that drew the cheque is the very pink of the proprieties, celebrated too, and (what makes it worse) one of your fellows who do what they call good. Black mail I suppose; an honest man paying through the nose for some of the capers of his youth. Black Mail House is what I call the place with the door, in consequence. Though even that, you know, is far from explaining all," he added, and with the words fell into a vein of musing.

From this he was recalled by Mr. Utterson asking rather suddenly: "And you don't know if the drawer of the cheque lives there?"

"A likely place, isn't it?" returned Mr. Enfield. "But I happen to have noticed his address; he lives in some square or other."

"And you never asked about the—place with the door?" said Mr. Utterson.

"No, sir: I had a delicacy," was the reply. "I feel very strongly about putting questions; it partakes too much of the style of the day of judgment. You start a question, and it's like starting a stone. You sit quietly on the top of a hill; and away the stone goes, starting others; and presently some bland old bird (the last you would have thought of) is knocked on the head in his own back garden and the family have to change their name. No sir, I make it a rule of mine: the more it looks like Queer Street,[13] the less I ask."

"A very good rule, too," said the lawyer.

"But I have studied the place for myself," continued Mr. Enfield. "It seems scarcely a house. There is no other door, and nobody goes in or out of that one but, once in a great while, the gentleman of my adventure. There are three windows looking on the court on the first floor; none below; the windows are always shut but they're clean. And then there is a chimney which is generally smoking; so somebody must live there. And yet it's not so sure; for the buildings are so packed together about the court, that it's hard to say where one ends and another begins."

The pair walked on again for a while in silence; and then— "Enfield," said Mr. Utterson, "that's a good rule of yours."

"Yes, I think it is," returned Enfield.

"But for all that," continued the lawyer, "there's one point I want to ask: I want to ask the name of that man who walked over the child."

"Well," said Mr. Enfield, "I can't see what harm it would do. It was a man of the name of Hyde."

"Hm," said Mr. Utterson. "What sort of a man is he to see?"

"He is not easy to describe. There is something wrong with his appearance; something displeasing, something down-right detestable. I never saw a man I so disliked, and yet I scarce know why. He must be deformed somewhere; he gives a strong feeling of deformity, although I couldn't specify the point. He's an extraordinary looking man, and yet I really can name nothing out of the way. No, sir; I can make no hand of it; I can't describe him. And it's not want of memory; for I declare I can see him this moment."

Mr. Utterson again walked some way in silence and obviously under a weight of consideration. "You are sure he used a key?" he inquired at last.

"My dear sir . . ." began Enfield, surprised out of himself.[14]

"Yes, I know," said Utterson; "I know it must seem strange. The fact is, if I do not ask you the name of the other party, it is because

---

[13] Slang: embarrassing situation, especially financial. Charles Dickens used the term in *Our Mutual Friend* (1865): "Queer Street is full of lodgers just at present." *Queer* was a new word in English slang for *homosexual,* and blackmail was a frequent peril (first used in the 16th c. for such accusations).

[14] This idiom is yet another image of self-division.

Fredric March in Rouben Mamoulian's *Dr. Jekyll and Mr. Hyde* (1932).

I know it already. You see, Richard, your tale has gone home. If you have been inexact in any point you had better correct it."

"I think you might have warned me," returned the other with a touch of sullenness. "But I have been pedantically exact, as you call it. The fellow had a key; and what's more, he has it still. I saw him use it not a week ago."

Mr. Utterson sighed deeply but said never a word; and the young man presently resumed. "Here is another lesson to say nothing," said he. "I am ashamed of my long tongue. Let us make a bargain never to refer to this again."

"With all my heart," said the lawyer. "I shake hands on that, Richard."

Search for Mr. Hyde[1]

THAT evening Mr. Utterson came home to his bachelor house in sombre spirits and sat down to dinner without relish. It was his custom of a Sunday, when this meal was over, to sit close by the fire, a volume of some dry divinity on his reading desk, until the clock of the neighbouring church rang out the hour of twelve, when he would go soberly and gratefully to bed. On this night however, as soon as the cloth was taken away, he took up a candle and went into his business room. There he opened his safe, took from the most private part of it a document endorsed on the envelope as Dr. Jekyll's Will, and sat down with a clouded brow to study its contents. The will was holograph,[2] for Mr. Utterson though he took charge of it now that it was made, had refused to lend the least assistance in the making of it; it provided not only that, in case of the decease of Henry Jekyll, M.D., D.C.L., L.L.D., F.R.S.,[3] etc., all his possessions were to pass into the hands of his "friend and benefactor Edward Hyde," but that in case of Dr. Jekyll's "disappearance or unexplained absence for any period exceeding three calendar months," the said Edward Hyde should step into the said Henry Jekyll's shoes without further delay, and free from any burthen or obligation, beyond the payment of a few small sums to the members of the doctor's household.[4] This document had long been the lawyer's

---

[1] A doubled syntax: *Search* may be a noun or a verb.

[2] In the signatory's own hand (not his lawyer's); this is the first mention of Dr. Jekyll and Mr. Hyde.

[3] Professional credentials: Medical Doctor, Doctor of Civil Law, Doctor of Law, Fellow of the Royal Society (of scientists).

[4] Editors Bradford Booth and Ernest Mehew (*Letters*, 5: 190n1) report that H. Rider Haggard (author of *She*) wrote to Stevenson after reading the novel to complain of only one "blot upon an attractive story": this will would never have been admitted to probate (that is, would have no legal standing).

eyesore. It offended him both as a lawyer and as a lover of the sane and customary sides of life, to whom the fanciful was the immodest. And hitherto it was his ignorance of Mr. Hyde that had swelled his indignation; now, by a sudden turn, it was his knowledge. It was already bad enough when the name was but a name of which he could learn no more. It was worse when it began to be clothed upon with detestable attributes; and out of the shifting, insubstantial mists that had so long baffled his eye, there leaped up the sudden, definite presentment of a fiend.

"I thought it was madness," he said, as he replaced the obnoxious paper in the safe, "and now I begin to fear it is disgrace."

With that he blew out his candle, put on a greatcoat, and set forth in the direction of Cavendish Square, that citadel of medicine, where his friend, the great Dr. Lanyon, had his house and received his crowding patients. "If anyone knows, it will be Lanyon," he had thought.

The solemn butler knew and welcomed him; he was subjected to no stage of delay, but ushered direct from the door to the dining-room where Dr. Lanyon sat alone over his wine. This was a hearty, healthy, dapper, red-faced gentleman, with a shock of hair prematurely white, and a boisterous and decided manner. At sight of Mr. Utterson, he sprang up from his chair and welcomed him with both hands. The geniality, as was the way of the man, was somewhat theatrical to the eye; but it reposed on genuine feeling. For these two were old friends, old mates both at school and college, both thorough respectors of themselves and of each other, and what does not always follow, men who thoroughly enjoyed each other's company.

After a little rambling talk, the lawyer led up to the subject which so disagreeably preoccupied his mind.

"I suppose, Lanyon," said he, "you and I must be the two oldest friends that Henry Jekyll has?"

"I wish the friends were younger," chuckled Dr. Lanyon. "But I suppose we are. And what of that? I see little of him now."

"Indeed?" said Utterson. "I thought you had a bond of common interest."

"We had," was the reply. "But it is more than ten years since Henry Jekyll became too fanciful for me. He began to go wrong, wrong in mind; and though of course I continue to take an interest in him for old sake's sake, as they say, I see and I have seen devilish little of the man. Such unscientific balderdash," added the doctor, flushing suddenly purple, "would have estranged Damon and Pythias."[5]

This little spirit of temper was somewhat of a relief to Mr. Utterson. "They have only differed on some point of science," he thought; and being a man of no scientific passions (except in the matter of conveyancing[6]), he even added: "It is nothing worse than that!" He gave his friend a few seconds to recover his composure, and then approached the question he had come to put. "Did you ever come across a *protégé*[7] of his—one Hyde?" he asked.

"Hyde?" repeated Lanyon. "No. Never heard of him. Since my time."

That was the amount of information that the lawyer carried back with him to the great, dark bed on which he tossed to and fro, until the small hours of the morning began to grow large. It was a night of little ease to his toiling mind, toiling in mere darkness and besieged by questions.

Six o'clock struck on the bells of the church that was so conveniently near to Mr. Utterson's dwelling, and still he was digging at the problem. Hitherto it had touched him on the intellectual side alone; but now his imagination also was engaged, or rather enslaved; and as he lay and tossed in the gross darkness of the night and the curtained room, Mr. Enfield's tale went by before his mind in a scroll of lighted pictures. He would be aware of the great field of lamps of a nocturnal city; then of the figure of a man walking swiftly; then of a child running from the doctor's; and then these met, and that human Juggernaut trod the child down and passed on regardless of her screams. Or else he would see a room in a rich house, where his friend lay asleep, dreaming and smiling at his dreams; and then the door of that room would be opened, the curtains of the bed plucked apart, the sleeper recalled, and lo! there would stand by his side a figure to whom power was given, and even at that dead hour, he must

---

[5] Classical Greek legend of exemplary friendship. When the friends visited Syracuse, Pythias was arrested and sentenced to death on trumped-up charges of spying and conspiracy against tyrant Dionysius. To allow him to return home to settle his affairs, Damon pledged his own life as security. Pythias was delayed and Damon was set for execution, but Pythias arrived in time to save him. So impressed was Dionysius by the friends' willingness to die for each other that he pardoned both.

[6] Drawing of deeds and other legal documents for the transfer of property, *conveyancing* also has a shady sense of swindling, sleight-of-hand, deceitful practice.

[7] French: one under the protection (more generally, sponsorship) of another.

rise and do its bidding.[8] The figure in these two phases haunted the lawyer all night; and if at any time he dozed over, it was but to see it glide more stealthily through sleeping houses, or move the more swiftly and still the more swiftly, even to dizziness, through wider labyrinths of lamp-lighted city, and at every street corner crush a child and leave her screaming. And still the figure had no face by which he might know it; even in his dreams, it had no face, or one that baffled him and melted before his eyes; and thus it was that there sprang up and grew apace in the lawyer's mind a singularly strong, almost an inordinate, curiosity to behold the features of the real Mr. Hyde. If he could but once set eyes on him, he thought the mystery would lighten and perhaps roll altogether away, as was the habit of mysterious things when well examined. He might see a reason for his friend's strange preference or bondage (call it which you please) and even for the startling clause of the will. At least it would be a face worth seeing: the face of a man who was without bowels of mercy: a face which had but to show itself to raise up, in the mind of the unimpressionable Enfield, a spirit of enduring hatred.

From that time forward, Mr. Utterson began to haunt the door in the by-street of shops. In the morning before office hours, at noon when business was plenty, and time scarce, at night under the face of the fogged city moon, by all lights and at all hours of solitude or concourse, the lawyer was to be found on his chosen post.

"If he be Mr. Hyde," he had thought, "I shall be Mr. Seek."

And at last his patience was rewarded. It was a fine dry night; frost in the air; the streets as clean as a ballroom floor; the lamps, unshaken by any wind, drawing a regular pattern of light and shadow. By ten o'clock, when the shops were closed the by-street was very solitary, in spite of the low growl of London from all round, very silent. Small sounds carried far; domestic sounds out of the houses were clearly audible on either side of the roadway; and the rumour of the approach of any passenger preceded him by a long time. Mr. Utterson had been some minutes at his post, when he was aware of an odd light footstep drawing near. In the course of

---

[8] This recalls a famous scene in *Frankenstein,* another tale of unorthodox science. Having fled his laboratory in horror at his Creature, Frankenstein faints away into sleep in his bedchamber, only to be interrupted: "by the dim and yellow light of the moon, as it forced its way through the window shutters, I beheld the wretch—the miserable monster whom I had created. He held up the curtain of the bed; and his eyes, if eyes they may be called, were fixed on me. . . . one hand was stretched out, seemingly to detain me" (1831, ch. 5).

his nightly patrols, he had long grown accustomed to the quaint effect with which the footfalls of a single person, while he is still a great way off, suddenly spring out distinct from the vast hum and clatter of the city. Yet his attention had never before been so sharply and decisively arrested; and it was with a strong, superstitious prevision of success that he withdrew into the entry of the court.

The steps drew swiftly nearer, and swelled out suddenly louder as they turned the end of the street. The lawyer, looking forth from the entry, could soon see what manner of man he had to deal with. He was small and very plainly dressed and the look of him, even at that distance, went somehow strongly against the watcher's inclination. But he made straight for the door, crossing the roadway to save time; and as he came, he drew a key from his pocket, like one approaching home.

Mr. Utterson stepped out and touched him on the shoulder as he passed. "Mr. Hyde, I think?"

Mr. Hyde shrank back with a hissing intake of the breath. But his fear was only momentary; and though he did not look the lawyer in the face, he answered coolly enough: "That is my name. What do you want?"

"I see you are going in," returned the lawyer. "I am an old friend of Dr. Jekyll's—Mr. Utterson of Gaunt Street—you must have heard of my name; and meeting you so conveniently, I thought you might admit me."

"You will not find Dr. Jekyll; he is from home," replied Mr. Hyde, blowing in the key. And then suddenly, but still without looking up, "How did you know me?" he asked.

"On your side," said Mr. Utterson, "will you do me a favour?"

"With pleasure," replied the other. "What shall it be?"

"Will you let me see your face?" asked the lawyer.

Mr. Hyde appeared to hesitate, and then, as if upon some sudden reflection, fronted about with an air of defiance; and the pair stared at each other pretty fixedly for a few seconds. "Now I shall know you again," said Mr. Utterson. "It may be useful."

"Yes," returned Mr. Hyde, "It is as well we have met; and *à propos*,[9] you should have my address." And he gave a number of a street in Soho.[10]

"Good God!" thought Mr. Utterson, "can he, too, have been thinking of the will?" But he kept his feelings to himself and only grunted in acknowledgment of the address.

[9] Latin: *to the purpose; at the right time.*
[10] Disreputable London district.

"And now," said the other, "how did you know me?"

"By description," was the reply.

"Whose description?"

"We have common friends," said Mr. Utterson.

"Common friends," echoed Mr. Hyde, a little hoarsely. "Who are they?"

"Jekyll, for instance," said the lawyer.

"He never told you," cried Mr. Hyde, with a flush of anger. "I did not think you would have lied."

"Come," said Mr. Utterson, "that is not fitting language."

The other snarled aloud into a savage laugh; and the next moment, with extraordinary quickness, he had unlocked the door and disappeared into the house.

The lawyer stood awhile when Mr. Hyde had left him, the picture of disquietude. Then he began slowly to mount the street, pausing every step or two and putting his hand to his brow like a man in mental perplexity. The problem he was thus debating as he walked, was one of a class that is rarely solved. Mr. Hyde was pale and dwarfish, he gave an impression of deformity without any nameable malformation, he had a displeasing smile, he had borne himself to the lawyer with a sort of murderous mixture of timidity and boldness, and he spoke with a husky, whispering and somewhat broken voice; all these were points against him, but not all of these together could explain the hitherto unknown disgust, loathing and fear with which Mr. Utterson regarded him. "There must be something else," said the perplexed gentleman. "There is something more, if I could find a name for it. God bless me, the man seems hardly human! Something troglodytic,[11] shall we say? or can it be the old story of Dr. Fell?[12] or is it the mere radiance of a foul soul that thus transpires through, and transfigures, its clay continent?

---

[11] Unsocialized, reclusive, brutish. The word stems from the Greek *trogle* (hole, cave) and *dyein* (to enter), referring to primitive cave-dwellers, evoking Mr. Utterson's "digging at the problem" (p. 70, above), and the Darwinian suggestion of a primitive self within, just under the veneer of civilization: "Perhaps we shall not be far wrong if we regard Troglodytism as the primitive state of all mankind" (*Chambers' Encyclopedia*, 1867).

[12] Dr. John Fell (1625–1686), English doctor, prelate, dean of Christ Church, Oxford, offered to cancel a sentence of expulsion on Thomas Brown (1663–1704) if he could translate extempore Martial's 23rd epigram: "*Non amo te, Sabidi, nec possum dicere quare; / Hoc tantum possum non amo te*" (I do not love you, Sabidi, nor can I say why; / This much I can—I do not love you). Brown's quatrain became famous: "I do not love thee Dr. Fell, / The reason why I cannot tell; / But this I know, and know full well, / I do not love thee Dr. Fell."

The last, I think; for, O my poor old Harry[13] Jekyll, if ever I read Satan's signature upon a face, it is on that of your new friend."

Round the corner from the by-street, there was a square of ancient, handsome houses, now for the most part decayed from their high estate and let in flats and chambers to all sorts and conditions of men; map-engravers, architects, shady lawyers and the agents of obscure enterprises. One house, however, second from the corner, was still occupied entire; and at the door of this, which wore a great air of wealth and comfort, though it was now plunged in darkness except for the fanlight,[14] Mr. Utterson stopped and knocked. A well-dressed, elderly servant opened the door.

"Is Dr. Jekyll at home, Poole?"[15] asked the lawyer.

"I will see, Mr. Utterson," said Poole, admitting the visitor, as he spoke, into a large, low-roofed, comfortable hall paved with flags, warmed (after the fashion of a country house) by a bright, open fire, and furnished with costly cabinets of oak. "Will you wait here by the fire, sir? or shall I give you a light in the dining-room?"

"Here, thank you," said the lawyer, and he drew near and leaned on the tall fender. This hall, in which he was now left alone, was a pet fancy of his friend the doctor's; and Utterson himself was wont to speak of it as the pleasantest room in London. But tonight there was a shudder in his blood; the face of Hyde sat heavy on his memory; he felt (what was rare with him) a nausea and distaste of life; and in the gloom of his spirits, he seemed to read a menace in the flickering of the firelight on the polished cabinets and the uneasy starting of the shadow on the roof. He was ashamed of his relief, when Poole presently returned to announce that Dr. Jekyll was gone out.

"I saw Mr. Hyde go in by the old dissecting room, Poole," he said. "Is that right, when Dr. Jekyll is from home?"

"Quite right, Mr. Utterson, sir," replied the servant. "Mr. Hyde has a key."

"Your master seems to repose a great deal of trust in that young man, Poole," resumed the other musingly.

"Yes, sir, he does indeed," said Poole. "We have all orders to obey him."

---

[13] Slang: the devil.

[14] Semicircular window (like an open fan) above the door.

[15] In Charlotte Brontë's *Jane Eyre* (1847), Grace Poole is the warden of Bertha Mason, Edward Rochester's mad wife, secretly lodged in the attic of Thornfield Hall.

"I do not think I ever met Mr. Hyde?" asked Utterson.

"O, dear no, sir. He never *dines* here," replied the butler. "Indeed we see very little of him on this side of the house; he mostly comes and goes by the laboratory."

"Well, good-night, Poole."

"Good-night, Mr. Utterson."

And the lawyer set out homeward with a very heavy heart. "Poor Harry Jekyll," he thought, "my mind misgives me he is in deep waters! He was wild when he was young; a long while ago to be sure; but in the law of God, there is no statute of limitations. Ay, it must be that; the ghost of some old sin, the cancer of some concealed disgrace: punishment coming, *pede claudo,*[16] years after memory has forgotten and self-love condoned the fault." And the lawyer, scared by the thought, brooded awhile on his own past, groping in all the corners of memory, lest by chance some Jack-in-the-Box of an old iniquity should leap to light there. His past was fairly blameless; few men could read the rolls of their life with less apprehension; yet he was humbled to the dust by the many ill things he had done, and raised up again into a sober and fearful gratitude by the many he had come so near to doing yet avoided. And then by a return on his former subject, he conceived a spark of hope. "This Master Hyde, if he were studied," thought he, "must have secrets of his own; black secrets, by the look of him; secrets compared to which poor Jekyll's worst would be like sunshine. Things cannot continue as they are. It turns me cold to think of this creature stealing like a thief to Harry's bedside; poor Harry, what a wakening! And the danger of it; for if this Hyde suspects the existence of the will, he may grow impatient to inherit. Ay, I must put my shoulders to the wheel—if Jekyll will but let me," he added, "if Jekyll will only let me." For once more he saw before his mind's eye, as clear as transparency, the strange clauses of the will.

Dr. Jekyll Was Quite at Ease

A FORTNIGHT later, by excellent good fortune, the doctor gave one of his pleasant dinners to some five or six old cronies, all intelligent, reputable men and all judges of good wine; and Mr. Utterson so contrived that he remained behind after the others had departed. This was no new arrangement, but a thing that had befallen many

[16] Latin: "on halting foot" (slowly, but surely).

scores of times. Where Utterson was liked, he was liked well. Hosts loved to detain the dry lawyer, when the light-hearted and loose-tongued had already their foot on the threshold; they liked to sit a while in his unobtrusive company, practising for solitude, sobering their minds in the man's rich silence after the expense and strain of gaiety. To this rule, Dr. Jekyll was no exception; and as he now sat on the opposite side of the fire—a large, well-made, smooth-faced man of fifty, with something of a stylish cast perhaps, but every mark of capacity and kindness—you could see by his looks that he cherished for Mr. Utterson a sincere and warm affection.

"I have been wanting to speak to you, Jekyll," began the latter. "You know that will of yours?"

A close observer might have gathered that the topic was distasteful; but the doctor carried it off gaily. "My poor Utterson," said he, "you are unfortunate in such a client. I never saw a man so distressed as you were by my will; unless it were that hide-bound pedant, Lanyon, at what he called my scientific heresies. O, I know he's a good fellow—you needn't frown—an excellent fellow, and I always mean to see more of him; but a hide-bound pedant for all that; an ignorant, blatant pedant. I was never more disappointed in any man than Lanyon."

"You know I never approved of it," pursued Utterson, ruthlessly disregarding the fresh topic.

"My will? Yes, certainly, I know that," said the doctor, a trifle sharply. "You have told me so."

"Well, I tell you so again," continued the lawyer. "I have been learning something of young Hyde."

The large handsome face of Dr. Jekyll grew pale to the very lips, and there came a blackness about his eyes. "I do not care to hear more," said he. "This is a matter I thought we had agreed to drop."

"What I heard was abominable," said Utterson.

"It can make no change. You do not understand my position," returned the doctor, with a certain incoherency of manner. "I am painfully situated, Utterson; my position is a very strange—a very strange one. It is one of those affairs that cannot be mended by talking."

"Jekyll," said Utterson, "you know me: I am a man to be trusted. Make a clean breast of this in confidence; and I make no doubt I can get you out of it."

"My good Utterson," said the doctor, "this is very good of you, this is downright good of you, and I cannot find words to thank you in. I believe you fully; I would trust you before any man alive, ay, before myself, if I could make the choice; but indeed it isn't what you fancy; it is not as bad as that; and just to put your good heart at rest, I will tell you one thing: the moment I choose, I can be rid of Mr. Hyde. I give you my hand upon that; and I thank you again and again; and I will just add one little word, Utterson, that I'm sure you'll take in good part: this is a private matter, and I beg of you to let it sleep."

Utterson reflected a little, looking in the fire.

"I have no doubt you are perfectly right," he said at last, getting to his feet.

"Well, but since we have touched upon this business, and for the last time I hope," continued the doctor, "there is one point I should like you to understand. I have really a very great interest in poor Hyde. I know you have seen him; he told me so; and I fear he was rude. But I do sincerely take a great, a very great interest in that young man; and if I am taken away, Utterson, I wish you to promise me that you will bear with him and get his rights for him. I think you would, if you knew all; and it would be a weight off my mind if you would promise."

"I can't pretend that I shall ever like him," said the lawyer.

"I don't ask that," pleaded Jekyll, laying his hand upon the other's arm; "I only ask for justice; I only ask you to help him for my sake, when I am no longer here."

Utterson heaved an irrepressible sigh. "Well," said he, "I promise."

The Carew Murder Case

NEARLY a year later, in the month of October, 18—, London was startled by a crime of singular ferocity and rendered all the more notable by the high position of the victim. The details were few and startling. A maid servant living alone in a house not far from the river, had gone upstairs to bed about eleven. Although a fog rolled over the city in the small hours, the early part of the night was cloudless, and the lane, which the maid's window overlooked, was brilliantly lit by the full moon. It seems she was romantically given, for she sat down upon her box, which stood immediately under the window, and fell into a dream of musing. Never (she used to say, with streaming tears, when she narrated that experience), never had she felt more at peace with all men or thought more kindly of the world. And as she so sat she became aware of an aged beautiful gentleman with white hair, drawing near along the lane; and advancing to meet him, another and very small gentleman, to whom at first she paid less attention. When they had come within speech (which was just under the maid's eyes) the older man bowed and accosted[1] the other with a very pretty manner of politeness. It did not seem as if the subject of his address were of great importance; indeed, from his pointing, it some times appeared as if he were only inquiring his way; but the moon shone on his face as he spoke, and the girl was pleased to watch it, it seemed to breathe such an innocent and old-world kindness of disposition, yet with something high too, as of a well-founded self-content. Presently her eye wandered to the other, and she was surprised to recognise in him a certain Mr. Hyde, who had once visited her master and for whom she had conceived a dislike. He had in his hand a heavy cane, with which he was trifling; but he answered never a word, and seemed to listen with an ill-contained impatience. And then all of a sudden he broke out in a great flame of anger, stamping with his foot, brandishing the cane, and carrying on (as the maid described it) like a madman. The old gentleman took a step back, with the air of one very much surprised and a trifle hurt; and at that Mr. Hyde broke out of all bounds and clubbed him to the earth. And next moment, with ape-like fury, he was trampling his victim under foot and hailing down a storm of blows, under which the bones were audibly shattered and the body jumped upon the roadway. At the horror of these sights and sounds, the maid fainted.

It was two o'clock when she came to herself[2] and called for the police. The murderer was gone long ago; but there lay his victim in the middle of the lane, incredibly mangled. The stick with which the deed had been done, although it was of some rare and very tough and heavy wood, had broken in the middle under the stress of this insensate cruelty; and one splintered half had rolled in the neighbouring gutter—the other, without doubt, had been carried away by the murderer. A purse and gold watch were found upon the victim: but no cards or papers, except a sealed and stamped envelope, which he had been probably carrying to the post, and which bore the name and address of Mr. Utterson.

[1] Addressed.

[2] It is as if she had been divided from herself by the force of Hyde.

Mr. Hyde's Murder of Sir Danvers Carew, from the First Illustrated Edition.

This was brought to the lawyer the next morning, before he was out of bed; and he had no sooner seen it and been told the circumstances, than he shot out a solemn lip. "I shall say nothing till I have seen the body," said he; "this may be very serious. Have the kindness to wait while I dress." And with the same grave countenance he hurried through his breakfast and drove to the police station, whither the body had been carried. As soon as he came into the cell, he nodded.

"Yes," said he, "I recognise him. I am sorry to say that this is Sir Danvers Carew."

"Good God, sir," exclaimed the officer, "is it possible?" And the next moment his eye lighted up with professional ambition. "This will make a deal of noise," he said. "And perhaps you can help us to the man." And he briefly narrated what the maid had seen, and showed the broken stick.

Mr. Utterson had already quailed at the name of Hyde; but when the stick was laid before him, he could doubt no longer; broken and battered as it was, he recognized it for one that he had himself presented many years before to Henry Jekyll.

"Is this Mr. Hyde a person of small stature?" he inquired.

"Particularly small and particularly wicked-looking, is what the maid calls him," said the officer.

Mr. Utterson reflected; and then, raising his head, "If you will come with me in my cab," he said, "I think I can take you to his house."

It was by this time about nine in the morning, and the first fog of the season. A great chocolate-coloured pall lowered over heaven, but the wind was continually charging and routing these embattled vapours; so that as the cab crawled from street to street, Mr. Utterson beheld a marvelous number of degrees and hues of twilight; for here it would be dark like the back-end of evening; and there would be a glow of a rich, lurid brown, like the light of some strange conflagration; and here, for a moment, the fog would be quite broken up, and a haggard shaft of daylight would glance in between the swirling wreaths. The dismal quarter of Soho seen under these changing glimpses, with its muddy ways, and slatternly passengers, and its lamps, which had never been extinguished or had been kindled afresh to combat this mournful reinvasion of darkness, seemed, in the lawyer's eyes, like a district of some city in a nightmare. The thoughts of his mind, besides, were of the gloomiest dye; and when he glanced at the companion of his drive, he was conscious of some touch of that terror of the law and the law's officers, which may at times assail the most honest.

As the cab drew up before the address indicated, the fog lifted a little and showed him a dingy street, a gin palace, a low French eating house, a shop for the retail of penny numbers[3] and twopenny salads, many ragged children huddled in the doorways, and many women of many different nationalities passing out, key in hand, to have a morning glass;[4] and the next moment the fog settled down

---

[3] The "penny dreadfuls" were cheap, mass-market magazines plump with sensation-fiction and lurid scandals.

[4] Some alcoholic drink.

again upon that part, as brown as umber, and cut him off from his blackguardly surroundings. This was the home of Henry Jekyll's favourite; of a man who was heir to a quarter of a million sterling.

An ivory-faced and silvery-haired old woman opened the door. She had an evil face, smoothed by hypocrisy: but her manners were excellent. Yes, she said, this was Mr. Hyde's, but he was not at home; he had been in that night very late, but he had gone away again in less than an hour; there was nothing strange in that; his habits were very irregular, and he was often absent; for instance, it was nearly two months since she had seen him till yesterday.

"Very well, then, we wish to see his rooms," said the lawyer; and when the woman began to declare it was impossible, "I had better tell you who this person is," he added. "This is Inspector Newcomen of Scotland Yard."

A flash of odious joy appeared upon the woman's face. "Ah!" said she, "he is in trouble! What has he done?"

Mr. Utterson and the inspector exchanged glances. "He don't seem a very popular character," observed the latter. "And now, my good woman, just let me and this gentleman have a look about us."

In the whole extent of the house, which but for the old woman remained otherwise empty, Mr. Hyde had only used a couple of rooms; but these were furnished with luxury and good taste. A closet[5] was filled with wine; the plate was of silver, the napery[6] elegant; a good picture hung upon the walls, a gift (as Utterson supposed) from Henry Jekyll, who was much of a connoisseur; and the carpets were of many plies and agreeable in colour. At this moment, however, the rooms bore every mark of having been recently and hurriedly ransacked; clothes lay about the floor, with their pockets inside out; lock-fast drawers stood open; and on the hearth there lay a pile of grey ashes, as though many papers had been burned. From these embers the inspector disinterred the butt end of a green cheque book, which had resisted the action of the fire; the other half of the stick was found behind the door; and as this clinched his suspicions, the officer declared himself delighted. A visit to the bank, where several thousand pounds were found to be lying to the murderer's credit, completed his gratification.

"You may depend upon it, sir," he told Mr. Utterson: "I have him in my hand. He must have lost his head, or he never would

[5] Small, private room.
[6] Table linens.

have left the stick or, above all, burned the cheque book. Why, money's life to the man. We have nothing to do but wait for him at the bank, and get out the handbills."

This last, however, was not so easy of accomplishment; for Mr. Hyde had numbered few familiars—even the master of the servant maid had only seen him twice; his family could nowhere be traced; he had never been photographed; and the few who could describe him differed widely, as common observers will. Only on one point were they agreed; and that was the haunting sense of unexpressed deformity with which the fugitive impressed his beholders.

Incident of the Letter

It was late in the afternoon, when Mr. Utterson found his way to Dr. Jekyll's door, where he was at once admitted by Poole, and carried down by the kitchen offices and across a yard which had once been a garden, to the building which was indifferently known as the laboratory or dissecting rooms. The doctor had bought the house from the heirs of a celebrated surgeon; and his own tastes being rather chemical than anatomical, had changed the destination of the block at the bottom of the garden. It was the first time that the lawyer had been received in that part of his friend's quarters; and he eyed the dingy, windowless structure with curiosity, and gazed round with a distasteful sense of strangeness as he crossed the theatre, once crowded with eager students and now lying gaunt and silent, the tables laden with chemical apparatus, the floor strewn with crates and littered with packing straw, and the light falling dimly through the foggy cupola. At the further end, a flight of stairs mounted to a door covered with red baize; and through this, Mr. Utterson was at last received into the doctor's cabinet.[1] It was a large room fitted round with glass presses, furnished, among other things, with a cheval-glass[2] and a business table, and looking out upon the court by three dusty windows barred with iron. The fire burned in the grate; a lamp was set lighted on the chimney shelf, for even in the houses the fog began to lie thickly; and there, close up to the warmth, sat Dr. Jekyll, looking deathly sick. He did not rise to meet his visitor, but held out a cold hand and bade him welcome in a changed voice.

[1] Private room.
[2] A full-length mirror hinged to a frame, so that it can be tilted up or down.

"And now," said Mr. Utterson, as soon as Poole had left them, "you have heard the news?"

The doctor shuddered. "They[3] were crying it in the square," he said. "I heard them in my dining-room."

"One word," said the lawyer. "Carew was my client, but so are you, and I want to know what I am doing. You have not been mad enough to hide this fellow?"

"Utterson, I swear to God," cried the doctor, "I swear to God I will never set eyes on him again. I bind my honour to you that I am done with him in this world. It is all at an end. And indeed he does not want my help; you do not know him as I do; he is safe, he is quite safe; mark my words, he will never more be heard of."

The lawyer listened gloomily; he did not like his friend's feverish manner. "You seem pretty sure of him," said he; "and for your sake, I hope you may be right. If it came to a trial, your name might appear."

"I am quite sure of him," replied Jekyll; "I have grounds for certainty that I cannot share with any one. But there is one thing on which you may advise me. I have—I have received a letter; and I am at a loss whether I should show it to the police. I should like to leave it in your hands, Utterson; you would judge wisely, I am sure; I have so great a trust in you."

"You fear, I suppose, that it might lead to his detection?" asked the lawyer.

"No," said the other. "I cannot say that I care what becomes of Hyde; I am quite done with him. I was thinking of my own character, which this hateful business has rather exposed."

Utterson ruminated awhile; he was surprised at his friend's selfishness, and yet relieved by it. "Well," said he, at last, "let me see the letter."

The letter was written in an odd, upright hand and signed "Edward Hyde": and it signified, briefly enough, that the writer's benefactor, Dr. Jekyll, whom he had long so unworthily repaid for a thousand generosities, need labour under no alarm for his safety, as he had means of escape on which he placed a sure dependence. The lawyer liked this letter well enough; it put a better colour on the intimacy than he had looked for; and he blamed himself for some of his past suspicions.

---

[3] Sellers of newspapers.

"Have you the envelope?" he asked.

"I burned it," replied Jekyll, "before I thought what I was about. But it bore no postmark. The note was handed in."

"Shall I keep this and sleep upon it?" asked Utterson.

"I wish you to judge for me entirely," was the reply. "I have lost confidence in myself."

"Well, I shall consider," returned the lawyer. "And now one word more: it was Hyde who dictated the terms in your will about that disappearance?"

The doctor seemed seized with a qualm of faintness; he shut his mouth tight and nodded.

"I knew it," said Utterson. "He meant to murder you. You had a fine escape."

"I have had what is far more to the purpose," returned the doctor solemnly: "I have had a lesson—O God, Utterson, what a lesson I have had!" And he covered his face for a moment with his hands.

On his way out, the lawyer stopped and had a word or two with Poole. "By the bye," said he, "there was a letter handed in to-day: what was the messenger like?" But Poole was positive nothing had come except by post; "and only circulars[4] by that," he added.

This news sent off the visitor with his fears renewed. Plainly the letter had come by the laboratory door; possibly, indeed, it had been written in the cabinet; and if that were so, it must be differently judged, and handled with the more caution. The newsboys, as he went, were crying themselves hoarse along the footways: "Special edition. Shocking murder of an M.P."[5] That was the funeral oration of one friend and client; and he could not help a certain apprehension lest the good name of another should be sucked down in the eddy of the scandal. It was, at least, a ticklish decision that he had to make; and self-reliant as he was by habit, he began to cherish a longing for advice. It was not to be had directly; but perhaps, he thought, it might be fished for.

Presently after, he sat on one side of his own hearth, with Mr. Guest, his head clerk, upon the other, and midway between, at a nicely calculated distance from the fire, a bottle of a particular old wine that had long dwelt unsunned in the foundations of his house. The fog still slept on the wing above the drowned city, where the

[4] Advertisements.

[5] Member of Parliament.

lamps glimmered like carbuncles;[6] and through the muffle and smother of these fallen clouds, the procession of the town's life was still rolling in through the great arteries with a sound as of a mighty wind. But the room was gay with firelight. In the bottle the acids were long ago resolved; the imperial dye had softened with time, as the colour grows richer in stained windows; and the glow of hot autumn afternoons on hillside vineyards, was ready to be set free and to disperse the fogs of London. Insensibly the lawyer melted. There was no man from whom he kept fewer secrets than Mr. Guest; and he was not always sure that he kept as many as he meant. Guest had often been on business to the doctor's; he knew Poole; he could scarce have failed to hear of Mr. Hyde's familiarity about the house; he might draw conclusions: was it not as well, then, that he should see a letter which put that mystery to right? and above all since Guest, being a great student and critic of handwriting, would consider the step natural and obliging? The clerk, besides, was a man of counsel; he could scarce read so strange a document without dropping a remark; and by that remark Mr. Utterson might shape his future course.

"This is a sad business about Sir Danvers," he said.

"Yes, sir, indeed. It has elicited a great deal of public feeling," returned Guest. "The man, of course, was mad."

"I should like to hear your views on that," replied Utterson. "I have a document here in his handwriting; it is between ourselves, for I scarce know what to do about it; it is an ugly business at the best. But there it is; quite in your way: a murderer's autograph."

Guest's eyes brightened, and he sat down at once and studied it with passion. "No sir," he said: "not mad; but it is an odd hand."

"And by all accounts a very odd writer," added the lawyer.

Just then the servant entered with a note.

"Is that from Dr. Jekyll, sir?" inquired the clerk. "I thought I knew the writing. Anything private, Mr. Utterson?"

"Only an invitation to dinner. Why? Do you want to see it?"

"One moment. I thank you, sir;" and the clerk laid the two sheets of paper alongside and sedulously compared their contents. "Thank you, sir," he said at last, returning both; "it's a very interesting autograph."

There was a pause, during which Mr. Utterson struggled with himself. "Why did you compare them, Guest?" he inquired suddenly.

---

[6] A ruby-like gem fabled to emit light.

"Well, sir," returned the clerk, "there's a rather singular resemblance; the two hands are in many points identical: only differently sloped."

"Rather quaint," said Utterson.

"It is, as you say, rather quaint," returned Guest.

"I wouldn't speak of this note, you know," said the master.

"No, sir," said the clerk. "I understand."

But no sooner was Mr. Utterson alone that night, than he locked the note into his safe, where it reposed from that time forward. "What!" he thought. "Henry Jekyll forge for a murderer!" And his blood ran cold in his veins.

Incident of Dr. Lanyon

TIME ran on; thousands of pounds were offered in reward, for the death of Sir Danvers was resented as a public injury; but Mr. Hyde had disappeared out of the ken of the police as though he had never existed. Much of his past was unearthed, indeed, and all disreputable: tales came out of the man's cruelty, at once so callous and violent; of his vile life, of his strange associates, of the hatred that seemed to have surrounded his career; but of his present whereabouts, not a whisper. From the time he had left the house in Soho on the morning of the murder, he was simply blotted out; and gradually, as time drew on, Mr. Utterson began to recover from the hotness of his alarm, and to grow more at quiet with himself. The death of Sir Danvers was, to his way of thinking, more than paid for by the disappearance of Mr. Hyde. Now that that evil influence had been withdrawn, a new life began for Dr. Jekyll. He came out of his seclusion, renewed relations with his friends, became once more their familiar guest and entertainer; and whilst he had always been known for charities, he was now no less distinguished for religion. He was busy, he was much in the open air, he did good; his face seemed to open and brighten, as if with an inward consciousness of service; and for more than two months, the doctor was at peace.

On the 8th of January Utterson had dined at the doctor's with a small party; Lanyon had been there; and the face of the host had looked from one to the other as in the old days when the trio were inseparable friends. On the 12th, and again on the 14th, the door was shut against the lawyer. "The doctor was confined to the house," Poole said, "and saw no one." On the 15th, he tried again, and was again refused; and having now been used for the last two months to see his friend almost daily, he found this return of solitude to weigh upon his spirits. The fifth night he had in Guest to dine with him; and the sixth he betook himself to Dr. Lanyon's.

There at least he was not denied admittance; but when he came in, he was shocked at the change which had taken place in the doctor's appearance. He had his death-warrant written legibly upon his face. The rosy man had grown pale; his flesh had fallen away; he was visibly balder and older; and yet it was not so much these tokens of a swift physical decay that arrested the lawyer's notice, as a look in the eye and quality of manner that seemed to testify to some deep-seated terror of the mind. It was unlikely that the doctor should fear death; and yet that was what Utterson was tempted to suspect. "Yes," he thought; "he is a doctor, he must know his own state and that his days are counted; and the knowledge is more than he can bear." And yet when Utterson remarked on his ill-looks, it was with an air of great firmness that Lanyon declared himself a doomed man.

"I have had a shock," he said, "and I shall never recover. It is a question of weeks. Well, life has been pleasant; I liked it; yes, sir, I used to like it. I sometimes think if we knew all, we should be more glad to get away."

"Jekyll is ill, too," observed Utterson. "Have you seen him?"

But Lanyon's face changed, and he held up a trembling hand. "I wish to see or hear no more of Dr. Jekyll," he said in a loud, unsteady voice. "I am quite done with that person; and I beg that you will spare me any allusion to one whom I regard as dead."

"Tut-tut," said Mr. Utterson; and then after a considerable pause, "Can't I do anything?" he inquired. "We are three very old friends, Lanyon; we shall not live to make others."

"Nothing can be done," returned Lanyon; "ask himself."

"He will not see me," said the lawyer.

"I am not surprised at that," was the reply. "Some day, Utterson, after I am dead, you may perhaps come to learn the right and wrong of this. I cannot tell you. And in the meantime, if you can sit and talk with me of other things, for God's sake, stay and do so; but if you cannot keep clear of this accursed topic, then in God's name, go, for I cannot bear it."

As soon as he got home, Utterson sat down and wrote to Jekyll, complaining of his exclusion from the house, and asking the cause of this unhappy break with Lanyon; and the next day brought him a long answer, often very pathetically worded, and sometimes darkly mysterious in drift. The quarrel with Lanyon was incurable. "I do not blame our old friend," Jekyll wrote, "but I share his view that we must never meet. I mean from henceforth to lead a life of extreme seclusion; you must not be surprised, nor must you doubt my friendship, if my door is often shut even to you. You must suffer me to go my own dark way. I have brought on myself a punishment and a danger that I cannot name. If I am the chief of sinners, I am the chief of sufferers also. I could not think that this earth contained a place for sufferings and terrors so unmanning; and you can do but one thing, Utterson, to lighten this destiny, and that is to respect my silence." Utterson was amazed; the dark influence of Hyde had been withdrawn, the doctor had returned to his old tasks and amities; a week ago, the prospect had smiled with every promise of a cheerful and an honoured age; and now in a moment, friendship, and peace of mind, and the whole tenor of his life were wrecked. So great and unprepared a change pointed to madness; but in view of Lanyon's manner and words, there must lie for it some deeper ground.

A week afterwards Dr. Lanyon took to his bed, and in something less than a fortnight he was dead. The night after the funeral, at which he had been sadly affected, Utterson locked the door of his business room, and sitting there by the light of a melancholy candle, drew out and set before him an envelope addressed by the hand and sealed with the seal of his dead friend. "PRIVATE: for the hands of G. J. Utterson ALONE, and in case of his predecease to be destroyed unread," so it was emphatically superscribed; and the lawyer dreaded to behold the contents. "I have buried one friend to-day," he thought: "what if this should cost me another?" And then he condemned the fear as a disloyalty, and broke the seal. Within there was another enclosure, likewise sealed, and marked upon the cover as "not to be opened till the death or disappearance of Dr. Henry Jekyll." Utterson could not trust his eyes. Yes, it was disappearance; here again, as in the mad will which he had long ago restored to its author, here again were the idea of a disappearance and the name of Henry Jekyll bracketed. But in the will, that idea had sprung from the sinister suggestion of the man Hyde; it was set there with a purpose all too plain and horrible. Written by the hand of Lanyon, what should it mean? A great curiosity came on the trustee, to disregard the prohibition and dive at once to the bottom of these mysteries; but professional honour and faith to his dead friend were stringent obligations; and the packet slept in the inmost corner of his private safe.

It is one thing to mortify curiosity, another to conquer it; and it may be doubted if, from that day forth, Utterson desired the society of his surviving friend with the same eagerness. He thought of him kindly; but his thoughts were disquieted and fearful. He went to call indeed; but he was perhaps relieved to be denied admittance; perhaps, in his heart, he preferred to speak with Poole upon the doorstep and surrounded by the air and sounds of the open city, rather than to be admitted into that house of voluntary bondage, and to sit and speak with its inscrutable recluse. Poole had, indeed, no very pleasant news to communicate. The doctor, it appeared, now more than ever confined himself to the cabinet over the laboratory, where he would sometimes even sleep; he was out of spirits, he had grown very silent, he did not read; it seemed as if he had something on his mind. Utterson became so used to the unvarying character of these reports, that he fell off little by little in the frequency of his visits.

Incident at the Window

It chanced on Sunday, when Mr. Utterson was on his usual walk with Mr. Enfield, that their way lay once again through the by-street; and that when they came in front of the door, both stopped to gaze on it.

"Well," said Enfield, "that story's at an end at least. We shall never see more of Mr. Hyde."

"I hope not," said Utterson. "Did I ever tell you that I once saw him, and shared your feeling of repulsion?"

"It was impossible to do the one without the other," returned Enfield. "And by the way, what an ass you must have thought me, not to know that this was a back way to Dr. Jekyll's! It was partly your own fault that I found it out, even when I did."

"So you found it out, did you?" said Utterson. "But if that be so, we may step into the court and take a look at the windows. To tell you the truth, I am uneasy about poor Jekyll; and even outside, I feel as if the presence of a friend might do him good."

The court was very cool and a little damp, and full of premature twilight, although the sky, high up overhead, was still bright with sunset. The middle one of the three windows was half-way open; and sitting close beside it, taking the air with an infinite sadness of mien, like some disconsolate prisoner, Utterson saw Dr. Jekyll.

"What! Jekyll!" he cried. "I trust you are better."

"I am very low, Utterson," replied the doctor drearily, "very low. It will not last long, thank God."

"You stay too much indoors," said the lawyer. "You should be out, whipping up the circulation' like Mr. Enfield and me. (This is my cousin—Mr. Enfield—Dr. Jekyll.) Come now; get your hat and take a quick turn with us."

"You are very good," sighed the other. "I should like to very much; but no, no, no, it is quite impossible; I dare not. But indeed, Utterson, I am very glad to see you; this is really a great pleasure; I would ask you and Mr. Enfield up, but the place is really not fit."

"Why, then," said the lawyer, good-naturedly, "the best thing we can do is to stay down here and speak with you from where we are."

"That is just what I was about to venture to propose," returned the doctor with a smile. But the words were hardly uttered, before the smile was struck out of his face and succeeded by an expression of such abject terror and despair, as froze the very blood of the two gentlemen below. They saw it but for a glimpse for the window was instantly thrust down; but that glimpse had been sufficient, and they turned and left the court without a word. In silence, too, they traversed the by-street; and it was not until they had come into a neighbouring thoroughfare, where even upon a Sunday there were still some stirrings of life, that Mr. Utterson at last turned and looked at his companion. They were both pale; and there was an answering horror in their eyes.

"God forgive us, God forgive us," said Mr. Utterson.

But Mr. Enfield only nodded his head very seriously, and walked on once more in silence.

The Last Night

MR. Utterson was sitting by his fireside one evening after dinner, when he was surprised to receive a visit from Poole.

"Bless me, Poole, what brings you here?" he cried; and then taking a second look at him, "What ails you?" he added; "is the doctor ill?"

"Mr. Utterson," said the man, "there is something wrong."

"Take a seat, and here is a glass of wine for you," said the lawyer. "Now, take your time, and tell me plainly what you want."

"You know the doctor's ways, sir," replied Poole, "and how he shuts himself up. Well, he's shut up again in the cabinet; and I don't like it, sir—I wish I may die if I like it. Mr. Utterson, sir, I'm afraid."

"Now, my good man," said the lawyer, "be explicit. What are you afraid of?"

"I've been afraid for about a week," returned Poole, doggedly disregarding the question, "and I can bear it no more."

The man's appearance amply bore out his words; his manner was altered for the worse; and except for the moment when he had first announced his terror, he had not once looked the lawyer in the face. Even now, he sat with the glass of wine untasted on his knee, and his eyes directed to a corner of the floor. "I can bear it no more," he repeated.

"Come," said the lawyer, "I see you have some good reason, Poole; I see there is something seriously amiss. Try to tell me what it is."

"I think there's been foul play," said Poole, hoarsely.

"Foul play!" cried the lawyer, a good deal frightened and rather inclined to be irritated in consequence. "What foul play! What does the man mean?"

"I daren't say, sir," was the answer; "but will you come along with me and see for yourself?"

Mr. Utterson's only answer was to rise and get his hat and great-coat; but he observed with wonder the greatness of the relief that appeared upon the butler's face, and perhaps with no less, that the wine was still untasted when he set it down to follow.

It was a wild, cold, seasonable night of March, with a pale moon, lying on her back as though the wind had tilted her, and fly-ing wrack of the most diaphanous and lawny texture. The wind made talking difficult, and flecked the blood into the face. It seemed to have swept the streets unusually bare of passengers, besides; for Mr. Utterson thought he had never seen that part of London so deserted. He could have wished it otherwise; never in his life had he been conscious of so sharp a wish to see and touch his fellow-creatures; for struggle as he might, there was borne in upon his mind a crushing anticipation of calamity. The square, when they got there, was full of wind and dust, and the thin trees in the garden were lashing themselves along the railing. Poole, who had kept all the way a pace or two ahead, now pulled up in the middle of the pavement, and in spite of the biting weather, took off his hat and mopped his brow with a red pocket-handkerchief. But for all the hurry of his coming, these were not the dews of exertion that he wiped away, but the moisture of some strangling anguish; for his face was white and his voice, when he spoke, harsh and broken.

"Well, sir," he said, "here we are, and God grant there be nothing wrong."

"Amen, Poole," said the lawyer.

Thereupon the servant knocked in a very guarded manner; the door was opened on the chain; and a voice asked from within, "Is that you, Poole?"

"It's all right," said Poole. "Open the door."

The hall, when they entered it, was brightly lighted up; the fire was built high; and about the hearth the whole of the servants, men and women, stood huddled together like a flock of sheep. At the sight of Mr. Utterson, the housemaid broke into hysterical whimpering; and the cook, crying out "Bless God! it's Mr. Utterson," ran forward as if to take him in her arms.

"What, what? Are you all here?" said the lawyer peevishly. "Very irregular, very unseemly; your master would be far from pleased."

"They're all afraid," said Poole.

Blank silence followed, no one protesting; only the maid lifted her voice and now wept loudly.

"Hold your tongue!" Poole said to her, with a ferocity of accent that testified to his own jangled nerves; and indeed, when the girl had so suddenly raised the note of her lamentation, they had all started and turned towards the inner door with faces of dreadful expectation. "And now," continued the butler, addressing the knife-boy, "reach me a candle, and we'll get this through hands[1] at once." And then he begged Mr. Utterson to follow him, and led the way to the back garden.

"Now, sir," said he, "you come as gently as you can. I want you to hear, and I don't want you to be heard. And see here, sir, if by any chance he was to ask you in, don't go."

Mr. Utterson's nerves, at this unlooked-for termination, gave a jerk that nearly threw him from his balance; but he recollected his courage and followed the butler into the laboratory building through the surgical theatre, with its lumber of crates and bottles, to the foot of the stair. Here Poole motioned him to stand on one side and listen; while he himself, setting down the candle and making a great and obvious call on his resolution, mounted the steps and knocked with a somewhat uncertain hand on the red baize of the cabinet door.

---

[1] Handled.

"Mr. Utterson, sir, asking to see you," he called; and even as he did so, once more violently signed to the lawyer to give ear.

A voice answered from within: "Tell him I cannot see anyone," it said complainingly.

"Thank you, sir," said Poole, with a note of something like triumph in his voice; and taking up his candle, he led Mr. Utterson back across the yard and into the great kitchen, where the fire was out and the beetles were leaping on the floor.

"Sir," he said, looking Mr. Utterson in the eyes, "Was that my master's voice?"

"It seems much changed," replied the lawyer, very pale, but giving look for look.

"Changed? Well, yes, I think so," said the butler. "Have I been twenty years in this man's house, to be deceived about his voice? No, sir; master's made away with; he was made away with eight days ago, when we heard him cry out upon the name of God; and who's in there instead of him, and why it stays there, is a thing that cries to Heaven, Mr. Utterson!"

"This is a very strange tale, Poole; this is rather a wild tale, my man," said Mr. Utterson, biting his finger. "Suppose it were as you suppose, supposing Dr. Jekyll to have been—well, murdered, what could induce the murderer to stay? That won't hold water; it doesn't commend itself to reason."

"Well, Mr. Utterson, you are a hard man to satisfy, but I'll do it yet," said Poole. "All this last week (you must know) him, or it, whatever it is that lives in that cabinet, has been crying night and day for some sort of medicine and cannot get it to his mind. It was sometimes his way—the master's, that is—to write his orders on a sheet of paper and throw it on the stair. We've had nothing else this week back; nothing but papers, and a closed door, and the very meals left there to be smuggled in when nobody was looking. Well, sir, every day, ay, and twice and thrice in the same day, there have been orders and complaints, and I have been sent flying to all the wholesale chemists in town. Every time I brought the stuff back, there would be another paper telling me to return it, because it was not pure, and another order to a different firm. This drug is wanted bitter bad, sir, whatever for."

"Have you any of these papers?" asked Mr. Utterson.

Poole felt in his pocket and handed out a crumpled note, which the lawyer, bending nearer to the candle, carefully examined. Its contents ran thus: "Dr. Jekyll presents his compliments to Messrs.

Maw. He assures them that their last sample is impure and quite useless for his present purpose. In the year 18—, Dr. J. purchased a somewhat large quantity from Messrs. M. He now begs them to search with most sedulous care, and should any of the same quality be left, forward it to him at once. Expense is no consideration. The importance of this to Dr. J. can hardly be exaggerated." So far the letter had run composedly enough, but here with a sudden splutter of the pen, the writer's emotion had broken loose. "For God's sake," he added, "find me some of the old."

"This is a strange note," said Mr. Utterson; and then sharply, "How do you come to have it open?"

"The man at Maw's was main angry, sir, and he threw it back to me like so much dirt," returned Poole.

"This is unquestionably the doctor's hand, do you know?" resumed the lawyer.

"I thought it looked like it," said the servant rather sulkily; and then, with another voice, "But what matters hand of write?" he said. "I've seen him!"

"Seen him?" repeated Mr. Utterson. "Well?"

"That's it!" said Poole. "It was this way. I came suddenly into the theatre from the garden. It seems he had slipped out to look for this drug or whatever it is; for the cabinet door was open, and there he was at the far end of the room digging among the crates. He looked up when I came in, gave a kind of cry, and whipped upstairs into the cabinet. It was but for one minute that I saw him, but the hair stood upon my head like quills. Sir, if that was my master, why had he a mask upon his face? If it was my master, why did he cry out like a rat, and run from me? I have served him long enough. And then . . ." The man paused and passed his hand over his face.

"These are all very strange circumstances," said Mr. Utterson, "but I think I begin to see daylight. Your master, Poole, is plainly seized with one of those maladies that both torture and deform the sufferer; hence, for aught I know, the alteration of his voice; hence the mask and the avoidance of his friends; hence his eagerness to find this drug, by means of which the poor soul retains some hope of ultimate recovery—God grant that he be not deceived! There is my explanation; it is sad enough, Poole, ay, and appalling to consider; but it is plain and natural, hangs well together, and delivers us from all exorbitant alarms."

"Sir," said the butler, turning to a sort of mottled pallor, "that thing was not my master, and there's the truth. My master"—here he looked round him and began to whisper—"is a tall, fine build of a man, and this was more of a dwarf." Utterson attempted to protest. "O, sir," cried Poole, "do you think I do not know my master after twenty years? Do you think I do not know where his head comes to in the cabinet door, where I saw him every morning of my life? No, sir, that thing in the mask was never Dr. Jekyll—God knows what it was, but it was never Dr. Jekyll; and it is the belief of my heart that there was murder done."

"Poole," replied the lawyer, "if you say that, it will become my duty to make certain. Much as I desire to spare your master's feelings, much as I am puzzled by this note which seems to prove him to be still alive, I shall consider it my duty to break in that door."

"Ah, Mr. Utterson, that's talking!" cried the butler.

"And now comes the second question," resumed Utterson: "Who is going to do it?"

"Why, you and me, sir," was the undaunted reply.

"That's very well said," returned the lawyer; "and whatever comes of it, I shall make it my business to see you are no loser."

"There is an axe in the theatre," continued Poole; "and you might take the kitchen poker for yourself."

The lawyer took that rude but weighty instrument into his hand, and balanced it. "Do you know, Poole," he said, looking up, "that you and I are about to place ourselves in a position of some peril?"

"You may say so, sir, indeed," returned the butler.

"It is well, then, that we should be frank," said the other. "We both think more than we have said; let us make a clean breast. This masked figure that you saw, did you recognise it?"

"Well, sir, it went so quick, and the creature was so doubled up, that I could hardly swear to that," was the answer. "But if you mean, was it Mr. Hyde?—why, yes, I think it was! You see, it was much of the same bigness; and it had the same quick, light way with it; and then who else could have got in by the laboratory door? You have not forgot, sir, that at the time of the murder he had still the key with him? But that's not all. I don't know, Mr. Utterson, if you ever met this Mr. Hyde?"

"Yes," said the lawyer, "I once spoke with him."

"Then you must know as well as the rest of us that there was something queer about that gentleman—something that gave a man a turn—I don't know rightly how to say it, sir, beyond this: that you felt in your marrow kind of cold and thin."

"I own I felt something of what you describe," said Mr. Utterson.

"Quite so, sir," returned Poole. "Well, when that masked thing like a monkey jumped from among the chemicals and whipped into the cabinet, it went down my spine like ice. O, I know it's not evidence, Mr. Utterson; I'm book-learned enough for that; but a man has his feelings, and I give you my bible-word it was Mr. Hyde!"

"Ay, ay," said the lawyer. "My fears incline to the same point. Evil, I fear, founded—evil was sure to come—of that connection. Ay truly, I believe you; I believe poor Harry is killed; and I believe his murderer (for what purpose, God alone can tell) is still lurking in his victim's room. Well, let our name be vengeance. Call Bradshaw."

The footman came at the summons, very white and nervous.

"Put yourself together, Bradshaw," said the lawyer. "This suspense, I know, is telling upon all of you; but it is now our intention to make an end of it. Poole, here, and I are going to force our way into the cabinet. If all is well, my shoulders are broad enough to bear the blame. Meanwhile, lest anything should really be amiss, or any malefactor seek to escape by the back, you and the boy must go round the corner with a pair of good sticks and take your post at the laboratory door. We give you ten minutes, to get to your stations."

As Bradshaw left, the lawyer looked at his watch. "And now, Poole, let us get to ours," he said; and taking the poker under his arm, led the way into the yard. The scud had banked over the moon, and it was now quite dark. The wind, which only broke in puffs and draughts into that deep well of building, tossed the light of the candle to and fro about their steps, until they came into the shelter of the theatre, where they sat down silently to wait. London hummed solemnly all around; but nearer at hand, the stillness was only broken by the sounds of a footfall moving to and fro along the cabinet floor.

"So it will walk all day, sir," whispered Poole; "ay, and the better part of the night. Only when a new sample comes from the chemist, there's a bit of a break. Ah, it's an ill conscience that's such an enemy to rest! Ah, sir, there's blood foully shed in every step of it! But hark again, a little closer—put your heart in your ears, Mr. Utterson, and tell me, is that the doctor's foot?"

The steps fell lightly and oddly, with a certain swing, for all they went so slowly; it was different indeed from the heavy creaking tread of Henry Jekyll. Utterson sighed. "Is there never anything else?" he asked.

Poole nodded. "Once," he said. "Once I heard it weeping!"

"Weeping? how that?" said the lawyer, conscious of a sudden chill of horror.

"Weeping like a woman or a lost soul," said the butler. "I came away with that upon my heart, that I could have wept too."

But now the ten minutes drew to an end. Poole disinterred the axe from under a stack of packing straw; the candle was set upon the nearest table to light them to the attack; and they drew near with bated breath to where that patient foot was still going up and down, up and down, in the quiet of the night. "Jekyll," cried Utterson, with a loud voice, "I demand to see you." He paused a moment, but there came no reply. "I give you fair warning, our suspicions are aroused, and I must and shall see you," he resumed; "if not by fair means, then by foul—if not of your consent, then by brute force!"

"Utterson," said the voice, "for God's sake, have mercy!"

"Ah, that's not Jekyll's voice—it's Hyde's!" cried Utterson. "Down with the door, Poole!"

Poole swung the axe over his shoulder; the blow shook the building, and the red baize door leaped against the lock and hinges. A dismal screech, as of mere animal terror, rang from the cabinet. Up went the axe again, and again the panels crashed and the frame bounded; four times the blow fell; but the wood was tough and the fittings were of excellent workmanship; and it was not until the fifth, that the lock burst and the wreck of the door fell inwards on the carpet.

The besiegers, appalled by their own riot and the stillness that had succeeded, stood back a little and peered in. There lay the cabinet before their eyes in the quiet lamplight, a good fire glowing and chattering on the hearth, the kettle singing its thin strain, a drawer or two open, papers neatly set forth on the business table, and nearer the fire, the things laid out for tea; the quietest room, you would have said, and, but for the glazed presses[2] full of chemicals, the most commonplace that night in London.

Right in the middle there lay the body of a man sorely contorted and still twitching. They drew near on tiptoe, turned it on its back and beheld the face of Edward Hyde. He was dressed in clothes far too large for him, clothes of the doctor's bigness; the cords of his face still moved with a semblance of life, but life was quite gone: and by the crushed phial in the hand and the strong smell of kernels that hung upon the air, Utterson knew that he was looking on the body of a self-destroyer.

---

[2] Cabinets with glass doors. The "cabinet" above is a private room.

"We have come too late," he said sternly, "whether to save or punish. Hyde is gone to his account; and it only remains for us to find the body of your master."

The far greater proportion of the building was occupied by the theatre, which filled almost the whole ground storey and was lighted from above, and by the cabinet, which formed an upper story at one end and looked upon the court. A corridor joined the theatre to the door on the by-street; and with this the cabinet communicated separately by a second flight of stairs. There were besides a few dark closets and a spacious cellar. All these they now thoroughly examined. Each closet needed but a glance, for all were empty, and all, by the dust that fell from their doors, had stood long unopened. The cellar, indeed, was filled with crazy lumber, mostly dating from the times of the surgeon who was Jekyll's predecessor; but even as they opened the door they were advertised of the uselessness of further search, by the fall of a perfect mat of cobweb which had for years sealed up the entrance. No where was there any trace of Henry Jekyll dead or alive.

Poole stamped on the flags of the corridor. "He must be buried here," he said, hearkening to the sound.

"Or he may have fled," said Utterson, and he turned to examine the door in the by-street. It was locked; and lying near by on the flags, they found the key, already stained with rust.

"This does not look like use," observed the lawyer.

"Use!" echoed Poole. "Do you not see, sir, it is broken? much as if a man had stamped on it."

"Ay," continued Utterson, "and the fractures, too, are rusty." The two men looked at each other with a scare. "This is beyond me, Poole," said the lawyer. "Let us go back to the cabinet."

They mounted the stair in silence, and still with an occasional awestruck glance at the dead body, proceeded more thoroughly to examine the contents of the cabinet. At one table, there were traces of chemical work, various measured heaps of some white salt being laid on glass saucers, as though for an experiment in which the unhappy man had been prevented.

"That is the same drug that I was always bringing him," said Poole; and even as he spoke, the kettle with a startling noise boiled over.

This brought them to the fireside, where the easy-chair was drawn cosily up, and the tea things stood ready to the sitter's elbow, the very sugar in the cup. There were several books on a shelf; one lay beside the tea things open, and Utterson was amazed to find it a copy of a pious work, for which Jekyll had several times expressed a great esteem, annotated, in his own hand with startling blasphemies.

Next, in the course of their review of the chamber, the searchers came to the cheval-glass, into whose depths they looked with an involuntary horror. But it was so turned as to show them nothing but the rosy glow playing on the roof, the fire sparkling in a hundred repetitions along the glazed front of the presses, and their own pale and fearful countenances stooping to look in.

"This glass has seen some strange things, sir," whispered Poole.

"And surely none stranger than itself," echoed the lawyer in the same tones. "For what did Jekyll"—he caught himself up at the word with a start, and then conquering the weakness—"what could Jekyll want with it?" he said.

"You may say that!" said Poole.

Next they turned to the business table. On the desk, among the neat array of papers, a large envelope was uppermost, and bore, in the doctor's hand, the name of Mr. Utterson. The lawyer unsealed it, and several enclosures fell to the floor. The first was a will, drawn in the same eccentric terms as the one which he had returned six months before, to serve as a testament in case of death and as a deed of gift in case of disappearance; but in place of the name of Edward Hyde, the lawyer, with indescribable amazement read the name of Gabriel John Utterson. He looked at Poole, and then back at the paper, and last of all at the dead malefactor stretched upon the carpet.

"My head goes round," he said. "He has been all these days in possession; he had no cause to like me; he must have raged to see himself displaced; and he has not destroyed this document."

He caught up the next paper; it was a brief note in the doctor's hand and dated at the top. "O Poole!" the lawyer cried, "he was alive and here this day. He cannot have been disposed of in so short a space; he must be still alive, he must have fled! And then, why fled? and how? and in that case, can we venture to declare this suicide? O, we must be careful. I foresee that we may yet involve your master in some dire catastrophe."

"Why don't you read it, sir?" asked Poole.

"Because I fear," replied the lawyer solemnly. "God grant I have no cause for it!" And with that he brought the paper to his eyes and read as follows:

"My dear Utterson,—When this shall fall into your hands, I shall have disappeared, under what circumstances I have not the penetration to foresee, but my instinct and all the circumstances of

my nameless situation tell me that the end is sure and must be
early. Go then, and first read the narrative which Lanyon warned
me he was to place in your hands; and if you care to hear more,
turn to the confession of

Your unworthy and unhappy friend,

HENRY JEKYLL.

"There was a third enclosure?" asked Utterson.

"Here, sir," said Poole, and gave into his hands a considerable
packet sealed in several places.

The lawyer put it in his pocket. "I would say nothing of this paper.
If your master has fled or is dead, we may at least save his credit. It is
now ten; I must go home and read these documents in quiet; but
I shall be back before midnight, when we shall send for the police."

They went out, locking the door of the theatre behind them;
and Utterson, once more leaving the servants gathered about the
fire in the hall, trudged back to his office to read the two narratives
in which this mystery was now to be explained.

Dr. Lanyon's Narrative

ON the ninth of January, now four days ago, I received by the
evening delivery a registered envelope, addressed in the hand of my
colleague and old school companion, Henry Jekyll. I was a good
deal surprised by this; for we were by no means in the habit of cor-
respondence; I had seen the man, dined with him, indeed, the night
before; and I could imagine nothing in our intercourse that should
justify formality of registration. The contents increased my wonder;
for this is how the letter ran:

10th December, 18—.

Dear Lanyon,—You are one of my oldest friends; and although
we may have differed at times on scientific questions, I cannot
remember, at least on my side, any break in our affection. There
was never a day when, if you had said to me, "Jekyll, my life, my
honour, my reason, depend upon you," I would not have sacri-
ficed my left hand to help you. Lanyon my life, my honour, my
reason, are all at your mercy; if you fail me to-night, I am lost.
You might suppose, after this preface, that I am going to ask you
for something dishonourable to grant. Judge for yourself.

I want you to postpone all other engagements for to-night—ay, even if you were summoned to the bedside of an emperor; to take a cab, unless your carriage should be actually at the door; and with this letter in your hand for consultation, to drive straight to my house. Poole, my butler, has his orders; you will find him waiting your arrival with a locksmith. The door of my cabinet is then to be forced: and you are to go in alone; to open the glazed press (letter E) on the left hand, breaking the lock if it be shut; and to draw out, with all its contents as they stand, the fourth drawer from the top or (which is the same thing) the third from the bottom. In my extreme distress of mind, I have a morbid fear of misdirecting you; but even if I am in error, you may know the right drawer by its contents: some powders, a phial and a paper book. This drawer I beg of you to carry back with you to Cavendish Square exactly as it stands.

That is the first part of the service: now for the second. You should be back, if you set out at once on the receipt of this, long before midnight; but I will leave you that amount of margin, not only in the fear of one of those obstacles that can neither be prevented nor foreseen, but because an hour when your servants are in bed is to be preferred for what will then remain to do. At midnight, then, I have to ask you to be alone in your consulting room, to admit with your own hand into the house a man who will present himself in my name, and to place in his hands the drawer that you will have brought with you from my cabinet. Then you will have played your part and earned my gratitude completely. Five minutes afterwards, if you insist upon an explanation, you will have understood that these arrangements are of capital importance; and that by the neglect of one of them, fantastic as they must appear, you might have charged your conscience with my death or the shipwreck of my reason.

Confident as I am that you will not trifle with this appeal, my heart sinks and my hand trembles at the bare thought of such a possibility. Think of me at this hour, in a strange place, labouring under a blackness of distress that no fancy can exaggerate, and yet well aware that, if you will but punctually serve me, my troubles will roll away like a story that is told. Serve me, my dear Lanyon and save

Your friend,

H. J.

P.S.—I had already sealed this up when a fresh terror struck upon my soul. It is possible that the post-office may fail me, and this letter not come into your hands until to-morrow morning. In that case, dear Lanyon, do my errand when it shall be most convenient for you in the course of the day; and once more expect my messenger at midnight. It may then already be too late; and if that night passes without event, you will know that you have seen the last of Henry Jekyll.

Upon the reading of this letter, I made sure my colleague was insane; but till that was proved beyond the possibility of doubt, I felt bound to do as he requested. The less I understood of this farrago, the less I was in a position to judge of its importance; and an appeal so worded could not be set aside without a grave responsibility. I rose accordingly from table, got into a hansom,[1] and drove straight to Jekyll's house. The butler was awaiting my arrival; he had received by the same post as mine a registered letter of instruction, and had sent at once for a locksmith and a carpenter. The tradesmen came while we were yet speaking; and we moved in a body to old Dr. Denman's surgical theatre, from which (as you are doubtless aware) Jekyll's private cabinet is most conveniently entered. The door was very strong, the lock excellent; the carpenter avowed he would have great trouble and have to do much damage, if force were to be used; and the locksmith was near despair. But this last was a handy fellow, and after two hour's work, the door stood open. The press marked E was unlocked; and I took out the drawer, had it filled up with straw and tied in a sheet, and returned with it to Cavendish Square.

Here I proceeded to examine its contents. The powders were neatly enough made up, but not with the nicety of the dispensing chemist; so that it was plain they were of Jekyll's private manufacture: and when I opened one of the wrappers I found what seemed to me a simple crystalline salt of a white colour. The phial, to which I next turned my attention, might have been about half full of a blood-red liquor, which was highly pungent to the sense of smell and seemed to me to contain phosphorus and some volatile ether. At the other ingredients I could make no guess. The book was an ordinary version book[2] and contained little but a series of dates. These covered a period of many years, but I observed that the entries ceased

---

[1] Hired carriage, cab.
[2] A bound book of blank pages.

nearly a year ago and quite abruptly. Here and there a brief remark was appended to a date, usually no more than a single word: "double" occurring perhaps six times in a total of several hundred entries; and once very early in the list and followed by several marks of exclamation, "total failure!!!" All this, though it whetted my curiosity, told me little that was definite. Here were a phial of some tincture,[3] a paper of some salt, and the record of a series of experiments that had led (like too many of Jekyll's investigations) to no end of practical usefulness. How could the presence of these articles in my house affect either the honour, the sanity, or the life of my flighty colleague? If his messenger could go to one place, why could he not go to another? And even granting some impediment, why was this gentleman to be received by me in secret? The more I reflected, the more convinced I grew that I was dealing with a case of cerebral disease; and though I dismissed my servants to bed, I loaded an old revolver, that I might be found in some posture of self-defence.

Twelve o'clock had scarce rung out over London, ere the knocker sounded very gently on the door. I went myself at the summons, and found a small man crouching against the pillars of the portico.

"Are you come from Dr. Jekyll?" I asked.

He told me "yes" by a constrained gesture; and when I had bidden him enter, he did not obey me without a searching backward glance into the darkness of the square. There was a policeman not far off, advancing with his bull's eye[4] open; and at the sight, I thought my visitor started and made greater haste.

These particulars struck me, I confess, disagreeably; and as I followed him into the bright light of the consulting room, I kept my hand ready on my weapon. Here, at last, I had a chance of clearly seeing him. I had never set eyes on him before, so much was certain. He was small, as I have said; I was struck besides with the shocking expression of his face, with his remarkable combination of great muscular activity and great apparent debility of constitution, and—last but not least—with the odd, subjective disturbance caused by his neighbourhood. This bore some resemblance to incipient rigour,[5] and was accompanied by a marked sinking of the pulse. At the time, I set it down to some idiosyncratic, personal distaste, and

---

[3] Solution in alcohol.

[4] Lantern.

[5] Paralysis.

merely wondered at the acuteness of the symptoms; but I have since had reason to believe the cause to lie much deeper in the nature of man, and to turn on some nobler hinge than the principle of hatred. This person (who had thus, from the first moment of his entrance, struck in me what I can only, describe as a disgustful curiosity) was dressed in a fashion that would have made an ordinary person laughable; his clothes, that is to say, although they were of rich and sober fabric, were enormously too large for him in every measurement—the trousers hanging on his legs and rolled up to keep them from the ground, the waist of the coat below his haunches, and the collar sprawling wide upon his shoulders. Strange to relate, this ludicrous accoutrement was far from moving me to laughter. Rather, as there was something abnormal and misbegotten in the very essence of the creature that now faced me—something seizing, surprising and revolting—this fresh disparity seemed but to fit in with and to reinforce it; so that to my interest in the man's nature and character, there was added a curiosity as to his origin, his life, his fortune and status in the world.

These observations, though they have taken so great a space to be set down in, were yet the work of a few seconds. My visitor was, indeed, on fire with sombre excitement.

"Have you got it?" he cried. "Have you got it?" And so lively was his impatience that he even laid his hand upon my arm and sought to shake me.

I put him back, conscious at his touch of a certain icy pang along my blood. "Come, sir," said I. "You forget that I have not yet the pleasure of your acquaintance. Be seated, if you please." And I showed him an example, and sat down myself in my customary seat and with as fair an imitation of my ordinary manner to a patient, as the lateness of the hour, the nature of my preoccupations, and the horror I had of my visitor, would suffer me to muster.

"I beg your pardon, Dr. Lanyon," he replied civilly enough. "What you say is very well founded; and my impatience has shown its heels to my politeness. I come here at the instance of your colleague, Dr. Henry Jekyll, on a piece of business of some moment; and I understood . . ." He paused and put his hand to his throat, and I could see, in spite of his collected manner, that he was wrestling against the approaches of the hysteria[6]—"I understood, a drawer . . ."

---

[6] Literally: "wandering womb." These extravagant anxieties were thought, in the Victorian era, symptoms of a female disease, and unmanning in men.

But here I took pity on my visitor's suspense, and some perhaps on my own growing curiosity.

"There it is, sir," said I, pointing to the drawer, where it lay on the floor behind a table and still covered with the sheet.

He sprang to it, and then paused, and laid his hand upon his heart: I could hear his teeth grate with the convulsive action of his jaws; and his face was so ghastly to see that I grew alarmed both for his life and reason.

"Compose yourself," said I.

He turned a dreadful smile to me, and as if with the decision of despair, plucked away the sheet. At sight of the contents, he uttered one loud sob of such immense relief that I sat petrified. And the next moment, in a voice that was already fairly well under control, "Have you a graduated glass?"[7] he asked.

I rose from my place with something of an effort and gave him what he asked.

He thanked me with a smiling nod, measured out a few minims of the red tincture and added one of the powders. The mixture, which was at first of a reddish hue, began, in proportion as the crystals melted, to brighten in colour, to effervesce audibly, and to throw off small fumes of vapour. Suddenly and at the same moment, the ebullition ceased and the compound changed to a dark purple, which faded again more slowly to a watery green. My visitor, who had watched these metamorphoses with a keen eye, smiled, set down the glass upon the table, and then turned and looked upon me with an air of scrutiny.

"And now," said he, "to settle what remains. Will you be wise? will you be guided? will you suffer me to take this glass in my hand and to go forth from your house without further parley? or has the greed of curiosity too much command of you? Think before you answer, for it shall be done as you decide. As you decide, you shall be left as you were before, and neither richer nor wiser, unless the sense of service rendered to a man in mortal distress may be counted as a kind of riches of the soul. Or, if you shall so prefer to choose, a new province of knowledge and new avenues to fame and power shall be laid open to you, here, in this room, upon the instant; and your sight shall be blasted by a prodigy to stagger the unbelief of Satan."

---

[7] With horizontal marks for quantities, like a measuring cup.

"Sir," said I, affecting a coolness that I was far from truly possessing, "you speak enigmas, and you will perhaps not wonder that I hear you with no very strong impression of belief. But I have gone too far in the way of inexplicable services to pause before I see the end."

"It is well," replied my visitor. "Lanyon, you remember your vows: what follows is under the seal of our profession. And now, you who have so long been bound to the most narrow and material views, you who have denied the virtue of transcendental medicine, you who have derided your superiors—behold!"

He put the glass to his lips and drank at one gulp. A cry followed; he reeled, staggered, clutched at the table and held on, staring with injected eyes, gasping with open mouth; and as I looked there came, I thought, a change—he seemed to swell—his face became suddenly black and the features seemed to melt and alter—and the next moment, I had sprung to my feet and leaped back against the wall, my arms raised to shield me from that prodigy, my mind submerged in terror.

"O God!" I screamed, and "O God!" again and again; for there before my eyes—pale and shaken, and half fainting, and groping before him with his hands, like a man restored from death—there stood Henry Jekyll!

What he told me in the next hour, I cannot bring my mind to set on paper. I saw what I saw, I heard what I heard, and my soul sickened at it; and yet now when that sight has faded from my eyes, I ask myself if I believe it, and I cannot answer. My life is shaken to its roots; sleep has left me; the deadliest terror sits by me at all hours of the day and night; and I feel that my days are numbered, and that I must die; and yet I shall die incredulous. As for the moral turpitude that man unveiled to me, even with tears of penitence, I can not, even in memory, dwell on it without a start of horror. I will say but one thing, Utterson, and that (if you can bring your mind to credit it) will be more than enough. The creature who crept into my house that night was, on Jekyll's own confession, known by the name of Hyde and hunted for in every corner of the land as the murderer of Carew.

HASTIE LANYON

Henry Jekyll's Full Statement of the Case[1]

I was born in the year 18— to a large fortune, endowed besides with excellent parts,[2] inclined by nature to industry, fond of the respect of the wise and good among my fellowmen, and thus, as might have been supposed, with every guarantee of an honourable and distinguished future. And indeed the worst of my faults was a certain impatient gaiety of disposition, such as has made the happiness of many, but such as I found it hard to reconcile with my imperious desire to carry my head high, and wear a more than commonly grave countenance before the public. Hence it came about that I concealed my pleasures; and that when I reached years of reflection, and began to look round me and take stock of my progress and position in the world, I stood already committed to a profound duplicity of life. Many a man would have even blazoned such irregularities as I was guilty of; but from the high views that I had set before me, I regarded and hid[3] them with an almost morbid sense of shame. It was thus rather the exacting nature of my aspirations than any particular degradation in my faults, that made me what I was, and, with even a deeper trench than in the majority of men, severed in me those provinces of good and ill which divide and compound man's dual nature. In this case, I was driven to reflect deeply and inveterately on that hard law of life, which lies at the root of religion and is one of the most plentiful springs of distress. Though so profound a double-dealer, I was in no sense a hypocrite; both sides of me were in dead earnest; I was no more myself when I laid aside restraint and plunged in shame, than when I laboured, in the eye of day, at the futherance of knowledge or the relief of sorrow and suffering. And it chanced that the direction of my scientific studies, which led wholly towards the mystic and the transcendental, reacted and shed a strong light on this consciousness of the perennial war among my members.[4] With every day, and from both sides of my intelligence, the moral and the intellectual, I thus drew

---

[1] Repeating a keyword from the title of the tale, *case* has a range of intriguing meaning; see pp. 123–24 below.

[2] Talents and abilities.

[3] An incipience (or retrospective discovery) of the name Hyde.

[4] Echoing the New Testament Epistle of James: "From whence come wars and fightings among you? come they not hence, even of your lusts that war in our members?" (4:1). For James, however, all these wars between members of the human race and within each human being are to be resolved by a turn of desire to God.

steadily nearer to that truth, by whose partial discovery I have been doomed to such a dreadful shipwreck: that man is not truly one, but truly two. I say two, because the state of my own knowledge does not pass beyond that point. Others will follow, others will outstrip me on the same lines; and I hazard the guess that man will be ultimately known for a mere polity of multifarious, incongruous and independent denizens. I, for my part, from the nature of my life, advanced infallibly in one direction and in one direction only. It was on the moral side, and in my own person, that I learned to recognise the thorough and primitive duality of man; I saw that, of the two natures that contended in the field of my consciousness, even if I could rightly be said to be either, it was only because I was radically both; and from an early date, even before the course of my scientific discoveries had begun to suggest the most naked possibility of such a miracle, I had learned to dwell with pleasure, as a beloved daydream, on the thought of the separation of these elements. If each, I told myself, could be housed in separate identities, life would be relieved of all that was unbearable; the unjust might go his way, delivered from the aspirations and remorse of his more upright twin; and the just could walk steadfastly and securely on his upward path, doing the good things in which he found his pleasure, and no longer exposed to disgrace and penitence by the hands of this extraneous evil. It was the curse of mankind that these incongruous faggots[5] were thus bound together—that in the agonised womb of consciousness, these polar twins should be continuously struggling. How, then were they dissociated?

I was so far in my reflections when, as I have said, a side light began to shine upon the subject from the laboratory table. I began to perceive more deeply than it has ever yet been stated, the trembling immateriality, the mistlike transience, of this seemingly so solid body in which we walk attired. Certain agents I found to have the power to shake and pluck back that fleshly vestment, even as a wind might toss the curtains of a pavilion. For two good reasons, I will not enter deeply into this scientific branch of my confession. First, because I have been made to learn that the doom and burthen of our life is bound for ever on man's shoulders, and when the attempt is made to cast it off, it but returns upon us with more unfamiliar and more awful pressure. Second, because, as my narrative will make, alas! too

[5] Bundles of sticks.

evident, my discoveries were incomplete. Enough then, that I not only recognised my natural body from the mere aura and effulgence of certain of the powers that made up my spirit, but managed to compound a drug by which these powers should be dethroned from their supremacy, and a second form and countenance substituted, none the less natural to me because they were the expression, and bore the stamp of lower elements in my soul.

I hesitated long before I put this theory to the test of practice. I knew well that I risked death; for any drug that so potently controlled and shook the very fortress of identity, might, by the least scruple[6] of an overdose or at the least inopportunity in the moment of exhibition, utterly blot out that immaterial tabernacle which I looked to it to change. But the temptation of a discovery so singular and profound at last overcame the suggestions of alarm. I had long since prepared my tincture; I purchased at once, from a firm of wholesale chemists, a large quantity of a particular salt which I knew, from my experiments, to be the last ingredient required; and late one accursed night, I compounded the elements, watched them boil and smoke together in the glass, and when the ebullition had subsided, with a strong glow of courage, drank off the potion.

The most racking pangs succeeded: a grinding in the bones, deadly nausea, and a horror of the spirit that cannot be exceeded at the hour of birth or death. Then these agonies began swiftly to subside, and I came to myself as if out of a great sickness. There was something strange in my sensations, something indescribably new and, from its very novelty, incredibly sweet. I felt younger, lighter, happier in body; within I was conscious of a heady recklessness, a current of disordered sensual images running like a millrace in my fancy, a solution[7] of the bonds of obligation, an unknown but not an innocent freedom of the soul. I knew myself, at the first breath of this new life, to be more wicked, tenfold more wicked, sold a slave to my original evil; and the thought, in that moment, braced and delighted me like wine. I stretched out my hands, exulting in the freshness of these sensations; and in the act, I was suddenly aware that I had lost in stature.

[6] Minute weight. From Latin for "small, sharp stone" (used on the scale), *scrupulus* is also the source of *scruple*, an inhibiting ethical principle (a sense noticeably excluded, even as it evoked here).

[7] This is a rich double-word, deriving from the Latin *solvere* (loosen, solve): *a loosening or dissolving of,* and *finding an answer to, solving the problem of.*

There was no mirror, at that date, in my room; that which stands beside me as I write,[8] was brought there later on and for the very purpose of these transformations. The night, however, was far gone into the morning—the morning, black as it was, was nearly ripe for the conception of the day—the inmates of my house were locked in the most rigorous hours of slumber; and I determined, flushed as I was with hope and triumph, to venture in my new shape as far as to my bedroom. I crossed the yard, wherein the constellations looked down upon me, I could have thought, with wonder, the first creature of that sort that their unsleeping vigilance had yet disclosed to them; I stole through the corridors, a stranger in my own house; and coming to my room, I saw for the first time the appearance of Edward Hyde.

I must here speak by theory alone, saying not that which I know, but that which I suppose to be most probable. The evil side of my nature, to which I had now transferred the stamping efficacy, was less robust and less developed than the good which I had just deposed. Again, in the course of my life, which had been, after all, nine tenths a life of effort, virtue and control, it had been much less exercised and much less exhausted. And hence, as I think, it came about that Edward Hyde was so much smaller, slighter and younger than Henry Jekyll. Even as good shone upon the countenance of the one, evil was written broadly and plainly on the face of the other. Evil besides (which I must still believe to be the lethal side of man) had left on that body an imprint of deformity and decay. And yet when I looked upon that ugly idol in the glass, I was conscious of no repugnance, rather of a leap of welcome. This, too, was myself. It seemed natural and human. In my eyes it bore a livelier image of the spirit, it seemed more express and single, than the imperfect and divided countenance I had been hitherto accustomed to call mine. And in so far I was doubtless right. I have observed that when I wore the semblance of Edward Hyde, none could come near to me at first without a visible misgiving of the flesh. This, as I take it, was because all human beings, as we meet them, are commingled out of good and evil: and Edward Hyde, alone in the ranks of mankind, was pure evil.

I lingered but a moment at the mirror: the second and conclusive experiment had yet to be attempted; it yet remained to be seen if I had lost my identity beyond redemption and must flee before

---

[8] That cheval-glass.

daylight from a house that was no longer mine; and hurrying back to my cabinet, I once more prepared and drank the cup, once more suffered the pangs of dissolution, and came to myself once more with the character, the stature and the face of Henry Jekyll. That night I had come to the fatal cross-roads.[9] Had I approached my discovery in a more noble spirit, had I risked the experiment while under the empire of generous or pious aspirations, all must have been otherwise, and from these agonies of death and birth, I had come forth an angel instead of a fiend. The drug had no discriminating action; it was neither diabolical nor divine; it but shook the doors of the prisonhouse of my disposition; and like the captives of Philippi, that which stood within ran forth.[10] At that time my virtue slumbered; my evil, kept awake by ambition, was alert and swift to seize the occasion; and the thing that was projected was Edward Hyde. Hence, although I had now two characters as well as two appearances, one was wholly evil, and the other was still the old Henry Jekyll, that incongruous compound of whose reformation and improvement I had already learned to despair. The movement was thus wholly toward the worse.

Even at that time, I had not conquered my aversions to the dryness of a life of study. I would still be merrily disposed at times; and as my pleasures were (to say the least) undignified, and I was not only well known and highly considered, but growing towards the elderly man, this incoherency of my life was daily growing more unwelcome. It was on this side that my new power tempted me until I fell in slavery. I had but to drink the cup, to doff at once the body of the noted professor, and to assume, like a thick cloak, that of Edward Hyde. I smiled at the notion; it seemed to me at the time to be humourous; and I made my preparations with the most studious care. I took and furnished that house in Soho, to which Hyde was tracked by the police; and engaged as a housekeeper a creature whom I knew well to be silent and unscrupulous. On the other side, I announced to my

---

[9] A metaphor for a moment of critical decision; the imagery evokes Oedipus, who (unknowingly) kills his father in a quarrel over priority at a crossroads. In 1909, Freud would use this fable to name the "Oedipus complex": the son's rebellion against paternal authority.

[10] The event is recounted in Acts 16: Evangelizing in Philippi, Paul and his followers are beaten, cast into prison, and bound in stocks. At midnight an earthquake shakes open the prison doors and loosens the prisoners' bands. Supposing the prisoners have all escaped, the warden is about to commit suicide, but is converted by Paul; the next day all are released.

servants that a Mr. Hyde (whom I described) was to have full liberty and power about my house in the square; and to parry mishaps, I even called and made myself a familiar object, in my second character. I next drew up that will to which you so much objected; so that if anything befell me in the person of Dr. Jekyll, I could enter on that of Edward Hyde without pecuniary loss. And thus fortified, as I supposed, on every side, I began to profit by the strange immunities of my position.

Men have before hired bravos to transact their crimes, while their own person and reputation sat under shelter. I was the first that ever did so for his pleasures. I was the first that could plod in the public eye with a load of genial respectability, and in a moment, like a schoolboy, strip off these lendings and spring headlong into the sea of liberty.[11] But for me, in my impenetrable mantle, the safety was complete. Think of it—I did not even exist! Let me but escape into my laboratory door, give me but a second or two to mix and swallow the draught that I had always standing ready; and whatever he had done, Edward Hyde would pass away like the stain of breath upon a mirror; and there in his stead, quietly at home, trimming the midnight lamp in his study, a man who could afford to laugh at suspicion, would be Henry Jekyll.

The pleasures which I made haste to seek in my disguise were, as I have said, undignified; I would scarce use a harder term. But in the hands of Edward Hyde, they soon began to turn toward the monstrous. When I would come back from these excursions, I was often plunged into a kind of wonder at my vicarious depravity. This familiar[12] that I called out of my own soul, and sent forth alone to do his good pleasure, was a being inherently malign and villainous; his every

---

[11] Startled at the sight of beggar "poor Tom" into a recognition that man is "no more but such a poor, bare, forked animal," King Lear tears off his clothes, crying "Off, off you lendings!" (Shakespeare, *King Lear*, 3.4.112). Stevenson also echoes poet John Keats, on whose biography his friend, Sidney Colvin, was working (published the year after *Jekyll and Hyde*, in 1887). Keats had labored on a long poem, *Endymion*, with great hopes of success, but shared the reviewers' judgment that it was mostly a failure. "Had I been nervous about it being a perfect piece, and with that view asked advice, and trembled over every page, it would not have been written," he told his publisher, adding, "I leaped headlong into the sea, and thereby have become better acquainted with the soundings, the quicksands, and the rocks, than if I had stayed upon the green shore, and piped a silly pipe, and took tea and comfortable advice" (October 8, 1818, from R. M. Milnes, *Life, Letters, and Literary Remains of John Keats*, 1848).

[12] An intimate attendant, with a folkloric sense of a spirit embodied in an animal companion, with a charge to serve and guard.

act and thought centered on self; drinking pleasure with bestial avidity from any degree of torture to another; relentless like a man of stone. Henry Jekyll stood at times aghast before the acts of Edward Hyde; but the situation was apart from ordinary laws, and insidiously relaxed the grasp of conscience. It was Hyde, after all, and Hyde alone, that was guilty. Jekyll was no worse; he woke again to his good qualities seemingly unimpaired; he would even make haste, where it was possible, to undo the evil done by Hyde. And thus his conscience slumbered.

Into the details of the infamy at which I thus connived (for even now I can scarce grant that I committed it) I have no design of entering; I mean but to point out the warnings and the successive steps with which my chastisement approached. I met with one accident which, as it brought on no consequence, I shall no more than mention. An act of cruelty to a child aroused against me the anger of a passer-by, whom I recognised the other day in the person of your kinsman; the doctor and the child's family joined him; there were moments when I feared for my life; and at last, in order to pacify their too just resentment, Edward Hyde had to bring them to the door, and pay them in a cheque drawn in the name of Henry Jekyll. But this danger was easily eliminated from the future, by opening an account at another bank in the name of Edward Hyde himself; and when, by sloping my own hand backward, I had supplied my double with a signature, I thought I sat beyond the reach of fate.

Some two months before the murder of Sir Danvers, I had been out for one of my adventures, had returned at a late hour, and woke the next day in bed with somewhat odd sensations. It was in vain I looked about me; in vain I saw the decent furniture and tall proportions of my room in the square; in vain that I recognised the pattern of the bed curtains and the design of the mahogany frame; something still kept insisting that I was not where I was, that I had not wakened where I seemed to be, but in the little room in Soho where I was accustomed to sleep in the body of Edward Hyde. I smiled to myself, and in my psychological way, began lazily to inquire into the elements of this illusion, occasionally, even as I did so, dropping back into a comfortable morning doze. I was still so engaged when, in one of my more wakeful moments, my eyes fell upon my hand. Now the hand of Henry Jekyll (as you have often remarked) was professional in shape and size: it was large, firm, white and comely. But the hand which I now saw, clearly enough, in the yellow light of a mid-London morning, lying half shut on the bedclothes, was lean, corded, knuckly, of a dusky pallor, and thickly shaded with a swart growth of hair. It was the hand of Edward Hyde.

I must have stared upon it for near half a minute, sunk as I was in the mere stupidity of wonder, before terror woke up in my breast as sudden and startling as the crash of cymbals; and bounding from my bed I rushed to the mirror. At the sight that met my eyes, my blood was changed into something exquisitely thin and icy. Yes, I had gone to bed Henry Jekyll, I had awakened Edward Hyde. How was this to be explained? I asked myself; and then, with another bound of terror—how was it to be remedied? It was well on in the morning; the servants were up; all my drugs were in the cabinet—a long journey down two pairs of stairs, through the back passage, across the open court and through the anatomical theatre, from where I was then standing horror-struck. It might indeed be possible to cover my face; but of what use was that, when I was unable to conceal the alteration in my stature? And then with an overpowering sweetness of relief, it came back upon my mind that the servants were already used to the coming and going of my second self. I had soon dressed, as well as I was able, in clothes of my own size: had soon passed through the house, where Bradshaw stared and drew back at seeing Mr. Hyde at such an hour and in such a strange array; and ten minutes later, Dr. Jekyll had returned to his own shape and was sitting down, with a darkened brow, to make a feint of breakfasting.

Small indeed was my appetite. This inexplicable incident, this reversal of my previous experience, seemed, like the Babylonian finger on the wall, to be spelling out the letters of my judgment;[13] and I began to reflect more seriously than ever before on the issues and possibilities of my double existence. That part of me which I had the power of projecting, had lately been much exercised and nourished; it had seemed to me of late as though the body of Edward Hyde had grown in stature, as though (when I wore that form) I were conscious of a more generous tide of blood; and I began to spy a danger that, if this were much prolonged, the balance of my nature might be permanently overthrown, the power of voluntary change be forfeited, and the character of Edward Hyde become irrevocably mine. The power of the drug had not been

---

[13] At the royal feast of Belshazzar, a mysterious hand appears, to write upon the palace wall. Daniel, famed for interpretive power, reads a prophecy to the king of Babylonia: "God hath numbered thy kingdom, and finished it. . . . Thou art weighed in the balances, and art found wanting. . . . Thy kingdom is divided and given to the Medes and Persians" (Daniel 5).

[handwritten margin notes: "Homophobic?", "I can stop whenever I want."]

always equally displayed. Once, very early in my career, it had totally failed me; since then I had been obliged on more than one occasion to double, and once, with infinite risk of death, to treble the amount; and these rare uncertainties had cast hitherto the sole shadow on my contentment. Now, however, and in the light of that morning's accident, I was led to remark that whereas, in the beginning, the difficulty had been to throw off the body of Jekyll, it had of late gradually but decidedly transferred itself to the other side. All things therefore seemed to point to this; that I was slowly losing hold of my original and better self, and becoming slowly incorporated with my second and worse.

Between these two, I now felt I had to choose. My two natures had memory in common, but all other faculties were most unequally shared between them. Jekyll (who was composite) now with the most sensitive apprehensions, now with a greedy gusto, projected and shared in the pleasures and adventures of Hyde; but Hyde was indifferent to Jekyll, or but remembered him as the mountain bandit remembers the cavern in which he conceals himself from pursuit. Jekyll had more than a father's interest; Hyde had more than a son's indifference. To cast in my lot with Jekyll, was to die to those appetites which I had long secretly indulged and had of late begun to pamper. To cast it in with Hyde, was to die to a thousand interests and aspirations, and to become, at a blow and forever, despised and friendless. The bargain might appear unequal; but there was still another consideration in the scales; for while Jekyll would suffer smartingly in the fires of abstinence, Hyde would be not even conscious of all that he had lost. Strange as my circumstances were, the terms of this debate are as old and commonplace as man; much the same inducements and alarms cast the die[14] for any tempted and trembling sinner; and it fell out with me, as it falls with so vast a majority of my fellows, that I chose the better part and was found wanting in the strength to keep to it.

Yes, I preferred the elderly and discontented doctor, surrounded by friends and cherishing honest hopes; and bade a resolute farewell to the liberty, the comparative youth, the light step, leaping impulses and secret pleasures, that I had enjoyed in the disguise of Hyde. I made this choice perhaps with some unconscious reservation, for I neither gave up the house in Soho, nor destroyed the clothes of Edward Hyde, which still lay ready in my cabinet. For two months,

---

[14] Singular of *dice;* metaphorically, played a chance or hazard.

however, I was true to my determination; for two months, I led a life of such severity as I had never before attained to, and enjoyed the compensations of an approving conscience. But time began at last to obliterate the freshness of my alarm; the praises of conscience began to grow into a thing of course; I began to be tortured with throes and longings, as of Hyde struggling after freedom; and at last, in an hour of moral weakness, I once again compounded and swallowed the transforming draught.

I do not suppose that, when a drunkard reasons with himself upon his vice, he is once out of five hundred times affected by the dangers that he runs through his brutish, physical insensibility; neither had I, long as I had considered my position, made enough allowance for the complete moral insensibility and insensate readiness to evil, which were the leading characters of Edward Hyde. Yet it was by these that I was punished. My devil had been long caged, he came out roaring. I was conscious, even when I took the draught, of a more unbridled, a more furious propensity to ill. It must have been this, I suppose, that stirred in my soul that tempest of impatience with which I listened to the civilities of my unhappy victim; I declare, at least, before God, no man morally sane could have been guilty of that crime upon so pitiful a provocation; and that I struck in no more reasonable spirit than that in which a sick child may break a plaything. But I had voluntarily stripped myself of all those balancing instincts by which even the worst of us continues to walk with some degree of steadiness among temptations; and in my case, to be tempted, however slightly, was to fall.

Instantly the spirit of hell awoke in me and raged. With a transport of glee, I mauled the unresisting body, tasting delight from every blow; and it was not till weariness had begun to succeed, that I was suddenly, in the top fit of my delirium, struck through the heart by a cold thrill of terror. A mist dispersed; I saw my life to be forfeit; and fled from the scene of these excesses, at once glorying and trembling, my lust of evil gratified and stimulated, my love of life screwed to the topmost peg. I ran to the house in Soho, and (to make assurance doubly sure[15]) destroyed my papers; thence I set out through the lamplit streets, in the same divided ecstasy of mind,

[15] Although he is assured by the witches that "none of woman born" can harm him, Macbeth decides to "make assurance double sure" and kill his enemy Macduff (*Macbeth,* 4.1.80–84). What the witches didn't tell him is that Macduff was not actually born, but "from his mother's womb / Untimely ripped" by cesarian section (5.8.15–16).

gloating on my crime, light-headedly devising others in the future, and yet still hastening and still hearkening in my wake for the steps of the avenger. Hyde had a song upon his lips as he compounded the draught, and as he drank it, pledged the dead man. The pangs of transformation had not done tearing him, before Henry Jekyll, with streaming tears of gratitude and remorse, had fallen upon his knees and lifted his clasped hands to God. The veil of self-indulgence was rent from head to foot. I saw my life as a whole: I followed it up from the days of childhood, when I had walked with my father's hand, and through the self-denying toils of my professional life, to arrive again and again, with the same sense of unreality, at the damned horrors of the evening. I could have screamed aloud; I sought with tears and prayers to smother down the crowd of hideous images and sounds with which my memory swarmed against me; and still, between the petitions, the ugly face of my iniquity stared into my soul. As the acuteness of this remorse began to die away, it was succeeded by a sense of joy. The problem of my conduct was solved. Hyde was thenceforth impossible; whether I would or not, I was now confined to the better part of my existence; and O, how I rejoiced to think of it! with what willing humility I embraced anew the restrictions of natural life! with what sincere renunciation I locked the door by which I had so often gone and come, and ground the key under my heel!

The next day, came the news that the murder had been over-looked,[16] that the guilt of Hyde was patent to the world, and that the victim was a man high in public estimation. It was not only a crime, it had been a tragic folly. I think I was glad to know it; I think I was glad to have my better impulses thus buttressed and guarded by the terrors of the scaffold. Jekyll was now my city of refuge; let but Hyde peep out an instant, and the hands of all men would be raised to take and slay him.

I resolved in my future conduct to redeem the past; and I can say with honesty that my resolve was fruitful of some good. You know yourself how earnestly, in the last months of the last year, I laboured to relieve suffering; you know that much was done for others, and that the days passed quietly, almost happily for myself. Nor can I truly say that I wearied of this beneficent and innocent life; I think instead that I daily enjoyed it more completely; but I was still cursed with my duality of purpose; and as the first edge of

---

[16] Witnessed (not, by dire pun, *ignored*).

my penitence wore off, the lower side of me, so long indulged, so recently chained down, began to growl for licence. Not that I dreamed of resuscitating Hyde; the bare idea of that would startle me to frenzy: no, it was in my own person that I was once more tempted to trifle with my conscience; and it was as an ordinary secret sinner that I at last fell before the assaults of temptation.

There comes an end to all things; the most capacious measure is filled at last; and this brief condescension to my evil finally destroyed the balance of my soul. And yet I was not alarmed; the fall seemed natural, like a return to the old days before I had made my discovery. It was a fine, clear, January day, wet under foot where the frost had melted, but cloudless overhead; and the Regent's Park was full of winter chirrupings and sweet with spring odours. I sat in the sun on a bench; the animal within me licking the chops of memory; the spiritual side a little drowsed, promising subsequent penitence, but not yet moved to begin. After all, I reflected, I was like my neighbours; and then I smiled, comparing myself with other men, comparing my active good-will with the lazy cruelty of their neglect. And at the very moment of that vainglorious thought, a qualm came over me, a horrid nausea and the most deadly shuddering. These passed away, and left me faint; and then as in its turn faintness subsided, I began to be aware of a change in the temper of my thoughts, a greater boldness, a contempt of danger, a solution of the bonds of obligation. I looked down; my clothes hung formlessly on my shrunken limbs; the hand that lay on my knee was corded and hairy. I was once more Edward Hyde. A moment before I had been safe of all men's respect, wealthy, beloved—the cloth laying for me in the dining-room at home; and now I was the common quarry of mankind, hunted, houseless, a known murderer, thrall to the gallows.

My reason wavered, but it did not fail me utterly. I have more than once observed that in my second character, my faculties seemed sharpened to a point and my spirits more tensely elastic; thus it came about that, where Jekyll perhaps might have succumbed, Hyde rose to the importance of the moment. My drugs were in one of the presses of my cabinet; how was I to reach them? That was the problem that (crushing my temples in my hands) I set myself to solve. The laboratory door I had closed. If I sought to enter by the house, my own servants would consign me to the gallows. I saw I must employ another hand, and thought of Lanyon. How was he to be reached? how persuaded? Supposing that I escaped capture in the streets, how was I to make my way into his presence? and how should I, an unknown and displeasing visitor, prevail on the famous physician to rifle the study of his colleague, Dr. Jekyll? Then I remembered that of my original character, one part remained to me: I could write my own hand; and once I had conceived that kindling spark, the way that I must follow became lighted up from end to end.

Thereupon, I arranged my clothes as best I could, and summoning a passing hansom, drove to an hotel in Portland Street, the name of which I chanced to remember. At my appearance (which was indeed comical enough, however tragic a fate these garments covered) the driver could not conceal his mirth. I gnashed my teeth upon him with a gust of devilish fury; and the smile withered from his face—happily for him—yet more happily for myself, for in another instant I had certainly dragged him from his perch. At the inn, as I entered, I looked about me with so black a countenance as made the attendants tremble; not a look did they exchange in my presence; but obsequiously took my orders, led me to a private room, and brought me wherewithal to write. Hyde in danger of his life was a creature new to me; shaken with inordinate anger, strung to the pitch of murder, lusting to inflict pain. Yet the creature was astute; mastered his fury with a great effort of the will; composed his two important letters, one to Lanyon and one to Poole; and that he might receive actual evidence of their being posted, sent them out with directions that they should be registered. Thenceforward, he sat all day over the fire in the private room, gnawing his nails; there he dined, sitting alone with his fears, the waiter visibly quailing before his eye; and thence, when the night was fully come, he set forth in the corner of a closed cab, and was driven to and fro about the streets of the city. He, I say—I cannot say, I. That child of Hell had nothing human; nothing lived in him but fear and hatred. And when at last, thinking the driver had begun to grow suspicious, he discharged the cab and ventured on foot, attired in his misfitting clothes, an object marked out for observation, into the midst of the nocturnal passengers, these two base passions raged within him like a tempest. He walked fast, hunted by his fears, chattering to himself, skulking through the less frequented thoroughfares, counting the minutes that still divided him from midnight. Once a woman spoke to him, offering, I think, a box of lights. He smote her in the face, and she fled.

When I came to myself at Lanyon's, the horror of my old friend perhaps affected me somewhat: I do not know; it was at least but a drop in the sea to the abhorrence with which I looked back upon these hours. A change had come over me. It was no longer the fear of the gallows, it was the horror of being Hyde that racked me. I received Lanyon's condemnation partly in a dream; it was partly in a dream that I came home to my own house and got into bed. I slept after the prostration of the day, with a stringent and profound slumber which not even the nightmares that wrung me could avail to break. I awoke in the morning shaken, weakened, but refreshed. I still hated and feared the thought of the brute that slept within me, and I had not of course forgotten the appalling dangers of the day before; but I was once more at home, in my own house and close to my drugs; and gratitude for my escape shone so strong in my soul that it almost rivalled the brightness of hope.

I was stepping leisurely across the court after breakfast, drinking the chill of the air with pleasure, when I was seized again with those indescribable sensations that heralded the change; and I had but the time to gain the shelter of my cabinet, before I was once again raging and freezing with the passions of Hyde. It took on this occasion a double dose to recall me to myself; and alas! six hours after, as I sat looking sadly in the fire, the pangs returned, and the drug had to be re-administered. In short, from that day forth it seemed only by a great effort as of gymnastics, and only under the immediate stimulation of the drug, that I was able to wear the countenance of Jekyll. At all hours of the day and night, I would be taken with the premonitory shudder; above all, if I slept, or even dozed for a moment in my chair, it was always as Hyde that I awakened. Under the strain of this continually impending doom and by the sleeplessness to which I now condemned myself, ay, even beyond what I had thought possible to man, I became, in my own person, a creature eaten up and emptied by fever, languidly weak both in body and mind, and solely occupied by one thought: the horror of my other self. But when I slept, or when the virtue of the medicine wore off, I would leap almost without transition (for the pangs of transformation grew daily less marked) into the possession of a fancy brimming with images of terror, a soul boiling with causeless hatreds, and a body that seemed not strong enough to contain the raging energies of life. The powers of Hyde seemed to have grown with the sickliness of Jekyll. And certainly the hate that now divided them was equal on each side. With Jekyll, it was a thing of vital instinct. He had now seen the full deformity of that creature that shared with him some of the phenomena of consciousness, and was co-heir with him to death: and beyond these links of community, which in themselves made the most poignant part of his distress, he thought of Hyde, for all his energy of life, as of something not only hellish but inorganic. This was the shocking thing; that the slime of the pit seemed to utter cries and voices; that the amorphous dust gesticulated and sinned; that what was dead, and had no shape, should usurp the offices of life. And this again, that that insurgent horror was knit to him closer than a wife, closer than an eye; lay caged in his flesh, where he heard it mutter and felt it struggle to be born; and at every hour of weakness, and in the confidence of slumber, prevailed against him, and deposed him out of life. The hatred of Hyde for Jekyll was of a different order. His terror of the gallows drove him continually to commit temporary suicide, and return to his subordinate station of a part instead of a person; but he loathed the necessity, he loathed the despondency into which Jekyll was now fallen, and he resented the dislike with which he was himself regarded. Hence the ape-like tricks that he would play me, scrawling in my own hand blasphemies on the pages of my books, burning the letters and destroying the portrait of my father; and indeed, had it not been for his fear of death, he would long ago have ruined himself in order to involve mc in the ruin. But his love of me is wonderful; I go further: I, who sicken and freeze at the mere thought of him, when I recall the abjection and passion of this attachment, and when I know how he fears my power to cut him off by suicide, I find it in my heart to pity him.

It is useless, and the time awfully fails me, to prolong this description; no one has ever suffered such torments, let that suffice; and yet even to these, habit brought—no, not alleviation—but a certain callousness of soul, a certain acquiescence of despair; and my punishment might have gone on for years, but for the last calamity which has now fallen, and which has finally severed me from my own face and nature. My provision of the salt, which had never been renewed since the date of the first experiment, began to run low. I sent out for a fresh supply and mixed the draught; the ebullition followed, and the first change of colour, not the second; I drank it and it was without efficiency. You will learn from Poole how I have had London ransacked; it was in vain; and I am now persuaded that my first supply was impure, and that it was that unknown impurity which lent efficacy to the draught.

About a week has passed, and I am now finishing this statement under the influence of the last of the old powders. This, then, is the last time, short of a miracle, that Henry Jekyll can think his own thoughts or see his own face (now how sadly altered!) in the glass.

Nor must I delay too long to bring my writing to an end; for if my narrative has hitherto escaped destruction, it has been by a combination of great prudence and great good luck. Should the throes of change take me in the act of writing it, Hyde will tear it in pieces; but if some time shall have elapsed after I have laid it by, his wonderful selfishness and circumscription to the moment will probably save it once again from the action of his ape-like spite. And indeed the doom that is closing on us both has already changed and crushed him. Half an hour from now, when I shall again and forever reindue that hated personality, I know how I shall sit shuddering and weeping in my chair, or continue, with the most strained and fearstruck ecstasy of listening, to pace up and down this room (my last earthly refuge) and give ear to every sound of menace. Will Hyde die upon the scaffold? or will he find courage to release himself at the last moment? God knows; I am careless; this is my true hour of death, and what is to follow concerns another than myself. Here then, as I lay down the pen and proceed to seal up my confession, I bring the life of that unhappy Henry Jekyll to an end.

Key Words: *Strange* and *Case*

In a tale in which words as well as people seem to double or multiply in meaning, what might be suggested by Strange Case? *The definitions below are adapted from* The Oxford English Dictionary, *a project that published its first volume in 1884. Because Stevenson spent a good deal of time in the United States, we include some nineteenth-century American senses as well.*

STRANGE

1. Of persons: of or belonging to another country; foreign, alien.
2. Belonging to some other place or neighbourhood.
3. Belonging to others; not of one's own kin or family.

    . . .

5. Added or introduced from outside, external. In surgery: foreign.
6. Alien, far removed; diverse, different (obsolete).
7. Unknown, unfamiliar; not known, met with, or experienced before.

8. Of a kind that is unfamiliar or rare; unusual, uncommon, exceptional, singular, out of the way.

   . . .

10. Unfamiliar, abnormal, or exceptional to a degree that excites wonder or astonishment; difficult to take in or account for; queer, surprising, unaccountable.

11. Of persons: (a) Unfriendly; having the feelings alienated. (b) Distant or cold in demeanour; reserved; not affable, familiar, or encouraging.

    . . .

14. A strange person, stranger.

CASE

(from Latin *casus: fall, chance*)

1. A thing that befalls or happens to any one; an event, occurrence, hap, or chance.

   . . .

3. (a) An instance or example of the occurrence or existence of a thing (fact, circumstance, etc.). (b) An infatuation; a situation in which two people fall in love (originally U.S. slang, 1860s, but migrating to England).

4. (a) The actual state or position of matters; (b) A state of matters relating to a particular person or thing. *in the case of:* as regards.

5. (a) Condition, state (of circumstances external or internal), plight. (b) esp. Physical condition, as in good case.

6. Law: the state of facts, juridically considered. (a) A cause or suit brought into court for decision. (b) A statement of the facts, drawn up for the consideration of a higher court. (c) A cause which has been decided: leading case, one that has settled some important point and is frequently cited as a precedent. (d) The case as presented or "put" to the Court by one of the parties in a suit; (e) A form of procedure in the Common Law. (f) An incident or set of circumstances requiring investigation by the police or other detective agency.

7. Case of conscience: A practical question concerning which conscience may be in doubt; a question as to the application

of recognized principles of faith and obedience to one's duty in a particular case or set of circumstances.

Here, a translation of Latin *casus conscientiæ* (French *cas de conscience*), according to Ames (1576–1633), "called *casus*, because it is wont to happen or occur (*cadere*) in life; and *casus conscientiæ*, because when it happens, conscience ought to give a judgment with the greatest carefulness." These cases or questions are divided into two classes, (1) those which concern a man's state before God, (2) those which concern his actions in that state. It is mainly to the second of these, or cases of conduct, that *casuistry* is understood to refer.

8. Medical: (a) The condition of disease in a person. (b) An instance of disease, or other condition requiring medical treatment; "a record of the progress of disease in an individual." Also (colloquial), a patient. (c) U.S. slang, of persons: A "specimen." See *Bartlett's Dictionary of American English* (1848–1860): Case, a character, a queer one.

9. Grammar. In inflected languages, one of the varied forms of a substantive, adjective, or pronoun, which express the varied relations in which it may stand to some other word in the sentence (subjective, objective, possessive).

CASE

(from Middle English *cas*, Latin *capsa: chest*)

1. A thing fitted to contain or enclose something else; a receptacle or holder; a box, chest, bag, sheath, covering.
2. The outer protective or covering part of anything.

   In book-binding, the boards and back, cloth-covered or otherwise, in which books are "cased" or "bound in cloth."

3. *Figurative:* (a) The body (as enclosing the soul, etc.). (b) The exterior (of a man). Obsolete.
4. *Obsolete:* The skin or hide of an animal. Applied to clothes or garments.
5. The frame in which a door or window is set (staircase, windowcase)
6. The outer part of a house or building; the shell or carcass.
7. A box or chest with its proper contents; often of definite character (e.g., a case of surgical instruments, a case of drawers.) Hence, a set. (a) couple, brace, a pair. (b) ? One of a pair, the fellow to another.

From *A Child's Garden of Verses*
(London, Longmans, Green and Co., 1885)

Dr. Jekyll recalls "the days of childhood, when I had walked with my father's hand," and reports the adult consequence: "Jekyll had more than a father's interest; Hyde had more than a son's indifference." It is with a reflection on his felt need to "conceal" (or hide) his pleasures, even as a child, that "Henry Jekyll's Full Statement of the Case" begins. The author behind this *Case* also knows that a child's imagination may slip loose, may turn with fascination to the night life, may even invent a second self to explore it. The poems that populate *A Child's Garden of Verses*—published in 1885, the year Stevenson was writing *Strange Case of Dr. Jekyll and Mr. Hyde*—cast a symbolic prelude to a double life, as though Mr. Hyde were the adult emanation of dark fantasies cultivated by the child, intuitively conscious that deepest thrills have to stay hidden. For every "good boy," or happy child prospering in the day-world of this garden of verses, there are bad boys and children eager for, and often captivated by, nocturnal adventures.

The child of *The Land of Nod* is divided between a daylight self, alienated and restless among his friends in the day-world, and a night self, happily alone and at liberty, with "none to tell [him] what to do." Yet it's not an easy division: his is also a suspended consciousness, unable to recapture fully, in waking life ("get back by day"), the strange, exotic, curious night music that still plays faintly in his brain. With a more tortured psychology, this self-division and alienation will become Dr. Jekyll's freedom and agony. This is the implicit threat to the self-described "Good Boy," who is a little too insistently defensive against the implied bad opposite. His "ugly dream" plays as an adhesive, phantom double, recalled even as it is denied. The child who tells of "Shadow March" not only has frightful sights, but also believes them to have substantial agency. The night that "stares" into the child's room, as if a malevolent Bogie, seems connected to the child who casts the shadows that his heartbeat animates with "wicked" purpose. Mr. Hyde arises from the lineage of this Bogie, a "bad boy" who is not quite the opposite, but rather the spectral double of the "good boy" who wins parental approval.

In Stevenson's garden, every child seems doubled by shadow creatures. The first poem in the subsection *The Child Alone* turns out not to be about a child alone. This "Unseen Playmate," as the poem's too-knowing voice intimates, is an intimate of a child's world. To say that he "inhabits the caves that you dig" is to link him to the fundamental nature of play, a genesis in any child's imagination. "Fiction is to the grown man what play is to the child," Stevenson wrote in his essay *A Gossip on Romance* (1882). In *The Child Alone,* the unseen double is mostly harmless, even at times protective. But there are intimations of a nascent Mr. Hyde in its mischief and stubborn adolescence ("he hates to be big") and in hints of transgressive impishness. The unseen playmate is always siding with the enemy (Frenchmen), for instance; and if, in the daylight of British internationalism, this is the losing side, the poem's last line casts another kind of victory: "'T is he will take care of your playthings himself!" While you are sleeping, this double may be your care-taker, but the syntax also suggests a taking over or taking possession, as Hyde does with Jekyll.

This dark antagonism is more visible in the most famous poem in this *Garden,* where, as in *Shadow March,* a self-projection becomes a companion. *My Shadow* obliquely forecasts Mr. Hyde: though not clearly demonic, "my shadow" takes unpredictable forms, and though these are tied to the "me," they are not quite subject to "me." Compared to the unseen playmate, this shadow is less controlable and more overtly transgressive. The antics of "My Shadow" are funny but also a little embarrassing, a little annoying in being too "like me," even a little shameful in his mimicry, and more than a little anarchic in the way that it disrupts and rebels against what is "proper" for children. It is lazy and arrant in a culture where children are raised to be industrious and obedient. What is the relationship between the "I" and this thing of darkness he acknowledges "my" own? Is this shadow most significant to the poem's speaker for being "very, very like," or for being "not at all like proper children"? The word *proper* involves the question: it not only denotes socially desired behavior (how "children ought to" act) but also puns on the Latin root: *proper* as one's *own* (*property* is a cognate). The illogical joke in the last stanza, about the separate will of one's shadow, occurs just at the point where the speaker starts to complain about the "shame" of a shadow that "sticks to" him a little too closely. Stevenson's "Child" never stops making up tales for alternate, ghostly, hidden, buried selves.

YOUNG NIGHT THOUGHT

ALL night long and every night,
When my mama puts out the light,
I see the people marching by,
As plain as day before my eye.

Armies and emperors and kings,
All carrying different kinds of things,
And marching in so grand a way,
You never saw the like by day.

So fine a show was never seen,
At the great circus on the green;
For every kind of beast and man
Is marching in that caravan.

As first they move a little slow,
But still the faster on they go,
And still beside me close I keep
Until we reach the town of Sleep.

WINDY NIGHTS

WHENEVER the moon and stars are set,
   Whenever the wind is high,
All night long in the dark and wet,
   A man goes riding by.
Late in the night when the fires are out,
Why does he gallop and gallop about?

Whenever the trees are crying aloud,
   And ships are tossed at sea,
By, on the highway, low and loud,
   By at the gallop goes he.
By at the gallop he goes, and then
By he comes back at the gallop again.

ESCAPE AT BEDTIME

THE lights from the parlour and kitchen shone out
   Through the blinds and the windows and bars;
And high overhead and all moving about,

There were thousands of millions of stars.
There ne'er were such thousands of leaves on a tree,
   Nor of people in church or the Park,
As the crowds of the stars that looked down upon me,
   And that glittered and winked in the dark.

The Dog, and the Plough, and the Hunter, and all,
   And the Star of the Sailor, and Mars,
These shown in the sky, and the pail by the wall
   Would be half full of water and stars.
They saw me at last, and they chased me with cries,
   And they soon had me packed into bed;
But the glory kept shining and bright in my eyes,
   And the stars going round in my head.

THE LAND OF NOD

FROM breakfast on through all the day
At home among my friends I stay;
But every night I go abroad
Afar into the land of Nod.

All by myself I have to go,
With none to tell me what to do—
All alone beside the streams
And up the mountain-sides of dreams.

The strangest things are these for me,
Both things to eat and things to see,
And many frightening sights abroad
Till morning in the land of Nod.

Try as I like to find the way,
I never can get back by day,
Nor can remember plain and clear
The curious music that I hear.

A GOOD BOY

I WOKE before the morning, I was happy all the day,
I never said an ugly word, but smiled and stuck to play.

And now at last the sun is going down behind the wood,
And I am very happy, for I know that I've been good.

My bed is waiting cool and fresh, with linen smooth
    and fair,
And I must be off to sleepsin-by, and not forget my prayer.

I know that, till to-morrow I shall see the sun arise,
No ugly dream shall fright my mind, no ugly sight my eyes,

But slumber hold me tightly till I waken in the dawn,
And hear the thrushes singing in the lilacs round the lawn.

SHADOW MARCH

ALL around the house is the jet-black night;
    It stares through the window-pane;
It crawls in the corners, hiding from the light,
    And it moves with the moving flame.

Now my little heart goes a-beating like a drum,
    With the breath of the Bogie in my hair;
And all around the candle and the crooked shadows come
    And go marching along up the stair.

The shadow of the balusters, the shadow of the lamp,
    The shadow of the child that goes to bed—
All the wicked shadows coming, tramp, tramp, tramp,
    With the black night overhead.

THE UNSEEN PLAYMATE

WHEN children are playing alone on the green,
In comes the playmate that never was seen.
When children are happy and lonely and good,
The Friend of the Children comes out of the wood.

Nobody heard him and nobody saw,
His is a picture you never could draw,

But he's sure to be present, abroad or at home,
When children are happy and playing alone.

He lies in the laurels, he runs on the grass,
He sings when you tinkle the musical glass;
Whene'er you are happy and cannot tell why,
The Friend of the Children is sure to be by!

He loves to be little, he hates to be big,
'T is he that inhabits the caves that you dig;
'T is he when you play with your soldiers of tin
That sides with the Frenchmen and never can win.

'T is he, when at night you go off to your bed,
Bids you go to sleep and not trouble your head;
For wherever they're lying, in cupboard or shelf,
'T is he will take care of your playthings himself!

MY SHADOW

I HAVE a little shadow that goes in and out with me,
And what can be the use of him is more than I can see.
He is very, very like me from the heels up to the head;
And I see him jump before me, when I jump into my bed.

The funniest thing about him is the way he likes to grow—
Not at all like proper children, which is always very slow;
For he sometimes shoots up taller like an india-rubber ball,
And he sometimes gets so little that there's none of him
    at all.

He hasn't got a notion of how children ought to play,
And can only make a fool of me in every sort of way.
He stays so close beside me, he's a coward you can see;
I'd think shame to stick to nursie as that shadow sticks
    to me!

One morning, very early, before the sun was up,
I rose and found the shining dew on every buttercup;

But my lazy little shadow, like an arrant sleepy-head,
Had stayed at home behind me and was fast asleep in bed.

THE DUMB SOLDIER

WHEN the grass was closely mown,
Walking on the lawn alone,
In the turf a hole I found,
And hid a soldier underground.

Spring and daisies came apace;
Grasses hide my hiding place;
Grasses run like a green sea
O'er the lawn up to my knee.

Under grass alone he lies,
Looking up with leaden eyes,
Scarlet coat and pointed gun,
To the stars and to the sun.

When the grass is ripe like grain,
When the scythe is stoned again,
When the lawn is shaven clear,
Then my hole shall reappear.

I shall find him, never fear,
I shall find my grenadier;
But for all that's gone and come,
I shall find my soldier dumb.

He has lived, a little thing,
In the grassy woods of spring;
Done, if he could tell me true,
Just as I should like to do.

He has seen the starry hours
And the springing of the flowers;
And the fairy things that pass
In the forests of the grass.

In the silence he has heard
Talking bee and ladybird,

And the butterfly has flown,
O'er him as he lay alone.

Not a word will he disclose,
Not a word of all he knows.
I must lay him on the shelf,
And make up the tale myself.

THE LAND OF STORY-BOOKS

AT evening when the lamp is lit,
Around the fire my parents sit;
They sit at home and talk and sing,
And do not play at anything.

Now, with my little gun, I crawl
All in the dark along the wall,
And follow round the forest track
Away behind the sofa back.

There, in the night, where none can spy,
All in my hunter's camp I lie,
And play at books that I have read
Till it is time to go to bed.

These are the hills, these are the woods,
These are my starry solitudes;
And there the river by whose brink
The roaring lions come to drink.

I see the others far away
As if in firelit camp they lay,
And I, like to an Indian scout,
Around their party prowled about.

So, when my nurse comes in for me,
Home I return across the sea,
And go to bed with backward looks
At my dear land of Story-books.

A Chapter on Dreams
(*Scribner's Magazine,* 3 January 1888)

The past is all of one texture—whether feigned or suffered—whether acted out in three dimensions, or only witnessed in that small theatre of the brain which we keep brightly lighted all night long, after the jets[1] are down, and darkness and sleep reign undisturbed in the remainder of the body. There is no distinction on the face of our experiences; one is vivid indeed, and one dull, and one pleasant, and another agonising to remember; but which of them is what we call true, and which a dream, there is not one hair to prove. The past stands on a precarious footing; another straw split in the field of metaphysic, and behold us robbed of it. There is scarce a family that can count four generations but lays a claim to some dormant title or some castle and estate: a claim not prosecutable in any court of law, but flattering to the fancy and a great alleviation of idle hours. A man's claim to his own past is yet less valid. A paper might turn up (in proper story-book fashion) in the secret drawer of an old ebony secretary,[2] and restore your family to its ancient honours, and reinstate mine in a certain West Indian islet (not far from St. Kitt's,[3] as beloved tradition hummed in my young ears) which was once ours, and is now unjustly some one else's, and for that matter (in the state of the sugar trade) is not worth anything to anybody. I do not say that these revolutions are likely; only no man can deny that they are possible; and the past, on the other hand, is lost for ever: our old days and deeds, our old selves, too, and the very world in which these scenes were acted, all brought down to the same faint residuum as a last night's dream, to some in continuous images, and an echo in the chambers of the brain. Not an hour, not a mood, not a glance of the eye, can we revoke; it is all gone, past conjuring. And yet conceive us robbed of it, conceive that little thread of memory that we trail behind us broken at the pocket's edge; and in what naked nullity should we be left! for we only guide ourselves, and only know ourselves, by these air-painted pictures of the past.

Upon these grounds, there are some among us who claim to have lived longer and more richly than their neighbours; when they

---

[1] Gaslight.

[2] Writing desk.

[3] Part of the British Empire in the Caribbean.

lay asleep they claim they were still active; and among the treasures of memory that all men review for their amusement, these count in no second place the harvests of their dreams. There is one of this kind whom I have in my eye, and whose case is perhaps unusual enough to be described. He was from a child an ardent and uncomfortable dreamer. When he had a touch of fever at night, and the room swelled and shrank, and his clothes, hanging on a nail, now loomed up instant to the bigness of a church, and now drew away into a horror of infinite distance and infinite littleness, the poor soul was very well aware of what must follow, and struggled hard against the approaches of that slumber which was the beginning of sorrows.

But his struggles were in vain; sooner or later the night-hag[4] would have him by the throat, and pluck him strangling and screaming, from his sleep. His dreams were at times commonplace enough, at times very strange, at times they were almost formless: he would be haunted, for instance, by nothing more definite than a certain hue of brown, which he did not mind in the least while he was awake, but feared and loathed while he was dreaming; at times, again, they took on every detail of circumstance, as when once he supposed he must swallow the populous world, and awoke screaming with the horror of the thought. The two chief troubles of his very narrow existence—the practical and everyday trouble of school tasks and the ultimate and airy one of hell and judgment—were often confounded together into one appalling nightmare. He seemed to himself to stand before the Great White Throne; he was called on, poor little devil, to recite some form of words, on which his destiny depended; his tongue stuck, his memory was blank, hell gaped for him; and he would awake, clinging to the curtain-rod with his knees to his chin.

These were extremely poor experiences, on the whole; and at that time of life my dreamer would have very willingly parted with his power of dreams. But presently, in the course of his growth, the cries and physical contortions passed away, seemingly for ever; his visions were still for the most part miserable, but they were more constantly supported; and he would awake with no more extreme symptom than a flying heart, a freezing scalp, cold sweats, and the speechless midnight fear. His dreams, too, as befitted a mind better stocked with particulars, became more circumstantial, and had more the air and continuity of life. The look of the world beginning to take hold on his

[4] An embodied nightmare (a cognate).

attention, scenery came to play a part in his sleeping as well as in his waking thoughts, so that he would take long, uneventful journeys and see strange towns and beautiful places as he lay in bed. And, what is more significant, an odd taste that he had for the Georgian costume and for stories laid in that period of English history,[5] began to rule the features of his dreams; so that he masqueraded there in a three-cornered hat and was much engaged with Jacobite conspiracy[6] between the hour for bed and that for breakfast. About the same time, he began to read in his dreams—tales, for the most part, and for the most part after the manner of G. P. R. James,[7] but so incredibly more vivid and moving than any printed book, that he has ever since been malcontent with literature.

And then, while he was yet a student, there came to him a dream-adventure which he has no anxiety to repeat; he began, that is to say, to dream in sequence and thus to lead a double life—one of the day, one of the night—one that he had every reason to believe was the true one, another that he had no means of proving to be false. I should have said he studied, or was by way of studying, at Edinburgh College, which (it may be supposed) was how I came to know him. Well, in his dream-life, he passed a long day in the surgical theatre, his heart in his mouth, his teeth on edge, seeing monstrous malformations and the abhorred dexterity of surgeons. In a heavy, rainy, foggy evening he came forth into the South Bridge, turned up the High Street, and entered the door of a tall LAND,[8] at the top of which he supposed himself to lodge. All night long, in his wet clothes, he climbed the stairs, stair after stair in endless series, and at every second flight a flaring lamp with a reflector. All night long, he brushed by single persons passing downward—beggarly women of the street, great, weary, muddy labourers, poor scarecrows of men, pale parodies of women—but all drowsy and weary like himself, and all single, and all brushing against him as they passed. In the end, out of a northern window, he would see day beginning to whiten over the Firth,[9] give up the ascent, turn to descend, and in a breath be back again upon the streets, in his

---

[5] Kings George I–IV ruled England in the 18th century and the first decades of the 19th.

[6] Stuart claimants (in Scotland) to the throne of England.

[7] George Payne Rainsford James (1799–1860), doctor by profession, was a historian, biographer, and writer of romance adventure novels.

[8] Scots dialect for a house subdivided into apartments.

[9] Long narrow inlet of the sea; the one near Edinburgh is the Firth of Forth.

wet clothes, in the wet, haggard dawn, trudging to another day of monstrosities and operations. Time went quicker in the life of dreams, some seven hours (as near as he can guess) to one; and it went, besides, more intensely, so that the gloom of these fancied experiences clouded the day, and he had not shaken off their shadow ere it was time to lie down and to renew them. I cannot tell how long it was that he endured this discipline; but it was long enough to leave a great black blot upon his memory, long enough to send him, trembling for his reason, to the doors of a certain doctor; whereupon with a simple draught he was restored to the common lot of man.

The poor gentleman has since been troubled by nothing of the sort; indeed, his nights were for some while like other men's, now blank, now chequered with dreams, and these sometimes charming, sometimes appalling, but except for an occasional vividness, of no extraordinary kind. I will just note one of these occasions, ere I pass on to what makes my dreamer truly interesting. It seemed to him that he was in the first floor of a rough hill-farm. The room showed some poor efforts at gentility, a carpet on the floor, a piano, I think, against the wall; but, for all these refinements, there was no mistaking he was in a moorland place, among hillside people, and set in miles of heather. He looked down from the window upon a bare farmyard, that seemed to have been long disused. A great, uneasy stillness lay upon the world. There was no sign of the farm-folk or of any live stock, save for an old, brown, curly dog of the retriever breed, who sat close in against the wall of the house and seemed to be dozing. Something about this dog disquieted the dreamer; it was quite a nameless feeling, for the beast looked right enough—indeed, he was so old and dull and dusty and broken-down, that he should rather have awakened pity; and yet the conviction came and grew upon the dreamer that this was no proper dog at all, but something hellish. A great many dozing summer flies hummed about the yard; and presently the dog thrust forth his paw, caught a fly in his open palm, carried it to his mouth like an ape, and looking suddenly up at the dreamer in the window, winked to him with one eye. The dream went on, it matters not how it went; it was a good dream as dreams go; but there was nothing in the sequel worthy of that devilish brown dog. And the point of interest for me lies partly in that very fact: that having found so singular an incident, my imperfect dreamer should prove unable to carry the tale to a fit end and fall back on indescribable noises and indiscriminate horrors. It would be different now; he knows his business better!

For, to approach at last the point: This honest fellow had long been in the custom of setting himself to sleep with tales, and so had his father before him; but these were irresponsible inventions, told for the teller's pleasure, with no eye to the crass public or the thwart[10] reviewer: tales where a thread might be dropped, or one adventure quitted for another, on fancy's least suggestion. So that the little people who manage man's internal theatre had not as yet received a very rigorous training; and played upon their stage like children who should have slipped into the house and found it empty, rather than like drilled actors performing a set piece to a huge hall of faces. But presently my dreamer began to turn his former amusement of story-telling to (what is called) account; by which I mean that he began to write and sell his tales. Here was he, and here were the little people who did that part of his business, in quite new conditions. The stories must now be trimmed and pared and set upon all fours, they must run from a beginning to an end and fit (after a manner) with the laws of life; the pleasure, in one word, had become a business; and that not only for the dreamer, but for the little people of his theatre. These understood the change as well as he. When he lay down to prepare himself for sleep, he no longer sought amusement, but printable and profitable tales; and after he had dozed off in his box-seat, his little people continued their evolutions with the same mercantile designs. All other forms of dream deserted him but two: he still occasionally reads the most delightful books, he still visits at times the most delightful places; and it is perhaps worthy of note that to these same places, and to one in particular, he returns at intervals of months and years, finding new field-paths, visiting new neighbours, beholding that happy valley under new effects of noon and dawn and sunset. But all the rest of the family of visions is quite lost to him: the common, mangled version of yesterday's affairs, the raw-head-and-bloody-bones nightmare, rumoured to be the child of toasted cheese—these and their like are gone; and, for the most part, whether awake or asleep, he is simply occupied—he or his little people—in consciously making stories for the market. This dreamer (like many other persons) has encountered some trifling vicissitudes of fortune. When the bank begins to send letters and the butcher to linger at the back gate, he sets to belabouring his brains after a story, for that is his readiest money-winner; and, behold! at once the little people begin to bestir themselves in the same quest, and labour all night long, and all night

---

[10] Unsympathetic.

long set before him truncheons of tales upon their lighted theatre. No fear of his being frightened now; the flying heart and the frozen scalp are things by-gone; applause, growing applause, growing interest, growing exultation in his own cleverness (for he takes all the credit), and at last a jubilant leap to wakefulness, with the cry, "I have it, that'll do!" upon his lips: with such and similar emotions he sits at these nocturnal dramas, with such outbreaks, like Claudius in the play, he scatters the performance in the midst.[11] Often enough the waking is a disappointment: he has been too deep asleep, as I explain the thing; drowsiness has gained his little people, they have gone stumbling and maundering through their parts; and the play, to the awakened mind, is seen to be a tissue of absurdities. And yet how often have these sleepless Brownies[12] done him honest service, and given him, as he sat idly taking his pleasure in the boxes, better tales than he could fashion for himself.

Here is one, exactly as it came to him. It seemed he was the son of a very rich and wicked man, the owner of broad acres and a most damnable temper. The dreamer (and that was the son) had lived much abroad, on purpose to avoid his parent; and when at length he returned to England, it was to find him married again to a young wife, who was supposed to suffer cruelly and to loathe her yoke. Because of this marriage (as the dreamer indistinctly understood) it was desirable for father and son to have a meeting; and yet both being proud and both angry, neither would condescend upon a visit. Meet they did accordingly, in a desolate, sandy country by the sea; and there they quarrelled, and the son, stung by some intolerable insult, struck down the father dead. No suspicion was aroused; the dead man was found and buried, and the dreamer succeeded to the broad estates, and found himself installed under the same roof with his father's widow, for whom no provision had been made. These two lived very much alone, as people may after a bereavement, sat down to table together, shared the long evenings, and grew daily better friends; until it seemed to him of a sudden that she was prying about dangerous matters, that she had conceived a notion of his guilt, that

---

[11] In Shakespeare's *Hamlet* (Act 3), Hamlet stages a play at court, patterned on the crime of which he suspects his uncle Claudius (now King of Denmark)—murdering his brother (Hamlet's father), to get to the throne and Queen Gertrude. If Claudius reacts, Hamlet supposes, this will confirm his guilt. Claudius does react, putting a stop to the play and storming out.

[12] A "wee brown man" in Scottish folklore, a benevolent spirit or goblin, said to haunt old houses, and to perform useful chores while the family is asleep.

she watched him and tried him with questions. He drew back from her company as men draw back from a precipice suddenly discovered; and yet so strong was the attraction that he would drift again and again into the old intimacy, and again and again be startled back by some suggestive question or some inexplicable meaning in her eye. So they lived at cross purposes, a life full of broken dialogue, challenging glances, and suppressed passion; until, one day, he saw the woman slipping from the house in a veil, followed her to the station, followed her in the train to the seaside country, and out over the sandhills to the very place where the murder was done. There she began to grope among the bents,[13] he watching her, flat upon his face; and presently she had something in her hand—I cannot remember what it was, but it was deadly evidence against the dreamer—and as she held it up to look at it, perhaps from the shock of the discovery, her foot slipped, and she hung at some peril on the brink of the tall sand-wreaths. He had no thought but to spring up and rescue her; and there they stood face to face, she with that deadly matter openly in her hand—his very presence on the spot another link of proof. It was plain she was about to speak, but this was more than he could bear—he could bear to be lost, but not to talk of it with his destroyer; and he cut her short with trivial conversation. Arm in arm, they returned together to the train, talking he knew not what, made the journey back in the same carriage, sat down to dinner, and passed the evening in the drawing-room as in the past. But suspense and fear drummed in the dreamer's bosom. "She has not denounced me yet"— so his thoughts ran—"when will she denounce me? Will it be to-morrow?" And it was not to-morrow, nor the next day, nor the next; and their life settled back on the old terms, only that she seemed kinder than before, and that, as for him, the burthen of his suspense and wonder grew daily more unbearable, so that he wasted away like a man with a disease. Once, indeed, he broke all bounds of decency, seized an occasion when she was abroad, ransacked her room, and at last, hidden away among her jewels, found the damning evidence. There he stood, holding this thing, which was his life, in the hollow of his hand, and marvelling at her inconsequent behaviour, that she should seek, and keep, and yet not use it; and then the door opened, and behold herself. So, once more, they stood, eye to eye, with the evidence between them; and once more she raised to him a face brimming with some communication; and once more he shied away

---

[13] Reeds.

from speech and cut her off. But before he left the room, which he had turned upside down, he laid back his death-warrant where he had found it; and at that, her face lighted up. The next thing he heard, she was explaining to her maid, with some ingenious falsehood, the disorder of her things. Flesh and blood could bear the strain no longer; and I think it was the next morning (though chronology is always hazy in the theatre of the mind) that he burst from his reserve. They had been breakfasting together in one corner of a great, par-queted, sparely-furnished room of many windows; all the time of the meal she had tortured him with sly allusions; and no sooner were the servants gone, and these two protagonists alone together, than he leaped to his feet. She too sprang up, with a pale face; with a pale face, she heard him as he raved out his complaint: Why did she torture him so? she knew all, she knew he was no enemy to her; why did she not denounce him at once? what signified her whole behaviour? why did she torture him? and yet again, why did she torture him? And when he had done, she fell upon her knees, and with out-stretched hands: "Do you not understand?" she cried. "I love you!"

Hereupon, with a pang of wonder and mercantile delight, the dreamer awoke. His mercantile delight was not of long endurance; for it soon became plain that in this spirited tale there were unmar-ketable elements; which is just the reason why you have it here so briefly told. But his wonder has still kept growing; and I think the reader's will also, if he consider it ripely. For now he sees why I speak of the little people as of substantive inventors and performers. To the end they had kept their secret. I will go bail for the dreamer (having excellent grounds for valuing his candour) that he had no guess whatever at the motive of the woman—the hinge of the whole well-invented plot—until the instant of that highly dramatic declaration. It was not his tale; it was the little people's! And observe: not only was the secret kept, the story was told with really guileful craftsman-ship. The conduct of both actors is (in the cant phrase) psychologi-cally correct, and the emotion aptly graduated up to the surprising climax. I am awake now, and I know this trade; and yet I cannot bet-ter it. I am awake, and I live by this business; and yet I could not outdo—could not perhaps equal—that crafty artifice (as of some old, experienced carpenter of plays, some Dennery or Sardou[14]) by

---

[14] French playwrights Adolphe Dennery (1811–1899) and Victorien Sardou (1831–1908). Sardou, who wrote the play on which the opera *Tosca* is based, was celebrated for his comedies.

which the same situation is twice presented and the two actors twice brought face to face over the evidence, only once it is in her hand, once in his—and these in their due order, the least dramatic first. The more I think of it, the more I am moved to press upon the world my question: Who are the Little People? They are near connections of the dreamer's, beyond doubt; they share in his financial worries and have an eye to the bank-book; they share plainly in his training; they have plainly learned like him to build the scheme of a considerate story and to arrange emotion in progressive order; only I think they have more talent; and one thing is beyond doubt, they can tell him a story piece by piece, like a serial, and keep him all the while in ignorance of where they aim. Who are they, then? and who is the dreamer?

Well, as regards the dreamer, I can answer that, for he is no less a person than myself;—as I might have told you from the beginning, only that the critics murmur over my consistent egotism;—and as I am positively forced to tell you now, or I could advance but little farther with my story. And for the Little People, what shall I say they are but just my Brownies, God bless them! who do one-half my work for me while I am fast asleep, and in all human likelihood, do the rest for me as well, when I am wide awake and fondly suppose I do it for myself. That part which is done while I am sleeping is the Brownies' part beyond contention; but that which is done when I am up and about is by no means necessarily mine, since all goes to show the Brownies have a hand in it even then. Here is a doubt that much concerns my conscience. For myself—what I call I, my conscious ego, the denizen of the pineal gland[15] unless he has changed his residence since Descartes,[16] the man with the conscience and the variable bank-account, the man with the hat and the boots, and the privilege of voting and not carrying his candidate at the general elections—I am sometimes tempted to suppose he is no story-teller at all, but a creature as matter of fact as any cheesemonger or any cheese, and a realist bemired up to the ears in actuality; so that, by that account, the whole of my published fiction should be the single-handed product of some Brownie, some

---

[15] This gland in the brain is sometimes called "the third eye" (in birds it seems to be photosensitive).

[16] 17th century French philosopher René Descartes's famous statement is "Cogito ergo sum" (I think therefore I am)—that is, everything may be doubted, except the thinking subject who doubts.

Familiar,[17] some unseen collaborator, whom I keep locked in a back garret, while I get all the praise and he but a share (which I cannot prevent him getting) of the pudding. I am an excellent adviser, something like Moliere's servant;[18] I pull back and I cut down; and I dress the whole in the best words and sentences that I can find and make; I hold the pen, too; and I do the sitting at the table, which is about the worst of it; and when all is done, I make up the manuscript and pay for the registration; so that, on the whole, I have some claim to share, though not so largely as I do, in the profits of our common enterprise.

I can but give an instance or so of what part is done sleeping and what part awake, and leave the reader to share what laurels there are, at his own nod, between myself and my collaborators; and to do this I will first take a book that a number of persons have been polite enough to read, the STRANGE CASE OF DR. JEKYLL AND MR. HYDE. I had long been trying to write a story on this subject, to find a body, a vehicle, for that strong sense of man's double being which must at times come in upon and overwhelm the mind of every thinking creature. I had even written one, THE TRAVELLING COMPANION, which was returned by an editor on the plea that it was a work of genius and indecent, and which I burned the other day on the ground that it was not a work of genius, and that JEKYLL had supplanted it. Then came one of those financial fluctuations to which (with an elegant modesty) I have hitherto referred in the third person. For two days I went about racking my brains for a plot of any sort; and on the second night I dreamed the scene at the window, and a scene afterward split in two, in which Hyde, pursued for some crime, took the powder and underwent the change in the presence of his pursuers. All the rest was made awake, and consciously, although I think I can trace in much of it the manner of my Brownies. The meaning of the tale is therefore mine, and had long pre-existed in my garden of Adonis,[19] and tried one body after another in vain; indeed, I do most of the

---

[17] Supernatural visitor.

[18] Premier 17th-century French dramatist, actor, director, famed for his comic satires.

[19] Adonis, a handsome young hunter killed by a boar, was beloved of Venus, who appealed to Jove for mercy. He decided that Venus could have him for half the year, in the upper world, and the other half he would spend dreaming in the abode of the dead. Keats's *Endymion* sets Adonis in a lush bower guarded by cupids.

morality, worse luck! and my Brownies have not a rudiment of what we call a conscience. Mine, too, is the setting, mine the characters. All that was given me was the matter of three scenes, and the central idea of a voluntary change becoming involuntary. Will it be thought ungenerous, after I have been so liberally ladling out praise to my unseen collaborators, if I here toss them over, bound hand and foot, into the arena of the critics? For the business of the powders, which so many have censured, is, I am relieved to say, not mine at all but the Brownies'. Of another tale, in case the reader should have glanced at it, I may say a word: the not very defensible story of OLALLA.[20] Here the court, the mother, the mother's niche, Olalla, Olalla's chamber, the meetings on the stair, the broken window, the ugly scene of the bite, were all given me in bulk and detail as I have tried to write them; to this I added only the external scenery (for in my dream I never was beyond the court), the portrait, the characters of Felipe and the priest, the moral, such as it is, and the last pages, such as, alas! they are. And I may even say that in this case the moral itself was given me; for it arose immediately on a comparison of the mother and the daughter, and from the hideous trick of atavism in the first. Sometimes a parabolic sense is still more undeniably present in a dream; sometimes I cannot but suppose my Brownies have been aping Bunyan,[21] and yet in no case with what would possibly be called a moral in a tract; never with the ethical narrowness; conveying hints instead of life's larger limitations and that sort of sense which we seem to perceive in the arabesque of time and space.

For the most part, it will be seen, my Brownies are somewhat fantastic, like their stories hot and hot, full of passion and the picturesque, alive with animating incident; and they have no prejudice against the supernatural. But the other day they gave me a surprise, entertaining me with a love-story, a little April comedy, which I ought certainly to hand over to the author of A CHANCE ACQUAINTANCE, for he could write it as it should be written, and I am sure (although

---

[20] Another of Stevenson's "double" tales (including vampirism and repressed selves), this one published in the Christmas 1885 number of *Court and Society Review*, and reprinted in *Merry Men and Other Fables* (1887).

[21] John Bunyan's autobiography, *Grace Abounding to the Chief of Sinners* (1666) and his immensely popular allegory, *The Pilgrim's Progress from This World to That Which Is to Come* (published in two parts 1678, 1674) were all written while he was in prison.

I mean to try) that I cannot.—But who would have supposed that a Brownie of mine should invent a tale for Mr. Howells?[22]

Robert Louis Stevenson and his friends on *The Strange Case of Dr. Jekyll and Mr. Hyde*

Stevenson's letters are from The Letters of Robert Louis Stevenson, *ed. Sidney Colvin (New York: Scribner's, 1921).*

FROM A LETTER TO WILL H. LOW, 2 JANUARY 1886

Stevenson's friend American artist Will Low (1853–1932)—who did the ceiling murals and decorations of New York's Waldorf Astoria Hotel, and was an inspiration to Louis Comfort Tiffany—has been illustrating the poems of Keats. Stevenson admired his work on Lamia, *in which a Greek nymph has been made invisible to thwart the sexual advances of suitors and satyrs.*

. . . I send you herewith a gothic gnome for your Greek nymph; but the gnome is interesting I think and he came out of a deep mine, where he guards the fountain of tears. It is not always the time to rejoice, Yours ever,

R. L. S.

The gnome's name is <u>Jekyll and Hyde;</u> I believe you will find he is likewise quite willing to answer to the name of Low or Stevenson.

J. A. SYMONDS, TO R. L. STEVENSON, 3 MARCH 1886

Scholar, biographer, and literary historian, Symonds (1840–1893) was tormented from schoolboy days on by his homoerotic passions.

---

[22] William Dean Howells (1837–1920), editor of *Atlantic Monthly Magazine*, published his novel, *A Chance Acquaintance*, in 1873, and had a best-seller with *The Rise of Silas Lapham* in 1885. In *A Chance Acquaintance* a young Bostonian falls in love with a worthy but unworldly inland girl; his inability to overcome his condescension to her drives them apart.

My dear Louis

At last I have read <u>Dr. Jekyll.</u> It makes me wonder whether a man has the right so to scrutinise "the abysmal deeps of personality."[1] It is indeed a dreadful book, most dreadful because of a certain moral callousness, a want of sympathy, a shutting out of hope. The art is burning and intense. The "Peau de Chagrin" disappears; Poe is as water.[2] As a piece of literary work, this seems to me the finest you have done—in all that regards style, invention, psychological analysis, exquisite fitting of parts, and admirable employment of motives to realize the abnormal. But it has left such a deeply painful impression on my heart that I do not know how I am ever to turn to it again.

The fact is that, viewed as an allegory, it touches one too closely. Most of us at some epoch of our lives have been upon the verge of developing a Mr. Hyde.

Physical and biological Science on a hundred lines is reducing individual freedom to zero, and weakening the sense of responsibility. I doubt whether the artist should lend his genius to this grim argument. Your Dr. Jekyll seems to me capable of loosening the last threads of self-control in one who should read it while wavering between his better and worse self. It is like the Cave of Despair in the "Faery Queen."[3]

I had the great biologist Lauder Brunton[4] with me a fortnight back. He was talking about Dr. Jekyll and a book by

---

[1] From Alfred Lord Tennyson's *The Palace of Art* (1853 version): "God, before whom ever lie bare / The abysmal deeps of personality / Plagued her with sore despair" (223–25).

[2] "Peau de chagrin" is a French idiom: an appearance of grievous care; with reference to Honoré de Balzac's *La Peau de Chagrin* (1831), a tale about a man who finds a strange curio in an old curiosity shop—an animal skin (*peau*) that grants wishes, but shrinks with each bequest and proves fatal to the wisher when it shrinks to nothing. Realizing the curse, the wisher tries not to wish for, or desire, anything. There are complex punnings with which Stevenson, fluent in French, plays: the skin in Balzac's tale is an ass's hide, called *shagreen*, a pun on *chagrin*. And *peau* as skin or hide, winks at Hyde, as well as echoes in *Poe*. The similarity between *Dr. Jekyll and Mr. Hyde* and Edgar Allen Poe's *Murders in the Rue Morgue* (1841), in which it is discovered that the murders were wrought by an escaped wild animal—a sailor's pet—had been observed in the first reviews.

[3] In his Cave, allegorical Despair soothingly counsels suicide as a cure for the pains of existence (Edmund Spenser, *The Faerie Queene*, I.ix.28–51).

[4] Sir Thomas Lauder Brunton (1844–1916), Scots-educated London pharmacologist, was famed for his research on blood pressure and circulation.

W. O. Holmes, in which atavism is played with.[5] I could see that, though a Christian, he held very feebly to the theory of human liberty; and these two works of fiction interested him, as Dr. Jekyll does me, upon that point at issue.

I understand now thoroughly how much a sprite you are. Really there is something not quite human in your genius!

The denouement would have been finer, I think, if Dr. Jekyll by a last supreme effort of his lucid self had given Mr. Hyde up to justice which might have been arranged after the scene in Lanyon's study. Did you ever read Raskolnikow?[6] How fine is that ending! Had you made your hero act thus, you would at least have saved the sense of human dignity. The doors of Broadmoor[7] would have closed on Mr. Hyde.

Goodbye. I seem quite to have lost you. But if I come to England I shall try to see you.

> Love to your wife.
> Ever yrs
> J. A. Symonds

STEVENSON'S REPLY TO SYMONDS,
EARLY MARCH 1886

My dear Symonds . . . Jekyll is a dreadful thing, I own; but the only thing I feel dreadful about is that damned old business of the war in the members.[8] This time it came out; I hope it will stay in, in future.

Raskolnikoff is the greatest book I have read easily in ten years; I am glad you took to it. Many find it dull; Henry James

[5] U.S. Supreme Court Justice Oliver Wendell Holmes Jr. (1841–1935), advocate of eugenics and race-based theories of degeneration: "instead of waiting to execute degenerate offspring for crime, or to let them starve for their imbecility," he advocated sterilization, to "prevent those who are manifestly unfit from continuing their kind. . . . Three generations of imbeciles are enough" (a later majority opinion for the Supreme Court in *Buck v. Bell*, supporting mandatory sterilization).

[6] The protagonist and German title of Dostoevsky's *Crime and Punishment* (Russia, 1866); Stevenson had read it in French in 1885 (*Le Crime et le Châtiment*), commenting to his friend W. E. Henley that "it is having a brain fever to read it" (*Letters*, 5:151). The English translation appeared in 1886. The self-tortured murderer Raskolnikov finally confesses, and is redeemed by the love of his mother and sister.

[7] The Broadmoor Asylum for the Criminally Insane was built in Berkshire in 1863.

[8] "Your lusts that war in your members" (James 4:1). See p. 107n4.

could not finish it: all I can say is, it nearly finished me. It was like having an illness. James did not care for it because the character of Raskolnikoff was not objective; and at that I divined a great gulf between us and, on further reflection, the existence of a certain impotence in many minds of today, which prevents them from living in a book or a character, and keeps them standing afar off, spectators of a puppet show. To such I suppose the book may seem empty in the centre; to the others it is a room, a house of life, into which they themselves enter, and are tortured and purified.

STEVENSON TO JOHN PAUL BOCOCK, NOVEMBER 1887

John Paul Bocock (1856–1903) wrote stories, essays, and poems for magazines in New York and Philadelphia, including Scribner's, *to which Stevenson refers here.*

Private

Dear Mr Bocock

. . . Your prominent dramatic critic, writing like a journalist, has written like a braying ass; what he meant is probably quite different and true enough—that the work is ugly and the allegory too like the usual pulpit judge and not just enough to the modesty of facts. You are right as to Mansfield[9]: Hyde was the younger of the two. He was not good looking however; and not, Great Gods! a mere voluptuary. There is no harm in a voluptuary; and none, with my hand on my heart and in the sight of God, none—no harm whatever—in what prurient fools call 'immorality.' The harm was in Jekyll, because he was a hypocrite—not because he was fond of women; he says so himself; but people are so filled full of folly and inverted lust, that they can think of nothing but sexuality. The Hypocrite let out the beast Hyde—who is no more sexual than another, but who is the essence of cruelty and malice, and selfishness and cowardice: and these are the diabolic in man—not this poor wish to have a woman, that they make such a cry about. I know,

[9] Richard Mansfield; see p. 42.

and I dare to say, you know as well as I, that bad and good, even to our human eyes, has no more connection with what is called dissipation than it has with flying kites. But the sexual field and the business field are perhaps the two best fitted for the display of cruelty and cowardice and selfishness. That is what people see; and then they confound. . . .

Yours truly Robert Louis Stevenson

I need not say this letter is not for publication; you can use my facts, not my language; but indeed the distinction is made here chiefly to explain the word private at the top, or you might suppose I was feeding you with an empty spoon.

R.L.S.

Critical Reactions to *The Strange Case of Dr. Jekyll and Mr. Hyde*

Andrew Lang
Saturday Review (London), 9 January 1886

Prolific Scots man of letters Andrew Lang (1844–1912) was a poet, novelist, literary critic, anthropologist, and collector of folk and fairy tales. His novel, The Mark of Cain, *was published in 1886, the same year as Stevenson's* Strange Case.

Mr. Stevenson's *Prince Otto* was, no doubt, somewhat disappointing to many of his readers.[1] They will be hard to please if they are disappointed in his *Strange Case of Dr. Jekyll and Mr. Hyde.* To adopt a recent definition of some of Mr. Stevenson's tales, this little shilling work is like "Poe with the addition of a moral sense." Or perhaps to say that would be to ignore the fact that Poe was extremely fond of one kind of moral, of allegories in which embodied Conscience plays its part with terrible efficacy. . . . Mr. Stevenson's

---

[1] Published in 1885, this novel received mixed reviews; said the *Saturday Review:* "we are given . . . an impossible prince ruling over an impossible territory at an indeterminate time."

idea, his secret (but a very open secret) is that of the double personality in every man. The mere conception is familiar enough. Poe
used it in *William Wilson* and Gautier in *Le Chevalier Double.* Yet
Mr. Stevenson's originality of treatment remains none the less
striking and astonishing. The double personality does not in his
romance take the form of a personified conscience, the *doppel
ganger* of the sinner, a "double" like his own double which Goethe
is fabled to have seen. No; the "separable self" in this "strange
case" is all unlike that in *William Wilson,* and, with its unlikeness
to its master, with its hideous caprices, and appalling vitality, and
terrible power of growth and increase, is, to our thinking, a notion
as novel as it is terrific. We would welcome a spectre, a ghoul, or
even a vampire gladly, rather than meet Mr. Edward Hyde. Without
telling the whole story, and to some extent spoiling the effect, we
cannot explain the exact nature of the relations between Jekyll and
Hyde, nor reveal the mode (itself, we think, original, though it
depends on resources of pseudoscience) in which they were developed. Let it suffice to say that Jekyll's emotions when, as he sits
wearily in the park, he finds that his hand is not his own hand, but
another's; and that other moment when Utterson, the lawyer, is
brought to Jekyll's door, and learns that his locked room is haunted
by something which moans and weeps; and, again, the process beheld
by Dr. Lanyon, are all of them as terrible as anything ever dreamed
of by Poe. They lack, too, that quality of merely earthly horror or of
physical corruption and decay which Poe was apt to introduce so
frequently and with such unpleasant and unholy enjoyment.

It is a proof of Mr. Stevenson's skill that he has chosen the scene
for his wild "Tragedy of a Body and a Soul," as it might have been
called, in the most ordinary and respectable quarters of London.
His heroes (surely *this* is original) are all successful middle-aged
professional men. No woman appears in the tale (as in *Treasure
Island*), and we incline to think that Mr. Stevenson always does
himself most justice in novels without a heroine. It may be regarded
by some critics as a drawback to the tale that it inevitably disen-
gages a powerful lesson in conduct. It is not a moral allegory, of
course; but you cannot help reading the moral into it, and recogniz-
ing that, just as every one of us, according to Mr. Stevenson, travels
through life with a donkey (as he himself did in the Cévennes), so
every Jekyll among us is haunted by his own Hyde. But it would be
most unfair to insist on this, as there is nothing a novel-reader hates

more than to be done good to unawares. Nor has Mr. Stevenson, obviously, any didactic purpose. The moral of the tale is its natural soul, and no more separable from it than, in ordinary life, Hyde is separable from Jekyll.

While one is thrilled and possessed by the horror of the central fancy, one may fail, at first reading, to recognize the delicate and restrained skill of the treatment of accessories, details, and character. Mr. Utterson, for example, Jekyll's friend, is an admirable portrait, and might occupy a place unchallenged among pictures by the best masters of sober fiction.

> At friendly meetings, and when the wine was to his taste, something eminently human beaconed from his eye; something indeed which never found its way into his talk; but which spoke not only in these silent symbols of the after-dinner face, but more often and loudly in the acts of his life. He was austere with himself, but tolerant to others, sometimes wondering, almost with envy, at the high pressure of spirits involved in their misdeeds.

It is fair to add that, while the style of the new romance is usually as plain as any style so full of compressed thought and incident can be, there is at least one passage in the threshold of the book where Mr. Stevenson yields to his old Tempter, "preciousness." Nay, we cannot restrain the fancy that, if the good and less good of Mr. Stevenson's literary personality could be divided like Dr. Jekyll's moral and physical personality, his literary Mr. Hyde would greatly resemble ———— the reader may fill in the blank at his own will. The idea is capable of development. Perhaps Canon McColl is Mr. Gladstone's Edward Hyde,[2] a solution of historical problems which may be applauded by future generations. This is wandering from the topic in hand. It is pleasant to acknowledge that the half-page of "preciousness" stands almost alone in this excellent and horrific and captivating romance, where Mr. Stevenson gives us of his very best and increases that debt of gratitude which we all owe him for so many and such rare pleasures.

There should be a limited edition of the *Strange Case* on Large Paper. It looks lost in a shilling edition—the only "bob'svorth," as

---

[2] William Gladstone, member of parliament, and at various times Prime Minister, agitated for extending the vote to working-class males, advocated Irish Home Rule, and in 1876 published a pamphlet on the violent Turkish oppression of Bulgaria. Canon McColl was virulently anti-Turkish.

the cabman said when he took up Mr. Pickwick,[3] which has real permanent literary merit.

James Ashcroft Noble
Academy, 23 January 1886

> *Poet, essayist, critic, and journalist James Ashcroft Noble (1844–1896) had published a critical study,* The Sonnet in England, *in 1880.*

The Strange Case of Dr. Jekyll and Mr. Hyde is not an orthodox three-volume novel; it is not even a one-volume novel of the ordinary type; it is simply a paper-covered shilling story, belonging, so far as external appearance goes, to a class of literature familiarity with which has bred in the minds of most readers a certain measure of contempt. Appearances, it has been once or twice remarked, are deceitful; and in this case they are very deceitful indeed, for, in spite of the paper cover and the popular price, Mr. Stevenson's story distances so unmistakably its three-volume and one-volume competitors, that its only fitting place is the place of honour. It is, indeed, many years since English fiction has been enriched by any work at once so weirdly imaginative in conception and so faultlessly ingenious in construction as this little tale, which can be read with ease in a couple of hours. Dr. Henry Jekyll is a medical man of high reputation, not only as regards his professional skill, but his general moral and social character; and this reputation is, in the main, well-deserved, for he has honourable instincts and high aspirations with which the greater part of his life of conduct is in harmony. He has also, however, "a certain impatient gaiety of disposition," which at times impels him to indulge in pleasures of a kind which, while they would bring to many men no sense of shame, and therefore no prompting to concealment, do bring to him such sense and such prompting, in virtue of their felt inconsistency with the visible tenor of his existence. The divorce between the two lives becomes so complete that he is haunted and tortured by the consciousness of a double identity which deprives each separate life of its full measure of satisfaction. It is at this point that he makes a wonderful discovery, which seems to cut triumphantly the knot of his perplexity. The discovery is of certain chemical agents, the

---

[3] A bob is a shilling; Samuel Pickwick is the founder and chairman of the whimsical Pickwick Club, in Charles Dickens' first novel, *The Pickwick Papers* (1836–1837).

application of which can give the needed wholeness and homogeneity of individuality by destroying for a time all consciousness of one set of conflicting impulses, so that when the experimenter pleases his lower instincts can absorb his whole being, and, knowing nothing of restraint from anything above them, manifest themselves in new and quite diabolical activities. But this is not all. The fateful drug acts with its strange transforming power upon the body as well as the mind; for when the first dose has been taken the unhappy victim finds that "soul is form and doth the body make," and that his new nature, of evil all compact, has found for itself a corresponding environment, the shrunken shape and loathsome expression of which bear no resemblance to the shape and expression of Dr. Jekyll. It is this monster who appears in the world as Mr. Hyde, a monster whose play is outrage and murder; but who, though known, can never be captured, because when he is apparently traced to the doctor's house, no one is found there but the benevolent and highly honoured doctor himself. The re-transformation has, of course, been affected by another dose of the drug; but as time goes by Dr. Jekyll notices a curious and fateful change in its operation. At first the dethronement of the higher nature has been difficult; sometimes a double portion of the chemical agent has been found necessary to bring about the result; but the lower nature gains a vitality of its own, and at times the transformation from Jekyll to Hyde takes place without any preceding act of volition. How the story ends I must not say. Too much of it has already been told; but without something of such telling it would have been impossible to write an intelligible review. And, indeed, the story has a much larger and deeper interest than that belonging to a mere skilful narrative. It is a marvellous exploration into the recesses of human nature; and though it is more than possible that Mr. Stevenson wrote with no ethical intent, its impressiveness as a parable is equal to its fascination as a work of art. I do not ignore the many differences between the genius of the author of *The Scarlet Letter* and that of the author of *Dr. Jekyll and Mr. Hyde* when I say that the latter story is worthy of Hawthorne.

The *(London) Times*, 25 January 1886

Nothing Mr. Stevenson has written as yet has so strongly impressed us with the versatility of his very original genius as this sparsely-printed little shilling volume. From the business point of view we can only marvel in these practical days at the lavish waste of admirable material, and what strikes us as a disproportionate expenditure on brain-power, in relation to the tangible results. Of two things, one. Either the story was a flash of intuitive psychological research, dashed off in a burst of inspiration; or else it is the product of the most elaborate forethought, fitting together all the parts of an intricate and inscrutable puzzle. The proof is, that every connoisseur who reads the story once, must certainly read it twice. He will read it the first time, passing from surprise to surprise, in a curiosity that keeps growing, because it is never satisfied. For the life of us, we cannot make out how such and such an incident can possibly be explained on grounds that are intelligible or in any way plausible. Yet all the time the seriousness of the tone assures us that explanations are forthcoming. In our impatience we are hurried towards the denouement, which accounts for everything upon strictly scientific grounds, though the science be the science of problematical futurity. Then, having drawn a sigh of relief at having found even a fantastically speculative issue from our embarrassments, we begin reflectively to call to mind how systematically the writer has been working towards it. Never for a moment, in the most startling situations, has he lost his grasp of the grand ground-facts of a wonderful and supernatural problem. Each apparently incredible or insignificant detail has been thoughtfully subordinated to his purpose. And if we say, after all, on a calm retrospect, that the strange case is absurdly and insanely improbable, Mr. Stevenson might answer in the words of Hamlet, that there are more things in heaven and in earth than are dreamed of in our philosophy.[4] For we are still groping by doubtful lights on the dim limits of boundless investigation; and it is always possible that we may be on the brink of a new revelation as to the unforeseen resources of the medical art. And, at all events, the answer should suffice for the purposes of Mr. Stevenson's sensational *tour d'esprit*.

The Strange Case of Dr. Jekyll is sensational enough in all conscience, and yet we do not promise it the wide popularity of *Called Back*.[5] The *brochure* that brought fame and profit to the late Mr. Fargus was pitched in a more commonplace key, and consequently appealed to more vulgar circles. But, for ourselves, we

---

[4] Hamlet's rebuke to his rational schoolmate Horatio, who doubts the version of events given by a midnight ghost, in Shakespeare's *Hamlet* Act I.

[5] This hugely popular novel by "Hugh Conway"—Frederick John Fargus (1847–85)—was published in 1883 and sold over 350,000 copies within its first 4 years. Fargus died of pulmonary disease.

should many times sooner have the credit of *Dr. Jekyll,* which appeals irresistibly to the most cultivated minds, and must be appreciated by the most competent critics. Naturally, we compare it with the sombre masterpieces of Poe, and we may say at once that Mr. Stevenson has gone far deeper. Poe embroidered richly in the gloomy grandeur of his imagination upon themes that were but too material, and not very novel—on the sinister destiny overshadowing a doomed family, on a living and breathing man kept prisoner in a coffin or vault, on the wild whirling of a human waif in the boiling eddies of the Maelstrom—while Mr. Stevenson evolves the ideas of his story from the world that is unseen, enveloping everything in weird mystery, till at last it pleases him to give us the password. We are not going to tell his strange story, though we might well do so, and only excite the curiosity of our readers. We shall only say that we are shown the shrewdest of lawyers hopelessly puzzled by the inexplicable conduct of a familiar friend. All the antecedents of a life of virtue and honour seem to be belied by the discreditable intimacy that has been formed with one of the most callous and atrocious of criminals. A crime committed under the eyes of a witness goes unavenged, though the notorious criminal has been identified, for he disappears as absolutely as if the earth had swallowed him. He reappears in due time where we should least expect to see him, and for some miserable days he leads a charmed life, while he excites the superstitious terrors of all about him. Indeed, the strongest nerves are shaken by stress of sinister circumstances, as well they may be, for the worthy Dr. Jekyll—the benevolent physician—has likewise vanished amid events that are enveloped in impalpable mysteries; nor can anyone surmise what has become of him. So with overwrought feelings and conflicting anticipations we are brought to the end, where all is accounted for, more or less credibly.

Nor is it the mere charm of the story, strange as it is, which fascinates and thrills us. Mr. Stevenson is known for a master of style, and never has he shown his resources more remarkably than on this occasion. We do not mean that the book is written in excellent English—that must be a matter of course; but he has weighed his words and turned his sentences so as to sustain and excite throughout the sense of mystery and of horror. The mere artful use of an "it" for a "he" may go far in that respect, and Mr. Stevenson has carefully chosen his language and missed no opportunity. And if his style is good, his motive is better, and shows a higher order of genius. Slight as is the story, and supremely sensational, we remember nothing better since George Eliot's *Romola* than this delineation of a feeble but kindly nature steadily and inevitably succumbing to the sinister influences of besetting weaknesses. With no formal preaching and without a touch of Pharisaism,[6] he works out the essential power of Evil, which, with its malignant patience and unwearying perseverance, gains ground with each casual yielding to temptation, till the once well-meaning man may actually become a fiend, or at least wear the reflection of the fiend's image. But we have said enough to show our opinion of the book, which should be read as a finished study in the art of fantastic literature.

Julia Wedgwood
Contemporary Review, April 1886 (xlix: 594–95)

> *Frances Julia Wedgwood (1833–1913), principled and passionate English feminist, novelist, biographer, historian, and literary critic, had noteworthy affiliations: kin to and friend of popular novelist Elizabeth Gaskell; great-granddaughter of English potter Josiah Wedgwood, patron of Coleridge's literary career; and granddaughter of Sir James Mackintosh (whose* Vindiciae Gallicae *advocated the principles of the French Revolution before the Terror).*

By far the most remarkable work we have to notice this time is "The Strange Case of Dr. Jekyll and Mr. Hyde," a shilling story, which the reader devours in an hour, but to which he may return again and again, to study a profound allegory and admire a model of style. It is a perfectly original production; it recalls, indeed, the work of Hawthorne, but this is by kindred power, not by imitative workmanship. We will not do so much injustice to any possible reader of this weird tale as to describe its motif, but we blunt no curiosity in saying that its motto might have been the sentence of a Latin father— "Omnis anima et rea et testis est."[7] Mr. Stevenson has set before himself the psychical problem of Hawthorne's "Transformations,"[8]

---

[6] The character and spirit of the Pharisees as depicted in the New Testament: self-righteous, legalistic, frequent hypocritical; "When we speak of Pharisaism we mean obedience petrified into formalism, religion degraded into ritual, morals cankered by casuistry" (F. W. Farrar, *Life & Work of St. Paul* [1879], 1.1.3.46). Eliot's novel *Romola* was serialized in *Cornhill Magazine,* 1862–63.

[7] Tertullian, *De Testimonio Animae* (*The Testimony of the Soul*): "Every soul is both a culprit and a witness."

[8] Nathaniel Hawthorne published his story *The Marble Faun* (1859) in England under this title (London: Smith and Elder, 1860), in order to secure copyright.

viewed from a different and perhaps an opposite point of view, and has dealt with it with more vigour if with less grace. Here it is not the child of Nature who becomes manly by experience of sin, but a fully-developed man who goes through a different form of the process, and if the delineation is less associated with beautiful imagery, the parable is deeper, and, we would venture to add, truer. Mr. Stevenson represents the individualizing influence of modern democracy in its more concentrated form. Whereas most fiction deals with the relation between man and woman (and the very fact that its scope is so much narrowed is a sign of the atomic character of our modern thought), the author of this strange tale takes an even narrower range, and sets himself to investigate the meaning of the word *self*. No woman's name occurs in the book, no romance is even suggested in it; it depends on the interest of an idea; but so powerfully is this interest worked out that the reader feels that the same material might have been spun out to cover double the space, and still have struck him as condensed and close-knit workmanship. It is one of those rare fictions which make one understand the value of temperance in art. If this tribute appears exaggerated, it is at least the estimate of one who began Mr. Stevenson's story with a prejudice against it, arising from a recent perusal of its predecessor, his strangely dull and tasteless "Prince Otto." It is a psychological curiosity that the same man should have written both, and if they were bound up together, the volume would form the most striking illustration of a warning necessary for others besides the critic—the warning to judge no man by any single utterance, how complete soever.

Gerard Manley Hopkins
Letter to Robert Bridges, 28 October 1886

> *Gerard Manley Hopkins (1844–1889) did not publish his poems, struggling not only with a war between his feverish love of writing poetry and his religious vocation, but also with homosexual impulses. On entering the Jesuit priesthood he burned his poetry, but he could not stop writing, even as he agonized over the conflict with his religious devotion. Robert Bridges (1844–1930) would become Poet Laureate in 1913; in 1918 his edition of Hopkins introduced this brilliant poetry and secured its reputation in the twentieth century.*

Jekyll and Hyde I have read. You speak of the "gross absurdity" of the interchange. Enough that it is impossible and might perhaps have been a little better masked: it must be connived at, and it gives rise to a fine situation. It is not more impossible than fairies, giants, heathen gods, and lots of things that literature teems with—and none more than yours. You are certainly wrong about Hyde being overdrawn: my Hyde is worse. The trampling scene is perhaps a convention: he was thinking of something unsuitable for fiction.

I can by no means grant that the characters are not characterised, though how deep the springs of their surface action are I am not yet clear. But the superficial touches of character are admirable: how can you be so blind as not to see them? e.g. Utterson frowning, biting the end of his finger, and saying to the butler "This is a strange tale you tell me, my man, a very strange tale." And Dr. Lanyon: "I used to like it [life], sir; yes, sir, I liked it. Sometimes I think if we knew all" etc. These are worthy of Shakespeare. Have you read the *Pavilion on the Links* in the volume of *Arabian Nights* (not one of them)? The absconding banker is admirably characterised, the horror is nature itself, and the whole piece is genius from beginning to end.

In my judgment the amount of gift and genius which goes into novels in the English literature of this generation is perhaps not much inferior to what made the Elizabethan drama, and unhappily it is in great part wasted. How admirable are Blackmore and Hardy! Their merits are much eclipsed by the overdone reputations of the Evans—Eliot—Lewis—Cross woman (poor creature! one ought not to speak slightingly, I know), half real power, half imposition.[9] Do you know the bonfire scenes in the *Return of the Native* and still better the sword-exercise scene in the *Madding Crowd,* breathing epic? or the wife-sale in the *Mayor of Casterbridge* (read by chance)? But these writers only rise to their great strokes; they do not write continuously well: now Stevenson is master of a consummate style, and each phrase is finished as in poetry. It will not do at all, your treatment of him. . . .

Henry James
Partial Portraits (1888)

American novelist Henry James (1843–1916) spent much of his life in Europe and eventually became a British subject. His signature mode is a language of interior psychology, often located in biased or unreliable

---

[9] R. D. Blackmore's best-selling novel was an historical romance, *Lorna Doone* (1869). Novelist George Eliot (Mary Ann Evans, 1819–1880) lived unmarried with writer and editor G. H. Lewes, and a few months before her death married Lewes's business partner John Cross. The next three titles are novels by Thomas Hardy.

narrators, struggling with the moral uncertainties of modern life. Partial Portraits collects essays written across the 1880s, mostly on English and American writers, among them Stevenson and Eliot. The most influential of them all is "The Art of Fiction," which contends (as Oscar Wilde would) that "The only obligation to which in advance we may hold a novel, without incurring the accusation of being arbitrary, is that it be interesting."

Is *Doctor Jekyll and Mr. Hyde* a work of high philosophic intention, or simply the most ingenious and irresponsible of fictions? It has the stamp of a really imaginative production, that we may take it in different ways; but I suppose it would generally be called the most serious of the author's tales. It deals with the relation of the baser parts of man to his nobler, of the capacity for evil that exists in the most generous natures; and it expresses these things in a fable which is a wonderfully happy invention. The subject is endlessly interesting, and rich in all sorts of provocation, and Mr. Stevenson is to be congratulated on having touched the core of it. I may do him injustice, but it is, however, here, not the profundity of the idea which strikes me so much as the art of the presentation—the extremely successful form. There is a genuine feeling for the perpetual moral question, a fresh sense of the difficulty of being good and the brutishness of being bad; but what there is above all is a singular ability in holding the interest. I confess that that, to my sense, is the most edifying thing in the short, rapid, concentrated story, which is really a masterpiece of concision. There is something almost impertinent in the way, as I have noticed, in which Mr. Stevenson achieves his best effects without the aid of the ladies, and *Doctor Jekyll* is a capital example of his heartless independence. It is usually supposed that a truly poignant impression cannot be made without them, but in the drama of Mr. Hyde's fatal ascendancy, they remain altogether in the wing. It is very obvious—I do not say it cynically— that they must have played an important part in his development. The gruesome tone of the tale is, no doubt, deepened by their absence: it is like the late afternoon light of a foggy winter Sunday, when even inanimate objects have a kind of wicked look. I remember few situations in the pages of mystifying fiction more to the purpose than the episode of Mr. Utterson's going to Doctor Jekyll's to confer with the butler when the Doctor is locked up in his laboratory, and the old servant, whose sagacity has hitherto encountered successfully the problems of the sideboard and the pantry, confesses that this time he is utterly baffled. The way the two men, at the door of the laboratory, discuss the identity of the mysterious personage inside, who has revealed himself in two or three inhuman glimpses to Poole, has those touches of which irresistible shudders are made. The butler's theory is that his master has been murdered, and that the murderer is in the room, personating him with a sort of clumsy diabolism. "Well, when that masked thing like a monkey jumped from among the chemicals and whipped into the cabinet, it went down my spine like ice." That is the effect upon the reader of most of the story. I say of most rather than of all, because the ice rather melts in the sequel, and I have some difficulty in accepting the business of the powders, which seems to me too explicit and explanatory. The powders constitute the machinery of the transformation, and it will probably have struck many readers that this uncanny process would be more conceivable (so far as one may speak of the conceivable in such a case), if the author had not made it so definite.

Oscar Wilde, from
The Decay of Lying (*The Nineteenth Century*,
January 1889)

> *Oscar Wilde (1854–1900) led a double life, respectably married and homosexually active. An extravagant mixture of brilliant wit and social folly, he never guessed that the Victorian morality he so briskly satirized would bring about his downfall. His famous tale of a double self is* The Picture of Dorian Gray *(1890–1891; now in a Longman Cultural Edition edited by Andrew Elfenbein). The Decay of Lying (1889) deploys the form of a platonic dialogue to invert Plato's view in* The Republic *that art is false representation, a mere shadow of eternal Ideals. Wilde turns this to paradox: art doesn't represent life, life imitates art. Art is a lie, a wonderful invention; it doesn't reflect life, and shouldn't. In fact, life reaches its highest truth when it imitates art.*

VIVIAN: Life imitates art far more than Art imitates life. . . . Literature always anticipates life. . . . Shortly after Mr. Stevenson published his curious psychological story of transformation, a friend of mine, called Mr. Hyde, was in the north of London, and being anxious to get to a railway station, took what he thought would be a short cut, lost his way, and found himself in a network of mean, evil-looking streets. Feeling rather nervous he began to walk extremely fast, when suddenly out of an archway ran a child right between his legs. It fell on the pavement, he tripped over it, and trampled upon it. Being, of course, very much frightened and a little hurt, it began to scream, and in a few seconds the whole street was full of rough people who came pouring out of the houses like ants. They surrounded him, and asked him his name. He was just about to give it when he suddenly remembered the opening incident in Mr. Stevenson's story. He was so filled with horror at having realized in his own person that terrible and well written scene, and at having done accidentally, though in fact, what the Mr. Hyde of fiction had done with deliberate intent, that he ran away as hard as he could go. He was, however, very closely followed, and finally he took refuge in a surgery, the door of which happened to be open, where he explained to a young assistant, who happened to be there, exactly what had occurred. The humanitarian crowd were induced to go away on his giving them a small sum of money, and as soon as the coast was clear he left. As he passed out, the name on the brass door-plate of the surgery caught his eye. It was "Jekyll." At least it should have been.

G. K. Chesterton, from *Robert Louis Stevenson* (1927)

> *Astonishingly prolific writer—journalist, poet, biographer, fabulist— Gilbert Keith Chesterton (1874–1936) was a famous "Prince of Paradox"—nickname of Sir Henry Wotton, Dorian Gray's mentor.*

[W]hat is especially to the point of the present argument, there is a sense in which that Puritanism is expressed even more in Mr. Hyde than in Dr. Jekyll. The sense of the sudden stink of evil, the immediate invitation to step into stark filth, the abruptness of the alternative between that prim and proper pavement and that black and reeking gutter—all this, though doubtless involved in the logic of the tale, is far too frankly and familiarly offered not to have had some basis in observation and reality. . . . The real stab of the story is not in the discovery that the one man is two men; but in the discovery that the two men are one man. After all the diverse wandering and warring of those two incompatible beings, there was still only one man born and only one man buried. . . . The point of the story is not that a man *can* cut himself off from his conscience, but that he cannot. The surgical operation is fatal in the story. It is an amputation of which both the parts die. Jekyll, even in dying, declares the conclusion of the matter; that the load of man's moral struggle cannot be thus escaped. The reason is that there can never be equality between the evil and the good. Jekyll and Hyde are not twin brothers. They are rather, as one of them truly remarks, like father and son. After all, Jekyll created Hyde; Hyde would never have created Jekyll; he only destroyed Jekyll.

Vladimir Nabokov, from "The Strange Case of Dr. Jekyll and Mr. Hyde"

Internationally acclaimed man of letters, chessmaster, and lepidopterist Nabokov (1899–1977) is famed for his experimental novels Lolita *(1955) and* Pale Fire *(1962). Born into Russian aristocracy, he learned English and French as a child, enjoying a life of elegance and luxury until the revolution in 1917, when the family left for Crimea, then relocated to England. After graduating from Cambridge University, Nabokov settled in Berlin; in 1940, as war loomed, he emigrated to the United States seeking employment as a university teacher. His longest appointment was at Cornell, where in 1950 he began a course in Masters of European Fiction, which grew across the decade from a few dozen students to huge popularity. After his death, his wife and son assembled his lectures from notes, manuscripts, and typescripts, and these were published in 1980–1981. His lecture on* Dr. Jekyll and Mr. Hyde *was a perennial favorite.*

Stevenson has set himself a difficult artistic problem, and we wonder very much if he is strong enough to solve it. Let us break it up into the following points:

1. In order to make the fantasy plausible he wishes to have it pass through the minds of matter-of-fact persons, Utterson and Enfield, who even for all their commonplace logic must be affected by something bizarre and nightmarish in Hyde.

2. These two stolid souls must convey to the reader something of the horror of Hyde, but at the same time they, being neither artists nor scientists, unlike Dr. Lanyon, cannot be allowed by the author to notice details.

3. Now if Stevenson makes Enfield and Utterson too commonplace and too plain, they will not be able to express even the vague discomfort Hyde causes them. On the other hand, the reader is curious not only about their reactions but he wishes also to see Hyde's face for himself.

4. But the author himself does not see Hyde's face clearly enough, and could only have it described by Enfield or Utterson in some oblique, imaginative, suggestive way, which, however, would not be a likely manner of expression on the part of these stolid souls.

I suggest that . . . the only way to solve the problem is to have the aspect of Hyde cause in Enfield and Utterson not only a shudder of repulsion but also something else. I suggest that the shock of Hyde's presence brings out the hidden artist in Utterson.

Leslie Fiedler, from *No! In Thunder* (1963)

Prolific American literary critic, novelist, essayist, journalist, and political activist Leslie Fiedler (1917–2003) made his debut with an arresting essay on male intimacy in that quintessential American novel, Huck Finn, *later a chapter in his groundbreaking critical study,* Love and Death in the American Novel *(1960).* No! In Thunder: Essays on Myth and Literature *was published soon after.*

The somber good man and the glittering rascal are both two and one; they war within Stevenson's single country and in his single soul. . . . In *Dr. Jekyll and Mr. Hyde,* which Stevenson himself called a "fable"—that is, a dream allegorized into a morality—the point is made explicit: "I saw that of the two natures that contended in the field of my consciousness, even if I could rightly be said to be either, it was only because I was radically both." It is the respectable and lonely Dr. Jekyll who gives life to the monstrous Mr. Hyde; and once good has given form to the ecstasy of evil, the good can only destroy what it has shaped by destroying itself. The death of evil requires the death of good. *Jekyll and Hyde* is a tragedy, one of the only two tragedies that Stevenson ever wrote; but its allegory is too schematic, too slightly realized in terms of fiction and character, and too obviously colored with easy terror to be completely convincing; while its explicit morality demands that evil be portrayed finally as an obvious monster.

Edwin M. Eigner, from *Robert Louis Stevenson and the Romantic Tradition* (1966)

Edwin M. Eigner is Professor Emeritus of English and Creative Writing at University of California, Riverside.

Jekyll was wrong in attempting to segregate the two sides of his life, and he was even more wrong in glorifying the one side while alternately condemning and indulging the other. His chemical experiment is simply a logical extension of this treatment. It is by no means a new departure. The Spencer Tracy movie . . . makes a great deal of Jekyll's noble attempt to eradicate the evil in man's nature, but Stevenson's Jekyll is at least as much interested in freeing his evil nature from restraint as he is in giving scope to the good in him. . . . each of the two natures is dear to him, and he sees himself as "radically both." . . . He does not mean, at the beginning at least, to reject either of his identities. And when Hyde, the evil nature, appears for the first time, the experiment may be thought of as incomplete, but it should certainly not be considered a failure. . . . Hyde does not appear purely evil in this adventure, but he does seem to bring out all the cruelty and malice in those who judge him. . . . Enfield, the bystanders, and the other narrators are rejecting a part of themselves when they reject Hyde, and the more thoroughly they excise him, the more thoroughly they come to resemble their notion of him, and the more profoundly they are affected by the encounter.

Jorge Luis Borges, from *Borges on Writing* (1973)

Argentine fabulist, essayist, and poet Jorge Luis Borges (1899–1986) is famed for his imaginative paradoxes and conundrums. "Borges and Myself" is a brief essay on his divided character—the private self and the public man, the famous writer. Borges concludes this wonderful little anatomy by conceding that he does not know which of these characters wrote the essay. "The Watcher" shapes a poem from the doubling of self as percipient subject and observed object.

In "Borges and Myself" I am concerned with the division between the private man and the public man. In "The Watcher" I am interested in the feeling I get every morning when I awake and find that I am Borges. The first thing I do is think of my many worries. Before awakening, I was nobody, or perhaps everybody and everything—one knows so little about sleep—but waking up, I feel cramped, and I have to go back to the drudgery of being Borges. So this is a contrast of a different kind. It is something deep down within myself—the fact that I feel constrained to be a particular individual, living in a particular city, in a particular time, and so on. This might be thought of as a variation on the Jekyll and Hyde motif. Stevenson thought of the division in ethical terms, but here the division is hardly ethical. It is between the high and fine idea of being all things or nothing in particular, and the fact of being changed into a single man. It is the difference between pantheism—for all we know, we are God when we are asleep—and being merely Mr. Borges in New York.

Masao Miyoshi, from *The Divided Self* (1969)

Born and raised in Tokyo, Masao Miyoshi taught Victorian fiction at the University of California for years. The Divided Self *treats fictions of alter egos and the resonance with Victorian social existence.*

The important men of the book . . . are all unmarried, intellectually barren, emotionally stifled, joyless. Nor are things much different in the city as a whole. The more prosperous business people fix up their homes and shops, but in a fashion without chic. Houses give an appearance of "coquetry," and store fronts invite one like "rows of smiling saleswomen" (Ch. 1). The rather handsome town houses in the back streets of Dr. Jekyll's neighborhood rented out to all sorts— "map-engravers, architects, shady lawyers, and the agents of obscure enterprises" (Ch. 2). Everywhere the fog of the dismal city is inescapable, even creeping under the doors and through the window jambs (Ch. 5). The setting hides a wasteland behind that secure and relatively comfortable respectability of its inhabitants. . . .

For the mastery of the book is the vision it conjures of the late Victorian wasteland, truly a de-Hyde-rated land unfit to sustain a human being simultaneously in an honorable public life and a joyful private one.

Irving Saposnik, from *Robert Louis Stevenson* (1974)

Irving Saposnik (1936–2000) received a Fulbright scholarship to study at the University of Edinburgh in 1964. An innovative teacher at the University of Wisconsin, he was denied tenure, perhaps because of activism in anti–Vietnam-war protests. His book on Stevenson is part of the Twayne Author Series.

Hyde is usually described in metaphors because essentially that is what he is: a metaphor of uncontrolled appetites, an amoral abstraction driven by a compelling will unrestrained by any moral halter. Such a creature is, of necessity, only figuratively describable; for his deformity is moral rather than physical. Purposely left vague, he is best described as Jekyll—deformed, dwarfish, stumping, ape-like—a frightening parody of a man unable to exist on the surface. He and Jekyll are inextricably joined because one without the other cannot function in society. As Hyde is Jekyll's initial disguise, so Jekyll is Hyde's refuge after the Carew murder. If Jekyll reflects respectability, then Hyde is his image "through the looking glass."

Hyde's literal power ends with his suicide, but his metaphorical power is seemingly infinite. Many things to his contemporaries, he has grown beyond Stevenson's story in an age of automatic Freudian response. As Hyde has grown, Jekyll has been overshadowed so that his role has shifted from culprit to victim. Accordingly, the original fable has assumed a meaning neither significant for the nineteenth century nor substantial for the twentieth. The time has come for Jekyll and Hyde to be put back together again.

Stephen Heath, from "Psychopathia Sexualis: Stevenson's *Strange Case*" (*Critical Quarterly*, 1986)

Austro-German psychiatrist Richard F. von Krafft-Ebing (1840–1902) intended his study of sexual perversity, Psychopathia Sexualis *(1886), as a forensic reference for doctors and judges. In his introduction he said that he chose "a scientific term for the name of the book," put several sections in Latin in order "to discourage lay readers," and overall hewed to a professional discourse. Lay readers were not discouraged, driving sales into multiple printings and wide translation—giving it a place on many a bookshelf alongside* The Strange Case of Dr. Jekyll and Mr. Hyde, *published the same year, in 1886.*

What we can see in all this is Stevenson's closeness to his age. It is at the end of the nineteenth century that is begun and developed the scientific study of the human sexual. Stevenson's time is the time of the pioneer sexologists. *Strange Case of Dr. Jekyll and Mr. Hyde* is published in the same year as Krafft-Ebing's *Psychopathia Sexualis* whose initial recognition of "the incompleteness of our knowledge concerning the pathology of the sexual life" might be taken as an insight into the difficulty Stevenson has in his story. . . . Hysteria had served in the nineteenth century as the representation of women and of sexuality, the latter dealt with in the former. . . . Now at the end of the century Stevenson provides a text—perhaps *the* text—for the representation of men and sexuality, excluding women and so the sexual and so hysteria and then finding the only language it can for what is therefore the emergence of the hidden male: the animal, the criminal, *perversion.* Perversion is men's narrative and their story. When the masks of hysteria are down and the system of representation it keeps going wavers, that is what they say. Not that perversion *is* the word on male sexuality, simply there is no other representation, and this one, at least, offers a reconstruction from within a masculine world of that masculine world: perversion replaces and complements hysteria, positive to negative, maintaining male and female, man and woman, at whatever cost, as the terms of identity. A *psychopathia sexualis* is no psychoanalysis.

Patrick Brantlinger and Richard Boyle, from "Stevenson's 'Gothic Gnome' and the Mass Readership of Late Victorian England," from *Dr. Jekyll and Mr. Hyde after One Hundred Years* (1988)

> *Emeritus professor of English at Indiana University and former editor of Victorian Studies, cultural historian Patrick Brantlinger is author of many critical studies of the Victorian era, including* Bread and Circuses: Themes of Mass Cultural Decay *(1983) and* Rule of Darkness: British Literature and Imperialism *(1988).*

Jekyll and Hyde is totally lacking in explicit political themes. The allegorization prompted by Fanny[10] apparently did not lead to any elaboration of its social content. Hyde is an emanation of Jekyll's "transcendental medicine" or of Stevenson's nightmare, rather than of either a social class system that spawned criminality or an imperial domination that had shackled Ireland for centuries. Whatever the "moral" of the story—and at first there was none—it has to do with good versus evil in the abstract, not with the politics or even the police of late-Victorian society. The novella's anachronistic style and ahistoricism help it to seem timeless and universal, while also obscuring the literary sleight of hand that sneaks Hyde into the heart of the respectable bourgeoisie. Jekyll's metamorphosis is a matter of certain unbelievable "powders," not of politics nor even of science. But the mass cultural format of the first edition promised topical reality enough to the "populace"—the same readers who would have responded to the newsboys whom Utterson hears "crying themselves hoarse along the footways: 'Special edition. Shocking murder of an M.P.'"

Peter K. Garrett, "Cries and Voices,"[11] . . . *after One Hundred Years* (1988)

> *Peter K. Garrett, professor of English at University of Illinois, Urbana, is the author of several critical studies of the novel, including* The Victorian Multiplot Novel *(1980) and* Gothic Reflections *(2003).*

. . . a subversive or sceptical reading can rejoin and reinterpret the common sense. Like any popular tale of terror, *Jekyll and Hyde*

---

[10] Stevenson's wife.

[11] The title plays on Ingmar Bergman's film *Cries and Whispers* (1974), in which two sisters experience conflicts of dread and desire as they attend the deathbed of a third sister.

exploits the drama of uncertain control, of mysterious threat, the struggle for mastery, and the spectacle of victimization. As Jekyll's triumphant discovery of "a new province of knowledge and new avenues to fame and power" leads to utter and terrifying loss of control, we recognize an appeal to impulses and anxieties more powerful than the tale's moral framework, to fantasies and fears of releasing desire from social restraints and responsibilities. Gothic fiction depends at least as much on producing such disturbance as on containing it; its characteristic complication of narrative form and multiplication of voices, whether in conflict or complementarity, always express the effort required to establish control of meaning and often suggest its uncertain success. The narrative of *Jekyll and Hyde* advances precisely through a series of such efforts, through Utterson's quest and Enfield's, Lanyon's, and Jekyll's narratives, and through the larger development of the mystery plot that includes them. To observe how the voices and positions of the tale shift and blur is to see how these efforts all fail. Like Jekyll, the tale releases a force that cannot be mastered—not because it simply overwhelms all resistance but because all efforts at resistance or containment themselves become further instances of its cruel logic.

Ronald R. Thomas, "The Strange Voices in the Strange Case," . . . *after One Hundred Years* (1988)

The author of critical studies on detective fiction and the Freudian unconscious in literary fiction, Ronald R. Thomas is now president of the University of Puget Sound in Tacoma, Washington.

The breakdown of the conventions of characters in this text corresponds to a breakdown of narrative conventions as well. The absence of coherent self here is joined to the absence of a coherent plot. The "case" is composed not of chapters but of ten disparate documents identified only as letters, incidents, cases, statements. These parts never succeed in becoming a whole story that makes sense out of events; like Jekyll's character, they fray into "elements" that have less and less connection. The first of the pieces of the case is auspiciously titled, "The Story of the Door." But the story referred to is called a "bad story" by its teller, Enfield, because it is "far from explaining" the mystery it raises. It is the first account we have of the actions of Mr. Hyde and yet in the story itself, Hyde is not even named. Enfield "can't mention" the name, he says, even "though it is one of the points of my story.". . . the point of the story cannot be named because it has no single point. The personalities in it cannot be clearly connected to one another and the events in it cannot be explained. . . . The remainder of the text is merely a repetition of this "story" gone "bad." . . . We move through its secret door into a world where names cannot be named, points cannot be reached, stories cannot be told. . . . The psychological infirmities with which the text is manifestly concerned always express themselves as narrative infirmities in *Jekyll and Hyde*.

William Veeder, from "Children of the Night," . . . *after One Hundred Years* (1988)

William Veeder, Professor Emeritus in the Department of English at the University of Chicago, is a specialist in nineteenth-century British and American literature.

At stake in *Jekyll and Hyde* is nothing less than patriarchy itself, the social organization whose ideals and customs, transmissions of property and title, and locations of power privilege the male. Understanding the Fathers in *Jekyll and Hyde* is helped by seeing patriarchy both traditionally and locally: first in terms of its age-old obligations, then in terms of its immediate configuration in late-Victorian Britain. Traditionally the obligations of patriarchs are three: to maintain the distinctions (master-servant, proper-improper) that ground patriarchy; to sustain the male ties (father-son, brother-brother) that constitute it; and to enter the wedlock (foregoing homosexuality) that perpetuates it. Exclusion and inclusion are the operative principles. Men must distinguish the patriarchal self from enemies, pretenders, competitors, corruptors; and they must affiliate through proper bonds at appropriate times. What Stevenson devastatingly demonstrates is that patriarchy behaves exactly counter to its obligations.

Elaine Showalter, from *Sexual Anarchy* (1990)

Elaine Showalter, Emerita Professor of English, Princeton University, was one of the pioneers of twentieth-century feminist literary criticism; this work evolved into gender criticism, with attention to the social construction and deformations of maleness and masculinity. One site of "sexual anarchy" was the last decade of the nineteenth century, the decade of the "New Woman," the homosexual, men and women with double lives. In subsequent books Showalter would study "hysteria"— the physical and psychical disorder produced by repression and

> trauma—not only in women (who were thought by male scientists to
> be genetically disposed to this *"disease of the womb"*) but also in men,
> for whom the diagnostic was *"melancholy"* or, after World War I,
> *"shell shock."*

Stevenson was the fin-de-siècle laureate of the double life. . . . In contrast to the way it has been represented in film and popular culture,
Jekyll and Hyde is a story about communities of men. From the
moment of its publication, many critics have remarked on the "maleness," even the monasticism, of the story. The characters are all
middle-aged bachelors who have no relationships with women except
as servants. Furthermore, they are celibates whose major emotional
contacts are with each other and with Henry Jekyll. A female reviewer
of the book expressed her surprise that "no woman's name occurs in
the book, no romance is even suggested in it." "Mr. Stevenson," wrote
the critic Alice Brown, "is a boy who has no mind to play with
girls."[12] The romance of Jekyll and Hyde is conveyed instead through
men's names, men's bodies, and men's psyches. . . .

In the multiplication of narrative viewpoints that makes up the
story, . . . one voice is missing: that of Hyde himself. We never hear
his account of the events, his memories of his strange birth, his pleasure and fear. Hyde's story would disturb the sexual economy of the
text, the sense of panic at having liberated an uncontrollable desire.
Hyde's hysterical narrative comes to us in two ways: in the representation of his feminine behavior, and in the body language of hysterical discourse. . . . Hyde's reality breaks through Jekyll's body in the
shape of his hand, the timbre of his voice, and the quality of his gait.

Joyce Carol Oates, from a "Forward" to *The Strange Case of Dr. Jekyll and Mr. Hyde* (1990)

> *Joyce Carol Oates, woman of letters, poet, novelist, playwright, and
> essayist, is Professor of Humanities at Princeton University, where she
> teaches creative writing. Her fiction has a love affair with the gothic—
> not so much in the apparatus of remote castles, mad monks, dungeons,
> and dragons, but in the terrors of everyday life. A frequent figure in her
> fiction is the twin, the dark double.*

---

[12] The reviewer is Julia Wedgwood (see above). American novelist, poet, and playwright Alice Brown (1856–1948) made these comments in *Robert Louis Stevenson*
(Copland and Day, 1895), p. 40.

The visionary starkness of *The Strange Case of Dr. Jekyll and Mr. Hyde* anticipates that of Freud in such late melancholy meditations as *Civilization and Its Discontents* (1929–1930): there is a split in man's psyche between ego and instinct, between civilization and "nature," and the split can never be healed. Freud saw ethics as a reluctant concession of the individual to the group, veneer of a sort overlaid upon an unregenerate primordial self. The various stratagems of culture—including, not incidentally, the "sublimation" of raw aggression by way of art and science—are ultimately powerless to contain the discontent, which must erupt at certain periodic times, on a collective scale, as war. Stevenson's quintessentially Victorian parable is unique in that the protagonist initiates his tragedy of doubleness out of a fully lucid sensibility—one might say a scientific sensibility. Dr. Jekyll knows what he is doing, and why he is doing it, though he cannot, of course, know how it will turn out. What is unquestioned throughout the narrative, by either Jekyll or his circle of friends, is mankind's fallen nature: sin is *original,* and *irremediable.* For Hyde, though hidden, will not remain so. And when Jekyll finally destroys him he must destroy Jekyll too.

Garrett Stewart, from *Dear Reader: The Conscripted Audience in Nineteenth-Century British Fiction* (1996)

Garrett Stewart, professor of literature and film studies at the University of Iowa, Iowa City, is a masterful reader of wordplay in literature, and of its consequences for plot, for the pleasures and challenges of reading, and the relays with cultural fractures and fictions at large. This selection is from his chapter on "The Gothic of Reading."

. . . Concerning the self-referential thread of Stevenson's story ["a text about perverse textual materialization"], the metaplot (of inscription as a mode of self-division) leads to a monstrous co-optive doubling. It reaches its destination with the death of the author in the last sentence, where grammar falls away from first to third person: "Here, then, as I lay down the pen, and proceed to seal up my confession,"—as if it were a tomb—"I bring the life of that unhappy Henry Jekyll to an end," with that a fatal deictic pointing only backward on a life. . . .

Like all textual conjuration, Hyde must be read into being—in his case, like an embodied double entendre. . . . Well before the transformation scene (in fact, as it first medical clue), the repeated entry of "the single word: double" in Jekyll's log book (in reference to the dosage of his magic antidote) evokes both the corrective po(r)tion and the specter of doubleness it is meant to quell. Beyond localized duplicities of this sort, echoes across the text institute their own doublings. A negligible idiom of split identity at one early point—the dead metaphor of dissociated personality in Enfield's being "surprised out of himself" in a first discussion of Hyde—can, returning in a variant form, seem burdened with the weight of the entire tale, as when Jekyll "came to myself once more with the character, the stature, and the face of Henry Jekyll." . . .

Where else but in language can the one be made two (or more)? In dream and nightmare, . . . for most of us, only in literary language; that is in language *recognized* for its layered and multivalent associations. . . . in *Dr. Jekyll and Mr. Hyde,* the pun, as a paradoxically duplex singular, generates a kind of metalinguistic matrix (multiple signification per se) for this narrative of the dual personality. . . .

If the loss of self-control, in some drastically literal sense, is exactly what constitutes the long-shrouded aberration named Hyde, then even [the recipient] of secrets is hereby tainted with the contagion into which he inquires too closely. . . . Indeed, it is Utterson's early "wondering, almost with envy" about the sins of the other which is answered by Jekyll's state of mind when "plunged into a kind of wonder at my vicarious depravity," a wonderment that cannot be separated from further insatiable speculation and enactment. Surprise, curiosity, engagement, dependency; eager gust, greedy gustation, addictive voracity, enslavement—the tainted metonymic shuttle of associations generates *in reading* the metaphoric link between a reader's internal projections and the supernal nightmare of their actual embodiment.

Max Simon Nordau (1849–1923)

Interrupting the Victorian ideal of progress and improvement, theories of degeneracy—devolution across successive generations—were being formulated by such prominent Darwinians as British zoologist Edwin Ray Lankester. A scientist of comparative anatomy and evolution, Lankester focused on lower vertebrae, but others were considering human nature and the fate of civilization. Caesar Lombroso's Criminal Man *(L'Uomo delinquente, 1876) proposed a biological basis for this criminality that could be discerned in "anatomical phenomena of degeneracy" (Nordau's paraphrase): a primitive brain from a more brutal epoch of human existence. It was not long before other threatening or politically insurgent classes (the poor, restless workers, ethnic groups, even "decadent" aesthetic artists) could be read into the story: degenerate, primitive, prone to crime, a threat to civilization. In the wake of Darwin, readers were fascinated and disturbed by* Degeneration *(Entartung), by the Jewish German-Hungarian doctor, journalist, and opponent of modern aesthetics, Max Nordau. His quarry is the new "degenerate" art of the* fin de siècle, *but he begins with a more general typology, in terms that seem as relevant to Dr. Jekyll as to his degenerate epipsyche, Mr. Hyde.*

From *Degeneration* (1892; English trans., 1895)
Chapter 3, "Diagnosis"

"The clearest notion we can form of degeneracy is to regard it as *a morbid deviation from an original type.* This deviation, even if, at the outset, it was ever so slight, contained transmissible elements of such a nature that anyone bearing in him the germs becomes more and more incapable of fulfilling his functions in the world; and mental progress, already checked in his own person, finds itself menaced also in his descendants."[1]

When under any kind of noxious influences an organism becomes debilitated, its successors will not resemble the healthy, normal type of the species, with capacities for development, but will form a new sub-species, which, like all others, possesses the capacity of transmitting to its offspring, in a continuously increasing degree, its peculiarities, these being morbid deviations from the normal form—gaps in development, malformations and infirmities. That which distinguishes degeneracy from the formation of new species (phylogeny) is, that the morbid variation does not continuously subsist and propagate itself, like one that is healthy, but, fortunately, is soon rendered sterile, and after a few generations often dies out before it reaches the lowest grade of organic degradation.[2]

Degeneracy betrays itself among men in certain physical characteristics, which are denominated "stigmata," or brand-marks—an unfortunate term derived from a false idea, as if degeneracy were necessarily the consequence of a fault, and the indication of it a punishment. Such stigmata consist of deformities. [. . .] Science, however, has found, together with these physical stigmata, others of a mental order, which betoken degeneracy quite as clearly as the former. [. . .]

That which nearly all degenerates lack is the sense of morality and of right and wrong.[3] For them there exists no law, no decency, no modesty. In order to satisfy any momentary impulse, inclination, or caprice, they commit crimes and trespass with the greatest calmness and self-complacency, and do not comprehend that other persons take offence thereat. When this phenomenon is present in a high degree, we speak of "moral insanity"; with Maudsley,[4] there are,

---

[1] *Traité des Dégénérescences physiques, intellectuelles et mortals d l' Espèce humanine et des Causes qui produisent ces Variétés maladives.* [*Treatise on physical, intellectual, and moral Degeneration in the human Species and the Causes that produce these Varieties of illness*]. Par le Dr. B. A. Morel. Paris 1857, p. 5. [Nordau's note]; this is the chief source of the term *degeneration.*

[2] Morel, p. 684. [Nordau]

[3] This is a Darwinian thesis: see p. 38.

[4] Nordau admired the work of pioneering British psychologist and fervent theorist of degeneration, Dr. Henry Maudsley (1835–1918), whose *Responsibility in Mental Disease* was published by the International Scientific Series in 1874. Like other Darwin-influenced psychologists, Maudsley contended that mind and body were one, and that heredity influenced the development or degeneration of the mind. Like Nordau, he also proposed genius as a symptom of madness.

nevertheless, low stages in which the degenerate does not, perhaps, himself commit any act which will bring him into conflict with the criminal code, but at least asserts the theoretical legitimacy of crime; seeks, with philosophically sounding fustian,[5] to prove that "good" and "evil," virtue and vice, are arbitrary distinctions; goes into raptures over evildoers and their deeds, professes to discover beauties in the lowest and most repulsive things; and tries to awaken interest in, and so-called "comprehension" of, every bestiality. The two psychological roots of moral insanity, in all its degrees of development, are, first unbounded egoism, and, secondly, impulsiveness—*i.e.,* inability to resist a sudden impulse to any deed; and these characteristics also constitute the chief intellectual stigmata of degenerates.[6] [. . .]

Another mental stigma of degenerates is their emotionalism. Morel has even wished to make this peculiarity their chief characteristic—erroneously, it seems to me, for it is present in the same degree among hysterics, and, indeed, is to be found in perfectly healthy persons, who, from any transient cause, such as illness, exhaustion, or any mental shock, have been temporarily weakened. Nevertheless it is a phenomenon rarely absent in a degenerate. He laughs until he sheds tears, or weeps copiously without adequate occasion; [. . .] he believes himself to be possessed by a peculiar insight lacking in other mortals, and he is fain to despise the vulgar herd for the dullness and narrowness of their minds. [. . .]

Besides moral insanity and emotionalism, there is to be observed in the degenerate a condition of mental weakness and despondency, which, according to the circumstances of his life, assumes the form of pessimism, a vague fear of all men, and of the entire phenomenon of the universe, or self-abhorrence. [. . .], he rejoices in his faculty of imagination, which he contrasts with the insipidity of the Philistine,[7] and devotes himself with predilection to all sorts of unlicensed pursuits permitted by the unshackled vagabondage of his mind [. . .] seeks for the basis of all phenomena,

[5] Bombast.

[6] Nordau cites J. Roubinovitch, *Hystérie male et Dégénérescense* (*Male Hysteria and Degeneracy;* Paris, 1890); Legrain, *Du Délire chez les Dégénérés* (*On Delirium in Degenerates;* Paris, 1886); and Henry Colin, *Essai sur l'État mental des Hystériques* (*Essay on the mental State of Hysterics;* Paris, 1890). Hysteria, the symptoms of which Dr. Jekyll exhibits, though originally naming a "female" disease, had become a cover-term for any exhibit of extreme, uncontrollable emotional or sensory reactions.

[7] A vulgar materialist, with no interest in cultural refinement.

especially those whose first causes are completely inaccessible to us, and is unhappy when his inquiries and ruminations lead, as is natural, to no result. He is ever supplying new recruits to the army of system-inventing metaphysicians, profound expositors of the riddle of the universe, seekers for the philosopher's stone, the squaring of the circle and perpetual motion.[8] [. . .] In view of Lombroso's researches, it can scarcely be doubted that the writings and acts of revolutionists and anarchists are also attributable to degeneracy. The degenerate is incapable of adapting himself to existing circumstances. This incapacity, indeed, is an indication of morbid variation in every species, and probably a primary cause of their sudden extinction. He therefore rebels against conditions and views of things which he necessarily feels to be painful, chiefly because they impose upon him the duty of self-control, of which he is incapable on account of his organic weakness of will. Thus he becomes an improver of the world, and devises plans for making mankind happy, which, without exception, are conspicuous quite as much by their fervent philanthropy, and often pathetic sincerity, as by their absurdity and monstrous ignorance of all real relations. [. . .]

"As regards their intellect, they can," says Roubinovitch, "attain to a high degree of development, but from a moral point of view their existence is completely deranged. . . . A degenerate will employ his brilliant faculties quite as well in the service of some grand object as in the satisfaction of the basest propensities."

---

[8] Famously impossible ideas; in alchemy, the "philosopher's stone" could supposedly transmute lead into gold and grant immortality.

Joseph Conrad
1857–1924

Joseph Conrad, who learned English only in his twenties, after learning French, was a lifelong exile from a country that had ceased to exist on the map of Europe. In 1857, when Józef Teodor Konrad Korzeniowski was born, Poland was divided between the Austro-Hungarian empire and czarist Russia. After an uprising against Russia in 1863, Józef and his Polish-patriots parents were exiled to a bleak northern Russian village, where his mother died of tuberculosis in 1865. His father was allowed to return to Kraków, where he died four years later, leaving Józef an orphan at age twelve. Now in the care of a cultured, cosmopolitan uncle, Tadeusz Bobrowski, Józef was unhappy, so bored and restless in the local school that he was sent to Switzerland with a private tutor, who couldn't manage more than a year with his contentious charge. Not quite seventeen, Józef persuaded his uncle to let him go to Marseilles to join the French merchant navy. He would spend the next twenty years at sea, as sailor, then captain. In 1878, to avoid conscription in the French navy when he came of age, Conrad joined the British merchant navy, guardian of the most extensive and mighty of powers at a time of international imperial rivalry. In twenty years at sea, tracking routes of trade and commerce, conquest and empire, Conrad saw the globe from East to West, from Indonesia and the Philippines, to Venezuela, the West Indies, and Africa. In 1886, he became a British subject, and after his uncle's death in 1894, Józef Teodor Konrad Korzeniowski changed his name. "Joseph Conrad" was born at age thirty-seven.

Settling in England to become a full-time writer in English, Conrad married an English woman, Jessie George, and joined British literary life, finding friends in Henry James and Ford Madox

Ford, and winning popularity, with George Bernard Shaw and H. G. Wells among his admirers. English was Conrad's third language, and he wrote it, David Denby remarks, with traces of that "high intellectual melodrama" and "rhymed abstraction . . . characteristic of his second language, French."[1] The style is at once English and exotic, wrought with a poetic intensity that makes it seem altogether modern and certainly new, sometimes as challenging to negotiate as a foreign language, and self-reflexively engaged with the struggle for meaning in a world of uncertain moral, psychological, even epistemological markers.

    The Secret Sharer, written in late 1909, emerged in the wake of *Almayer's Folly* (1896), *An Outcast of the Islands* (1896), *The Nigger of the "Narcissus"* (1897), *Youth* (1898), *Heart of Darkness* (1899), *Lord Jim* (1900), and *Nostromo* (1904), works that constitute a sustained, intense experiment with events, sensations and introspection not only conveyed by, but located in words, syntax, and narrative form. In his 1898 preface to *The Nigger of the "Narcissus,"* Conrad describes his art as "an impression conveyed through the senses" and in the medium is language: "My task . . . is, by the power of the written word, to make you hear, to make you feel—it is, before all, to make you see. That—and no more, and it is everything." The register is typically a narrator or a protagonist (such as the young untested captain in *The Secret Sharer*) at a crisis, a summons to act in a world of radical uncertainties. Dramatic pressure is conveyed in the very rhythms of language, the narrators seeming to relive experience in telling it, feeling again its pulse in repetitions, imagistic details and spellbinding syntax, incremental, chiastic, expansive. To the central story-teller of *The Heart of Darkness* (Charlie Marlow), "the meaning of an episode was not inside like a kernel but outside, enveloping the tale which brought it out only as a glow brings out a haze, in the likeness of one of these misty halos that are sometimes made visible by the spectral illumination of moonshine." The "inspiring secret," writes Conrad in that 1898 preface, is something to "disclose" in "the stress and passion within the core of each convincing moment." If secrets are inspiration, another simile is offered by *The Secret Sharer:* "The Scorpion in the Inkwell." This is the first shipboard invader, a sharer of the chief-mate's cabin that also shares the medium of Conrad's imagination: "it managed to drown itself in the inkwell of his writing-desk," ending the threat of the sting but

[1] "A Critic at Large: Jungle Fever." *The New Yorker,* November 1995, p. 120.

infecting the ink, as if a poisonous muse and delegate. "My double gave me an inkling of his thoughts," says the unnamed narrator of the first conversation with this secret sharer, as if half-punning on the text of oneself that another can present in the delegation of ink.

Conrad's very title (as in *Transformation*) is an inkling and inking of key words in double-play. In the first, two-part serial in *Harper's Monthly Magazine* (Aug.–Sept. 1910) the title was *The Secret-Sharer*, the hyphen configuring someone who shares a secret. Canceling the hyphen for the version in *'Twixt Land and Sea* (1912; our text), Conrad releases further suggestions. While *Secret* may still be read as a noun (naming but not disclosing what is shared), it can also shimmer as an adjective for *Sharer* (the mode of this person), denoting a hidden, intimate share-holder in actions that others impute to single agency. *Secret* originates in the Latin verb, *secernere: to separate, divide off;* hence, the evolved sense of something hidden and concealed—even a radically private, inmost self (a secret anguish, a secret heart, a secret life). This sense stretches to invisible, unseen: a secret course, a secret weapon, a secret door, a secret drawer, a secret link, a secret passage (or sexual access: Hamlet scorns two spies as privates "in the secret parts" of Dame Fortune; 2.2.236ff). Conrad gave the title *The Secret Agent* to a novel he published just a few years before *The Secret Sharer* (1907): one who works in secret, by stealth, sometimes as a beneficiary, most often as an adversary. It is "under conscious Night / Secret" that Satan and the rebel angels prepare for war (*Paradise Lost,* 6.521–22), and Satan is the "secret foe" of Adam and Eve (4.7). Shakespeare's Prospero confesses his rapture with "secret studies" (*The Tempest,* 1.2.77), a sense that slides into secret society: the witches in *Macbeth* are "secret, black, & midnight Hags" (4.1.48); in *Paradise Lost,* the fallen angels "In close recess and secret conclave sat" (1.795).

As such confederacy suggests, secrets get *shared* with a confidant, one who "keeps" a secret (one of the oldest usages, dating from the fourteenth century). Thus a "secret" person (or sharer) is reserved in conduct and conversation, uncommunicative, hence trustworthy in private matters. As a noun, *secret* refers to any thing, situation, or knowledge withheld from general access, ranging from divine revelation, to occult or coterie knowledge, to perilous information. Victor Frankenstein's scientific studies put him in possession of an "astonishing . . . secret" (I.3). Though he refuses to share it, a secret is significant for its potential for communication, and its being held (shared) in confidence. The voices that narrate *Transformation* and *The Secret Sharer* can't share what they know—or they speak only to a confessor sworn to secrecy, or to the reader, who becomes the secret-sharer. *Secret* gathers further ranges of meaning in its compounds (say, *secret-sharer*): "to share the confidence or secrets of (a person); to let (a person) into the secret, to confide (to him) the secret (of an affair, trade)" (*OED*).

Share similarly shifts from individual to interpersonal. The verb emerged as a variant of *shear,* meaning *to cut into parts, to cut off (to shear off)*. Thus, Satan first knew pain when Archangel Michael's sword "deep entering shared / All his right side" (*Paradise Lost,* 6.326–27)—a shearing that is also intimate sharing. It is from *shear* that *share* gets the sense of *divide* (into parts or shares; a cut-off part is a *share*). So even as *sharer* holds the sense of a *holder* or *keeper* with another, it may indicate someone who divides or takes a part of something, property, benefit. A *sharer* has a claim on, or grants a claim to another. Or from the get-go, a *sharer* may be a co-participant in expenses, risks, benefits, experiences, and enterprises. Believing herself to have gained higher knowledge from eating the forbidden apple, Eve decides not to keep but to share the secret: "Adam shall share with me in bliss or woe" (*Paradise Lost,* 9.831). When their sons, Cain and Abel, are divided by unequal shares of God's "respect," Cain is driven to murderous rage (the first radical shearing). When God interrogates him about Abel's whereabouts, he protests he is not his brother's keeper (a kind of sharer). God sentences Cain to a negation of sympathy, dooming him to a life on earth as "a fugitive and a vagabond," shearing him off from human community by the mark that at once brands him and protects him from all but divine vengeance—a narrative from Genesis, chapter 4, that haunts Conrad's narrator.

All these doublings of meaning—*secret* as something held private, or communicated in confidence, or betrayed from confidence; *sharer* as divider or participant—are linguistic enigmas that remain in the voice of Conrad's narrator as he reports, in vivid recollection, "the secret sharer of my cabin and my thoughts."

The Secret Sharer

I

On my right hand there were lines of fishing stakes resembling a mysterious system of half-submerged bamboo fences, incomprehensible in its division of the domain of tropical fishes, and crazy of aspect as if abandoned forever by some nomad tribe of fishermen now gone to the other end of the ocean; for there was no sign of human habitation as far as the eye could reach. To the left a group of barren islets, suggesting ruins of stone walls, towers, and block-houses, had its foundations set in a blue sea that itself looked solid, so still and stable did it lie below my feet; even the track of light from the westering sun shone smoothly, without that animated glitter which tells of an imperceptible ripple. And when I turned my head to take a parting glance at the tug which had just left us anchored outside the bar, I saw the straight line of the flat shore joined to the stable sea, edge to edge, with a perfect and unmarked closeness, in one leveled floor half brown, half blue under the enormous dome of the sky. Corresponding in their insignificance to the islets of the sea, two small clumps of trees, one on each side of the only fault in the impeccable joint, marked the mouth of the river Meinam we had just left on the first preparatory stage of our homeward journey; and, far back on the inland level, a larger and loftier mass, the grove surrounding the great Paknam pagoda, was the only thing on which the eye could rest from the vain task of exploring the monotonous sweep of the horizon. Here and there gleams as of a few scattered pieces of silver marked the windings of the great river; and on the nearest of them, just within the bar, the tug steaming right into the land became lost to my sight, hull and funnel and masts, as though the impassive earth had swallowed her up without an effort, without a tremor. My eye followed the light cloud of her smoke, now here, now there, above the plain, according to the devious curves of the stream, but always fainter and farther away, till I lost it at last behind the miter-shaped hill of the great pagoda. And then I was left alone with my ship, anchored at the head of the Gulf of Siam.[1]

She floated at the starting point of a long journey, very still in an immense stillness, the shadows of her spars flung far to the eastward by the setting sun. At that moment I was alone on her decks. There was not a sound in her—and around us nothing moved, nothing lived, not a canoe on the water, not a bird in the air, not a cloud in the sky. In this breathless pause at the threshold of a long passage we seemed to be measuring our fitness for a long and arduous enterprise, the appointed task of both our existences to be carried out, far from all human eyes, with only sky and sea for spectators and for judges.

There must have been some glare in the air to interfere with one's sight, because it was only just before the sun left us that my roaming eyes made out beyond the highest ridges of the principal islet of the group something which did away with the solemnity of perfect solitude. The tide of darkness flowed on swiftly; and with tropical suddenness a swarm of stars came out above the shadowy earth, while I lingered yet, my hand resting lightly on my ship's rail as if on the shoulder of a trusted friend. But, with all that multitude of celestial bodies staring down at one, the comfort of quiet communion with her was gone for good. And there were also disturbing sounds by this time—voices, footsteps forward; the steward flitted along the main-deck, a busily ministering spirit; a hand bell tinkled urgently under the poop deck.

I found my two officers waiting for me near the supper table, in the lighted cuddy.[2] We sat down at once, and as I helped the chief mate, I said:

"Are you aware that there is a ship anchored inside the islands? I saw her mastheads above the ridge as the sun went down."

He raised sharply his simple face, overcharged by a terrible growth of whisker, and emitted his usual ejaculations: "Bless my soul, sir! You don't say so!"

My second mate was a round-cheeked, silent young man, grave beyond his years, I thought; but as our eyes happened to meet I detected a slight quiver on his lips. I looked down at once. It was not my part to encourage sneering on board my ship. It must be said, too, that I knew very little of my officers. In consequence of certain events of no particular significance, except to myself, I had

[1] Gulf of Thailand; an inlet of the South China Sea, mostly bordering on Thailand.
[2] Cabin.

been appointed to the command only a fortnight before. Neither did I know much of the hands forward. All these people had been together for eighteen months or so, and my position was that of the only stranger on board. I mention this because it has some bearing on what is to follow. But what I felt most was my being a stranger to the ship; and if all the truth must be told, I was somewhat of a stranger to myself. The youngest man on board (barring the second mate), and untried as yet by a position of the fullest responsibility, I was willing to take the adequacy of the others for granted. They had simply to be equal to their tasks; but I wondered how far I should turn out faithful to that ideal conception of one's own personality every man sets up for himself secretly.

Meantime the chief mate, with an almost visible effect of collaboration on the part of his round eyes and frightful whiskers, was trying to evolve a theory of the anchored ship. His dominant trait was to take all things into earnest consideration. He was of a painstaking turn of mind. As he used to say, he "liked to account to himself" for practically everything that came in his way, down to a miserable scorpion he had found in his cabin a week before. The why and the wherefore of that scorpion—how it got on board and came to select his room rather than the pantry (which was a dark place and more what a scorpion would be partial to), and how on earth it managed to drown itself in the inkwell of his writing desk—had exercised him infinitely. The ship within the islands was much more easily accounted for; and just as we were about to rise from table he made his pronouncement. She was, he doubted not, a ship from home lately arrived. Probably she drew too much water to cross the bar except at the top of spring tides. Therefore she went into that natural harbor to wait for a few days in preference to remaining in an open roadstead.

"That's so," confirmed the second mate, suddenly, in his slightly hoarse voice. "She draws over twenty feet. She's the Liverpool ship *Sephora* with a cargo of coal. Hundred and twenty-three days from Cardiff."

We looked at him in surprise.

"The tugboat skipper told me when he came on board for your letters, sir," explained the young man. "He expects to take her up the river the day after tomorrow."

After thus overwhelming us with the extent of his information he slipped out of the cabin. The mate observed regretfully that he "could not account for that young fellow's whims." What prevented him telling us all about it at once, he wanted to know.

I detained him as he was making a move. For the last two days the crew had had plenty of hard work, and the night before they had very little sleep. I felt painfully that I—a stranger—was doing something unusual when I directed him to let all hands turn in without setting an anchor watch. I proposed to keep on deck myself till one o'clock or thereabouts. I would get the second mate to relieve me at that hour.

"He will turn out the cook and the steward at four," I concluded, "and then give you a call. Of course at the slightest sign of any sort of wind we'll have the hands up and make a start at once."

He concealed his astonishment. "Very well, sir." Outside the cuddy he put his head in the second mate's door to inform him of my unheard-of caprice to take a five hours' anchor watch on myself. I heard the other raise his voice incredulously—"What? The Captain himself?" Then a few more murmurs, a door closed, then another. A few moments later I went on deck.

My strangeness, which had made me sleepless, had prompted that unconventional arrangement, as if I had expected in those solitary hours of the night to get on terms with the ship of which I knew nothing, manned by men of whom I knew very little more. Fast alongside a wharf, littered like any ship in port with a tangle of unrelated things, invaded by unrelated shore people, I had hardly seen her yet properly. Now, as she lay cleared for sea, the stretch of her main-deck seemed to me very fine under the stars. Very fine, very roomy for her size, and very inviting. I descended the poop and paced the waist, my mind picturing to myself the coming passage through the Malay Archipelago,[3] down the Indian Ocean, and up the Atlantic. All its phases were familiar enough to me, every characteristic, all the alternatives which were likely to face me on the high seas—everything! . . . except the novel responsibility of command. But I took heart from the reasonable thought that the ship was like other ships, the men like other men, and that the sea was not likely to keep any special surprises expressly for my discomfiture.

Arrived at that comforting conclusion, I bethought myself of a cigar and went below to get it. All was still down there. Everybody at the after end of the ship was sleeping profoundly. I came out again on the quarter-deck, agreeably at ease in my sleeping suit on that warm breathless night, barefooted, a glowing cigar in my teeth, and, going forward, I was met by the profound silence of the fore end of the ship. Only as I passed the door of the forecastle, I heard a deep, quiet, trustful sigh of some sleeper inside. And suddenly I rejoiced in the

[3] Islands between Australia and southeast Asia, including Indonesia and the Philippines.

great security of the sea as compared with the unrest of the land, in my choice of that untempted life presenting no disquieting problems, invested with an elementary moral beauty by the absolute straightforwardness of its appeal and by the singleness of its purpose.

The riding light in the forerigging burned with a clear, untroubled, as if symbolic, flame, confident and bright in the mysterious shades of the night. Passing on my way aft along the other side of the ship, I observed that the rope side ladder, put over, no doubt, for the master of the tug when he came to fetch away our letters, had not been hauled in as it should have been. I became annoyed at this, for exactitude in some small matters is the very soul of discipline. Then I reflected that I had myself peremptorily dismissed my officers from duty, and by my own act had prevented the anchor watch being formally set and things properly attended to. I asked myself whether it was wise ever to interfere with the established routine of duties even from the kindest of motives. My action might have made me appear eccentric. Goodness only knew how that absurdly whiskered mate would "account" for my conduct, and what the whole ship thought of that informality of their new captain. I was vexed with myself.

Not from compunction certainly, but, as it were mechanically, I proceeded to get the ladder in myself. Now a side ladder of that sort is a light affair and comes in easily, yet my vigorous tug, which should have brought it flying on board, merely recoiled upon my body in a totally unexpected jerk. What the devil! . . . I was so astounded by the immovableness of that ladder that I remained stockstill, trying to account for it to myself like that imbecile mate of mine. In the end, of course, I put my head over the rail.

The side of the ship made an opaque belt of shadow on the darkling glassy shimmer of the sea. But I saw at once something elongated and pale floating very close to the ladder. Before I could form a guess a faint flash of phosphorescent light, which seemed to issue suddenly from the naked body of a man, flickered in the sleeping water with the elusive, silent play of summer lightning in a night sky. With a gasp I saw revealed to my stare a pair of feet, the long legs, a broad livid back immersed right up to the neck in a greenish cadaverous glow. One hand, awash, clutched the bottom rung of the ladder. He was complete but for the head. A headless corpse![4] The cigar dropped out of my gaping mouth with a tiny plop and a short hiss quite audible in the absolute stillness of all things under heaven. At that I suppose he raised up his face, a dimly pale oval in the shadow

---

[4] The image is related to the anxiety of the new *Captain* (from the Latin, *capit: head*).

of the ship's side. But even then I could only barely make out down there the shape of his black-haired head. However, it was enough for the horrid, frost-bound sensation which had gripped me about the chest to pass off. The moment of vain exclamations was past, too. I only climbed on the spare spar and leaned over the rail as far as I could, to bring my eyes nearer to that mystery floating alongside.

As he hung by the ladder, like a resting swimmer, the sea lightning played about his limbs at every stir; and he appeared in it ghastly, silvery, fishlike. He remained as mute as a fish, too. He made no motion to get out of the water, either. It was inconceivable that he should not attempt to come on board, and strangely troubling to suspect that perhaps he did not want to. And my first words were prompted by just that troubled incertitude.

"What's the matter?" I asked in my ordinary tone, speaking down to the face upturned exactly under mine.

"Cramp," it answered, no louder. Then slightly anxious, "I say, no need to call anyone."

"I was not going to," I said.

"Are you alone on deck?"

"Yes."

I had somehow the impression that he was on the point of letting go the ladder to swim away beyond my ken—mysterious as he came. But, for the moment, this being appearing as if he had risen from the bottom of the sea (it was certainly the nearest land to the ship) wanted only to know the time. I told him. And he, down there, tentatively:

"I suppose your captain's turned in?"

"I am sure he isn't," I said.

He seemed to struggle with himself, for I heard something like the low, bitter murmur of doubt.[5] "What's the good?" His next words came out with a hesitating effort.

"Look here, my man. Could you call him out quietly?"

I thought the time had come to declare myself.

"I am the captain."

I heard a "By Jove!" whispered at the level of the water. The phosphorescence flashed in the swirl of the water all about his limbs, his other hand seized the ladder.

[5] In a tale of doubling, the play of *doubt* and *no doubt* is always pertinent; the Latin infinitive *dubitare* means *to be of two minds*.

"My name's Leggatt."[6]

The voice was calm and resolute. A good voice. The self-possession of that man had somehow induced a corresponding state in myself. It was very quietly that I remarked:

"You must be a good swimmer."

"Yes. I've been in the water practically since nine o'clock. The question for me now is whether I am to let go this ladder and go on swimming till I sink from exhaustion, or—to come on board here."

I felt this was no mere formula of desperate speech, but a real alternative in the view of a strong soul. I should have gathered from this that he was young; indeed, it is only the young who are ever confronted by such clear issues. But at the time it was pure intuition on my part. A mysterious communication was established already between us two—in the face of that silent, darkened tropical sea. I was young, too; young enough to make no comment. The man in the water began suddenly to climb up the ladder, and I hastened away from the rail to fetch some clothes.

Before entering the cabin I stood still, listening in the lobby at the foot of the stairs. A faint snore came through the closed door of the chief mate's room. The second mate's door was on the hook, but the darkness in there was absolutely soundless. He, too, was young and could sleep like a stone. Remained the steward, but he was not likely to wake up before he was called. I got a sleeping suit out of my room and, coming back on deck, saw the naked man from the sea sitting on the main hatch, glimmering white in the darkness, his elbows on his knees and his head in his hands. In a moment he had concealed his damp body in a sleeping suit of the same gray-stripe pattern as the one I was wearing and followed me like my double on the poop. Together we moved right aft, barefooted, silent.

"What is it?" I asked in a deadened voice, taking the lighted lamp out of the binnacle,[7] and raising it to his face.

"An ugly business."

He had rather regular features; a good mouth; light eyes under somewhat heavy, dark eyebrows; a smooth, square forehead; no

[6] J. H. Miller notes that the (thematically apt) doubled letters fashion a proper name out of the same-sounding word *legate* (emissary; from the Latin *legare*, to depute). Leggatt seems "an emissary of some sort." Kin to *legal* and *legislate* (from Latin *lex*), *legate* involves a sense of law ("Sharing Secrets" p. 233, n2). Note, too, the Captain's sympathy with aggravation when "there are no means of legal repression" (p. 189).

[7] An encasing for a compass.

growth on his cheeks; a small, brown mustache, and a well-shaped, round chin. His expression was concentrated, meditative, under the inspecting light of the lamp I held up to his face; such as a man thinking hard in solitude might wear. My sleeping suit was just right for his size. A well-knit young fellow of twenty-five at most. He caught his lower lip with the edge of white, even teeth.

"Yes," I said, replacing the lamp in the binnacle. The warm, heavy tropical night closed upon his head again.

"There's a ship over there," he murmured.

"Yes, I know. The Sephora. Did you know of us?"

"Hadn't the slightest idea. I am the mate of her—." He paused and corrected himself. "I should say I was."

"Aha! Something wrong?"

"Yes. Very wrong indeed. I've killed a man."

"What do you mean? Just now?"

"No, on the passage. Weeks ago. Thirty-nine south. When I say a man—"

"Fit of temper," I suggested, confidently.

The shadowy, dark head, like mine, seemed to nod imperceptibly above the ghostly gray of my sleeping suit. It was, in the night, as though I had been faced by my own reflection in the depths of a somber and immense mirror.

"A pretty thing to have to own up to for a Conway[8] boy," murmured my double, distinctly.

"You're a Conway boy?"

"I am," he said, as if startled. Then, slowly . . . "Perhaps you too—"

It was so; but being a couple of years older I had left before he joined. After a quick interchange of dates a silence fell; and I thought suddenly of my absurd mate with his terrific whiskers and the "Bless my soul—you don't say so" type of intellect. My double gave me an inkling of his thoughts by saying: "My father's a parson in Norfolk. Do you see me before a judge and jury on that charge? For myself I can't see the necessity. There are fellows that an angel from heaven— And I am not that. He was one of those creatures that are just simmering all the time with a silly sort of wickedness. Miserable devils that have no business to live at all. He wouldn't do his duty and wouldn't let anybody else do theirs. But what's the good of talking! You know well enough the sort of ill-conditioned snarling cur—"

---

[8] The training ship for officers in the British Merchant Marine.

He appealed to me as if our experiences had been as identical as our clothes. And I knew well enough the pestiferous danger of such a character where there are no means of legal repression. And I knew well enough also that my double there was no homicidal ruffian. I did not think of asking him for details, and he told me the story roughly in brusque, disconnected sentences. I needed no more. I saw it all going on as though I were myself inside that other sleeping suit.

"It happened while we were setting a reefed foresail, at dusk. Reefed foresail! You understand the sort of weather. The only sail we had left to keep the ship running; so you may guess what it had been like for days. Anxious sort of job, that. He gave me some of his cursed insolence at the sheet. I tell you I was overdone with this terrific weather that seemed to have no end to it. Terrific, I tell you—and a deep ship. I believe the fellow himself was half crazed with funk. It was no time for gentlemanly reproof, so I turned round and felled him like an ox. He up and at me. We closed just as an awful sea made for the ship. All hands saw it coming and took to the rigging, but I had him by the throat, and went on shaking him like a rat, the men above us yelling, 'Look out! look out!' Then a crash as if the sky had fallen on my head. They say that for over ten minutes hardly anything was to be seen of the ship—just the three masts and a bit of the forecastle head and of the poop all awash driving along in a smother of foam. It was a miracle that they found us, jammed together behind the forebitts. It's clear that I meant business, because I was holding him by the throat still when they picked us up. He was black in the face. It was too much for them. It seems they rushed us aft together, gripped as we were, screaming 'Murder!' like a lot of lunatics, and broke into the cuddy. And the ship running for her life, touch and go all the time, any minute her last in a sea fit to turn your hair gray only a-looking at it. I understand that the skipper, too, started raving like the rest of them. The man had been deprived of sleep for more than a week, and to have this sprung on him at the height of a furious gale nearly drove him out of his mind. I wonder they didn't fling me overboard after getting the carcass of their precious shipmate out of my fingers. They had rather a job to separate us, I've been told. A sufficiently fierce story to make an old judge and a respectable jury sit up a bit. The first thing I heard when I came to myself was the maddening howling of that endless gale, and on that the voice of the old man. He was hanging on to my bunk, staring into my face out of his sou'wester.

"'Mr. Leggatt, you have killed a man. You can act no longer as chief mate of this ship.'"

His care to subdue his voice made it sound monotonous. He rested a hand on the end of the skylight to steady himself with, and all that time did not stir a limb, so far as I could see. "Nice little tale for a quiet tea party," he concluded in the same tone.

One of my hands, too, rested on the end of the skylight; neither did I stir a limb, so far as I knew. We stood less than a foot from each other. It occurred to me that if old "Bless my soul—you don't say so" were to put his head up the companion and catch sight of us, he would think he was seeing double, or imagine himself come upon a scene of weird witchcraft; the strange captain having a quiet confabulation by the wheel with his own gray ghost. I became very much concerned to prevent anything of the sort. I heard the other's soothing undertone.

"My father's a parson in Norfolk," it said. Evidently he had forgotten he had told me this important fact before. Truly a nice little tale.

"You had better slip down into my stateroom now," I said, moving off stealthily. My double followed my movements; our bare feet made no sound; I let him in, closed the door with care, and, after giving a call to the second mate, returned on deck for my relief.

"Not much sign of any wind yet," I remarked when he approached.

"No, sir. Not much," he assented, sleepily, in his hoarse voice, with just enough deference, no more, and barely suppressing a yawn.

"Well, that's all you have to look out for. You have got your orders."

"Yes, sir."

I paced a turn or two on the poop and saw him take up his position face forward with his elbow in the ratlines of the mizzen rigging before I went below. The mate's faint snoring was still going on peacefully. The cuddy lamp was burning over the table on which stood a vase with flowers, a polite attention from the ship's provision merchant—the last flowers we should see for the next three months at the very least. Two bunches of bananas hung from the beam symmetrically, one on each side of the rudder casing. Everything was as before in the ship—except that two of her captain's sleeping suits were simultaneously in use, one motionless in the cuddy, the other keeping very still in the captain's stateroom.

It must be explained here that my cabin had the form of the capital letter L, the door being within the angle and opening into the

Drawn by W. J. Aylward

"NICE LITTLE TALE FOR A QUIET TEA-PARTY," HE CONCLUDED

Illustration by W. J. Aylward (*Harper's Monthly Magazine,* August, 1910).

short part of the letter. A couch was to the left, the bed place to the right; my writing desk and the chronometers' table faced the door. But anyone opening it, unless he stepped right inside, had no view of what I call the long (or vertical) part of the letter. It contained some lockers surmounted by a bookcase; and a few clothes, a thick jacket or two, caps, oilskin coat, and such like, hung on hooks. There was at the bottom of that part a door opening into my bathroom, which could be entered also directly from the saloon. But that way was never used.

The mysterious arrival had discovered the advantage of this particular shape. Entering my room, lighted strongly by a big bulkhead lamp swung on gimbals[9] above my writing desk, I did not see him anywhere till he stepped out quietly from behind the coats hung in the recessed part.

"I heard somebody moving about, and went in there at once," he whispered.

I, too, spoke under my breath.

"Nobody is likely to come in here without knocking and getting permission."

He nodded. His face was thin and the sunburn faded, as though he had been ill. And no wonder. He had been, I heard presently, kept under arrest in his cabin for nearly seven weeks. But there was nothing sickly in his eyes or in his expression. He was not a bit like me, really; yet, as we stood leaning over my bed place, whispering side by side, with our dark heads together and our backs to the door, anybody bold enough to open it stealthily would have been treated to the uncanny[10] sight of a double captain busy talking in whispers with his other self.

"But all this doesn't tell me how you came to hang on to our side ladder," I inquired, in the hardly audible murmurs we used, after he had told me something more of the proceedings on board the Sephora once the bad weather was over.

"When we sighted Java Head I had had time to think all those matters out several times over. I had six weeks of doing nothing else, and with only an hour or so every evening for a tramp on the quarter-deck."

[9] A pair of rings that keep objects suspended on them—a lamp or compass—horizontal during movements of a ship.

[10] This is a word of double, antithetical meanings: strange, eerie, unfamiliar / strangely familiar, eerily prescient, preternaturally perceptive.

He whispered, his arms folded on the side of my bed place, staring through the open port. And I could imagine perfectly the manner of this thinking out—a stubborn if not a steadfast operation; something of which I should have been perfectly incapable.

"I reckoned it would be dark before we closed with the land," he continued, so low that I had to strain my hearing near as we were to each other, shoulder touching shoulder almost. "So I asked to speak to the old man. He always seemed very sick when he came to see me—as if he could not look me in the face. You know, that foresail saved the ship. She was too deep to have run long under bare poles. And it was I that managed to set it for him. Anyway, he came. When I had him in my cabin—he stood by the door looking at me as if I had the halter round my neck already—I asked him right away to leave my cabin door unlocked at night while the ship was going through Sunda Straits. There would be the Java coast within two or three miles, off Angier Point. I wanted nothing more. I've had a prize for swimming my second year in the Conway."

"I can believe it," I breathed out.

"God only knows why they locked me in every night. To see some of their faces you'd have thought they were afraid I'd go about at night strangling people. Am I a murdering brute? Do I look it? By Jove! If I had been he[11] wouldn't have trusted himself like that into my room. You'll say I might have chucked him aside and bolted out, there and then—it was dark already. Well, no. And for the same reason I wouldn't think of trying to smash the door. There would have been a rush to stop me at the noise, and I did not mean to get into a confounded scrimmage. Somebody else might have got killed—for I would not have broken out only to get chucked back, and I did not want any more of that work. He refused, looking more sick than ever. He was afraid of the men, and also of that old second mate of his who had been sailing with him for years—a gray-headed old humbug; and his steward, too, had been with him devil knows how long—seventeen years or more—a dogmatic sort of loafer who hated me like poison, just because I was the chief mate. No chief mate ever made more than one voyage in the Sephora, you know. Those two old chaps ran the ship. Devil only knows what the skipper wasn't afraid of (all his nerve went to pieces altogether in that hellish spell of bad weather we had)—of

[11] Declining to punctuate with a comma after *been*, Conrad allows the fleeting phantom syntax of superimposed identities: *If I had been he*. . . .

what the law would do to him—of his wife, perhaps. Oh, yes! she's on board. Though I don't think she would have meddled. She would have been only too glad to have me out of the ship in any way. The 'brand of Cain' business, don't you see. That's all right. I was ready enough to go off wandering on the face of the earth— and that was price enough to pay for an Abel of that sort.[12] Anyhow, he wouldn't listen to me. 'This thing must take its course. I represent the law here.' He was shaking like a leaf. 'So you won't?' 'No!' 'Then I hope you will be able to sleep on that,' I said, and turned my back on him. 'I wonder that you can,' cries he, and locks the door.

"Well after that, I couldn't. Not very well. That was three weeks ago. We have had a slow passage through the Java Sea; drifted about Carimata for ten days. When we anchored here they thought, I suppose, it was all right. The nearest land (and that's five miles) is the ship's destination; the consul would soon set about catching me; and there would have been no object in bolding to these islets there. I don't suppose there's a drop of water on them. I don't know how it was, but tonight that steward, after bringing me my supper, went out to let me eat it, and left the door unlocked. And I ate it—all there was, too. After I had finished I strolled out on the quarter-deck. I don't know that I meant to do anything. A breath of fresh air was all I wanted, I believe. Then a sudden temptation came over me. I kicked off my slippers and was in the water before I had made up my mind fairly. Somebody heard the splash and they raised an awful hullabaloo. 'He's gone! Lower the boats! He's committed suicide! No, he's swimming.' Certainly I was swimming. It's not so easy for a swimmer like me to commit suicide by drowning. I landed on the nearest islet before the boat left the ship's side. I heard them pulling about in the dark, hailing, and so on, but after a bit they gave up. Everything quieted down and the anchorage became still as death. I sat down on a stone and began to think. I felt certain they would start searching for me at daylight. There was no place to hide on those stony things—and if there had been, what would have been the good? But now I was clear of that ship, I was not going back. So after a while I took off all my clothes, tied

---

[12] For slaying his brother Abel, God curses Cain to be a "fugitive and vagabond in the earth." To answer Cain's fear that he will be so despised "that every one that findeth me shall slay me," God sets a mark upon his forehead to prevent this, and threatens vengeance sevenfold on "whoever slayeth Cain" (Genesis 4: 8–15).

them up in a bundle with a stone inside, and dropped them in the deep water on the outer side of that islet. That was suicide enough for me. Let them think what they liked, but I didn't mean to drown myself. I meant to swim till I sank—but that's not the same thing. I struck out for another of these little islands, and it was from that one that I first saw your riding light. Something to swim for. I went on easily, and on the way I came upon a flat rock a foot or two above water. In the daytime, I dare say, you might make it out with a glass from your poop. I scrambled up on it and rested myself for a bit. Then I made another start. That last spell must have been over a mile."

His whisper was getting fainter and fainter, and all the time he stared straight out through the porthole, in which there was not even a star to be seen. I had not interrupted him. There was something that made comment impossible in his narrative, or perhaps in himself; a sort of feeling, a quality, which I can't find a name for. And when he ceased, all I found was a futile whisper: "So you swam for our light?"

"Yes—straight for it. It was something to swim for. I couldn't see any stars low down because the coast was in the way, and I couldn't see the land, either. The water was like glass. One might have been swimming in a confounded thousand-feet deep cistern with no place for scrambling out anywhere; but what I didn't like was the notion of swimming round and round like a crazed bullock before I gave out; and as I didn't mean to go back . . . No. Do you see me being hauled back, stark naked, off one of these little islands by the scruff of the neck and fighting like a wild beast? Somebody would have got killed for certain, and I did not want any of that. So I went on. Then your ladder—"

"Why didn't you hail the ship?" I asked, a little louder.

He touched my shoulder lightly. Lazy footsteps came right over our heads and stopped. The second mate had crossed from the other side of the poop and might have been hanging over the rail for all we knew.

"He couldn't hear us talking—could he?" My double breathed into my very ear, anxiously.

His anxiety was in answer, a sufficient answer, to the question I had put to him. An answer containing all the difficulty of that situation. I closed the porthole quietly, to make sure. A louder word might have been overheard.

"Who's that?" he whispered then.

"My second mate. But I don't know much more of the fellow than you do."

And I told him a little about myself. I had been appointed to take charge while I least expected anything of the sort, not quite a fortnight ago. I didn't know either the ship or the people. Hadn't had the time in port to look about me or size anybody up. And as to the crew, all they knew was that I was appointed to take the ship home. For the rest, I was almost as much of a stranger on board as himself, I said. And at the moment I felt it most acutely. I felt that it would take very little to make me a suspect person in the eyes of the ship's company.

He had turned about meantime; and we, the two strangers in the ship, faced each other in identical attitudes.

"Your ladder—" he murmured, after a silence. "Who'd have thought of finding a ladder hanging over at night in a ship anchored out here! I felt just then a very unpleasant faintness. After the life I've been leading for nine weeks, anybody would have got out of condition. I wasn't capable of swimming round as far as your rudder chains. And, lo and behold! there was a ladder to get hold of. After I gripped it I said to myself, 'What's the good?' When I saw a man's head looking over I thought I would swim away presently and leave him shouting—in whatever language it was. I didn't mind being looked at. I—I liked it. And then you speaking to me so quietly—as if you had expected me—made me hold on a little longer. It had been a confounded lonely time—I don't mean while swimming. I was glad to talk a little to somebody that didn't belong to the Sephora. As to asking for the captain, that was a mere impulse. It could have been no use, with all the ship knowing about me and the other people pretty certain to be round here in the morning. I don't know—I wanted to be seen, to talk with somebody, before I went on. I don't know what I would have said. . . . 'Fine night, isn't it?' or something of the sort."

"Do you think they will be round here presently?" I asked with some incredulity.

"Quite likely," he said, faintly.

He looked extremely haggard all of a sudden. His head rolled on his shoulders.

"H'm. We shall see then. Meantime get into that bed," I whispered. "Want help? There."

It was a rather high bed place with a set of drawers underneath. This amazing swimmer really needed the lift I gave him by seizing his leg. He tumbled in, rolled over on his back, and flung one arm across his eyes. And then, with his face nearly hidden, he must have looked exactly as I used to look in that bed. I gazed upon my other self for a while before drawing across carefully the two green serge curtains which ran on a brass rod. I thought for a moment of pinning them together for greater safety, but I sat down on the couch, and once there I felt unwilling to rise and hunt for a pin. I would do it in a moment. I was extremely tired, in a peculiarly intimate way, by the strain of stealthiness, by the effort of whispering and the general secrecy of this excitement. It was three o'clock by now and I had been on my feet since nine, but I was not sleepy; I could not have gone to sleep. I sat there, fagged out, looking at the curtains, trying to clear my mind of the confused sensation of being in two places at once, and greatly bothered by an exasperating knocking in my head. It was a relief to discover suddenly that it was not in my head at all, but on the outside of the door. Before I could collect myself the words "Come in" were out of my mouth, and the steward entered with a tray, bringing in my morning coffee. I had slept, after all, and I was so frightened that I shouted, "This way! I am here, steward," as though he had been miles away. He put down the tray on the table next the couch and only then said, very quietly, "I can see you are here, sir." I felt him give me a keen look, but I dared not meet his eyes just then. He must have wondered why I had drawn the curtains of my bed before going to sleep on the couch. He went out, hooking the door open as usual.

I heard the crew washing decks above me. I knew I would have been told at once if there had been any wind. Calm, I thought, and I was doubly vexed. Indeed, I felt dual more than ever. The steward reappeared suddenly in the doorway. I jumped up from the couch so quickly that he gave a start.

"What do you want here?"

"Close your port, sir—they are washing decks."

"It is closed," I said, reddening.

"Very well, sir." But he did not move from the doorway and returned my stare in an extraordinary, equivocal manner for a time. Then his eyes wavered, all his expression changed, and in a voice unusually gentle, almost coaxingly:

"May I come in to take the empty cup away, sir?"

"Of course!" I turned my back on him while he popped in and out. Then I unhooked and closed the door and even pushed the bolt. This sort of thing could not go on very long. The cabin was as hot as an oven, too. I took a peep at my double, and discovered that he had not moved, his arm was still over his eyes; but his chest heaved; his hair was wet; his chin glistened with perspiration. I reached over him and opened the port.

"I must show myself on deck," I reflected.

Of course, theoretically, I could do what I liked, with no one to say nay to me within the whole circle of the horizon; but to lock my cabin door and take the key away I did not dare. Directly I put my head out of the companion I saw the group of my two officers, the second mate barefooted, the chief mate in long India-rubber boots, near the break of the poop, and the steward halfway down the poop ladder talking to them eagerly. He happened to catch sight of me and dived, the second ran down on the main-deck shouting some order or other, and the chief mate came to meet me, touching his cap.

There was a sort of curiosity in his eye that I did not like. I don't know whether the steward had told them that I was "queer" only, or downright drunk, but I know the man meant to have a good look at me. I watched him coming with a smile which, as he got into point-blank range, took effect and froze his very whiskers. I did not give him time to open his lips.

"Square the yards by lifts and braces before the hands go to breakfast."

It was the first particular order I had given on board that ship; and I stayed on deck to see it executed, too. I had felt the need of asserting myself without loss of time. That sneering young cub got taken down a peg or two on that occasion, and I also seized the opportunity of having a good look at the face of every foremast man as they filed past me to go to the after braces. At breakfast time, eating nothing myself, I presided with such frigid dignity that the two mates were only too glad to escape from the cabin as soon as decency permitted; and all the time the dual working of my mind distracted me almost to the point of insanity. I was constantly watching myself, my secret self, as dependent on my actions as my own personality, sleeping in that bed, behind that door which faced me as I sat at the head of the table. It was very much like being mad, only it was worse because one was aware of it.

I had to shake him for a solid minute, but when at last he opened his eyes it was in the full possession of his senses, with an inquiring look.

"All's well so far," I whispered. "Now you must vanish into the bathroom."

He did so, as noiseless as a ghost, and then I rang for the steward, and facing him boldly, directed him to tidy up my stateroom while I was having my bath—"and be quick about it." As my tone admitted of no excuses, he said, "Yes, sir," and ran off to fetch his dustpan and brushes. I took a bath and did most of my dressing, splashing, and whistling softly for the steward's edification, while the secret sharer of my life stood drawn up bolt upright in that little space, his face looking very sunken in daylight, his eyelids lowered under the stern, dark line of his eyebrows drawn together by a slight frown.

When I left him there to go back to my room the steward was finishing dusting. I sent for the mate and engaged him in some insignificant conversation. It was, as it were, trifling with the terrific character of his whiskers; but my object was to give him an opportunity for a good look at my cabin. And then I could at last shut, with a clear conscience, the door of my stateroom and get my double back into the recessed part. There was nothing else for it. He had to sit still on a small folding stool, half smothered by the heavy coats hanging there. We listened to the steward going into the bathroom out of the saloon, filling the water bottles there, scrubbing the bath, setting things to rights, whisk, bang, clatter—out again into the saloon—turn the key—click. Such was my scheme for keeping my second self invisible. Nothing better could be contrived under the circumstances. And there we sat; I at my writing desk ready to appear busy with some papers, he behind me out of sight of the door. It would not have been prudent to talk in daytime; and I could not have stood the excitement of that queer sense of whispering to myself. Now and then, glancing over my shoulder, I saw him far back there, sitting rigidly on the low stool, his bare feet close together, his arms folded, his head hanging on his breast—and perfectly still. Anybody would have taken him for me.

I was fascinated by it myself. Every moment I had to glance over my shoulder. I was looking at him when a voice outside the door said:

"Beg pardon, sir."

"Well!" . . . I kept my eyes on him, and so when the voice outside the door announced, "There's a ship's boat coming our way, sir," I saw him give a start—the first movement he had made for hours. But he did not raise his bowed head.

"All right. Get the ladder over."

I hesitated. Should I whisper something to him? But what? His immobility seemed to have been never disturbed. What could I tell him he did not know already? . . . Finally I went on deck.

II

The skipper of the Sephora had a thin red whisker all round his face, and the sort of complexion that goes with hair of that color; also the particular, rather smeary shade of blue in the eyes. He was not exactly a showy figure; his shoulders were high, his stature but middling—one leg slightly more bandy than the other. He shook hands, looking vaguely around. A spiritless tenacity was his main characteristic, I judged. I behaved with a politeness which seemed to disconcert him. Perhaps he was shy. He mumbled to me as if he were ashamed of what he was saying; gave his name (it was something like Archbold—but at this distance of years I hardly am sure), his ship's name, and a few other particulars of that sort, in the manner of a criminal making a reluctant and doleful confession. He had had terrible weather on the passage out—terrible—terrible—wife aboard, too.

By this time we were seated in the cabin and the steward brought in a tray with a bottle and glasses. "Thanks! No." Never took liquor. Would have some water, though. He drank two tumblerfuls. Terrible thirsty work. Ever since daylight had been exploring the islands round his ship.

"What was that for—fun?" I asked, with an appearance of polite interest.

"No!" He sighed. "Painful duty."

As he persisted in his mumbling and I wanted my double to hear every word, I hit upon the notion of informing him that I regretted to say I was hard of hearing.

"Such a young man, too!" he nodded, keeping his smeary blue, unintelligent eyes fastened upon me. "What was the cause of it—some disease?" he inquired, without the least sympathy and as if he thought that, if so, I'd got no more than I deserved.

"Yes; disease," I admitted in a cheerful tone which seemed to shock him. But my point was gained, because he had to raise his voice to give me his tale. It is not worth while to record his version. It was just over two months since all this had happened, and he had thought so much about it that he seemed completely muddled as to its bearings, but still immensely impressed.

"What would you think of such a thing happening on board your own ship? I've had the Sephora for these fifteen years. I am a well-known shipmaster."

He was densely distressed—and perhaps I should have sympathized with him if I had been able to detach my mental vision from the unsuspected sharer of my cabin as though he were my second self. There he was on the other side of the bulkhead, four or five feet from us, no more, as we sat in the saloon. I looked politely at Captain Archbold (if that was his name), but it was the other I saw, in a gray sleeping suit, seated on a low stool, his bare feet close together, his arms folded, and every word said between us falling into the ears of his dark head bowed on his chest.

"I have been at sea now, man and boy, for seven-and-thirty years, and I've never heard of such a thing happening in an English ship. And that it should be my ship. Wife on board, too."

I was hardly listening to him.

"Don't you think," I said, "that the heavy sea which, you told me, came aboard just then might have killed the man? I have seen the sheer weight of a sea kill a man very neatly, by simply breaking his neck."

"Good God!" he uttered, impressively, fixing his smeary blue eyes on me. "The sea! No man killed by the sea ever looked like that." He seemed positively scandalized at my suggestion. And as I gazed at him certainly not prepared for anything original on his part, he advanced his head close to mine and thrust his tongue out at me so suddenly that I couldn't help starting back.

After scoring over my calmness in this graphic way he nodded wisely. If I had seen the sight, he assured me, I would never forget it as long as I lived. The weather was too bad to give the corpse a proper sea burial. So next day at dawn they took it up on the poop, covering its face with a bit of bunting; he read a short prayer, and then, just as it was, in its oilskins and long boots, they launched it amongst those mountainous seas that seemed ready every moment to swallow up the ship herself and the terrified lives on board of her.

"That reefed foresail saved you," I threw in.

"Under God—it did," he exclaimed fervently. "It was by a special mercy, I firmly believe, that it stood some of those hurricane squalls."

"It was the setting of that sail which—" I began.

"God's own hand in it," he interrupted me. "Nothing less could have done it. I don't mind telling you that I hardly dared give the order. It seemed impossible that we could touch anything without losing it, and then our last hope would have been gone."

The terror of that gale was on him yet. I let him go on for a bit, then said, casually—as if returning to a minor subject:

"You were very anxious to give up your mate to the shore people, I believe?"

He was. To the law. His obscure tenacity on that point had in it something incomprehensible and a little awful; something, as it were, mystical, quite apart from his anxiety that he should not be suspected of "countenancing any doings of that sort." Seven-and-thirty virtuous years at sea, of which over twenty of immaculate command, and the last fifteen in the Sephora, seemed to have laid him under some pitiless obligation.

"And you know," he went on, groping shame-facedly amongst his feelings, "I did not engage that young fellow. His people had some interest with my owners. I was in a way forced to take him on. He looked very smart, very gentlemanly, and all that. But do you know—I never liked him, somehow. I am a plain man. You see, he wasn't exactly the sort for the chief mate of a ship like the Sephora."

I had become so connected in thoughts and impressions with the secret sharer of my cabin that I felt as if I, personally, were being given to understand that I, too, was not the sort that would have done for the chief mate of a ship like the Sephora. I had no doubt of it in my mind.

"Not at all the style of man. You understand," he insisted, superfluously, looking hard at me.

I smiled urbanely. He seemed at a loss for a while.

"I suppose I must report a suicide."

"Beg pardon?"

"Suicide! That's what I'll have to write to my owners directly I get in."

"Unless you manage to recover him before tomorrow," I assented, dispassionately. . . . "I mean, alive."

He mumbled something which I really did not catch, and I turned my ear to him in a puzzled manner. He fairly bawled:

"The land—I say, the mainland is at least seven miles off my anchorage."

"About that."

My lack of excitement, of curiosity, of surprise, of any sort of pronounced interest, began to arouse his distrust. But except for the felicitous pretense of deafness I had not tried to pretend anything. I had felt utterly incapable of playing the part of ignorance properly, and therefore was afraid to try. It is also certain that he had brought some ready-made suspicions with him, and that he viewed my politeness as a strange and unnatural phenomenon. And yet how else could I have received him? Not heartily! That was impossible for psychological reasons, which I need not state here. My only object was to keep off his inquiries. Surlily? Yes, but surliness might have provoked a point-blank question. From its novelty to him and from its nature, punctilious courtesy was the manner best calculated to restrain the man. But there was the danger of his breaking through my defense bluntly. I could not, I think, have met him by a direct lie, also for psychological (not moral) reasons. If he had only known how afraid I was of his putting my feeling of identity with the other to the test! But, strangely enough—(I thought of it only afterwards)—I believe that he was not a little disconcerted by the reverse side of that weird situation, by something in me that reminded him of the man he was seeking—suggested a mysterious similitude to the young fellow he had distrusted and disliked from the first.

However that might have been, the silence was not very prolonged. He took another oblique step.

"I reckon I had no more than a two-mile pull to your ship. Not a bit more."

"And quite enough, too, in this awful heat," I said.

Another pause full of mistrust followed. Necessity, they say, is mother of invention, but fear, too, is not barren of ingenious suggestions. And I was afraid he would ask me point-blank for news of my other self.

"Nice little saloon, isn't it?" I remarked, as if noticing for the first time the way his eyes roamed from one closed door to the other. "And very well fitted out, too. Here, for instance," I continued, reaching over the back of my seat negligently and flinging the door open, "is my bathroom."

He made an eager movement, but hardly gave it a glance. I got up, shut the door of the bathroom, and invited him to have a look round, as if I were very proud of my accommodation. He had to rise and be shown round, but he went through the business without any raptures whatever.

"And now we'll have a look at my stateroom," I declared, in a voice as loud as I dared to make it, crossing the cabin to the starboard side with purposely heavy steps.

He followed me in and gazed around. My intelligent double had vanished. I played my part.

"Very convenient—isn't it?"

"Very nice. Very comf . . ." He didn't finish and went out brusquely as if to escape from some unrighteous wiles of mine. But it was not to be. I had been too frightened not to feel vengeful; I felt

I had him on the run, and I meant to keep him on the run. My polite insistence must have had something menacing in it, because he gave in suddenly. And I did not let him off a single item; mate's room, pantry, storerooms, the very sail locker which was also under the poop—he had to look into them all. When at last I showed him out on the quarter-deck he drew a long, spiritless sigh, and mumbled dismally that he must really be going back to his ship now. I desired my mate, who had joined us, to see to the captain's boat.

The man of whiskers gave a blast on the whistle which he used to wear hanging round his neck, and yelled, "Sephora's away!" My double down there in my cabin must have heard, and certainly could not feel more relieved than I. Four fellows came running out from somewhere forward and went over the side, while my own men, appearing on deck too, lined the rail. I escorted my visitor to the gangway ceremoniously, and nearly overdid it. He was a tenacious beast. On the very ladder he lingered, and in that unique, guiltily conscientious manner of sticking to the point:

"I say . . . you . . . you don't think that—"

I covered his voice loudly:

"Certainly not. . . . I am delighted. Good-by."

I had an idea of what he meant to say, and just saved myself by the privilege of defective hearing. He was too shaken generally to insist, but my mate, close witness of that parting, looked mystified and his face took on a thoughtful cast. As I did not want to appear as if I wished to avoid all communication with my officers, he had the opportunity to address me.

"Seems a very nice man. His boat's crew told our chaps a very extraordinary story, if what I am told by the steward is true. I suppose you had it from the captain, sir?"

"Yes. I had a story from the captain."

"A very horrible affair—isn't it, sir?"

"It is."

"Beats all these tales we hear about murders in Yankee ships."

"I don't think it beats them. I don't think it resembles them in the least."

"Bless my soul—you don't say so! But of course I've no acquaintance whatever with American ships, not I so I couldn't go against your knowledge. It's horrible enough for me. . . . But the queerest part is that those fellows seemed to have some idea the man was hidden aboard here. They had really. Did you ever hear of such a thing?"

"Preposterous—isn't it?"

We were walking to and fro athwart the quarter-deck. No one of the crew forward could be seen (the day was Sunday), and the mate pursued:

"There was some little dispute about it. Our chaps took offense. 'As if we would harbor a thing like that,' they said. 'Wouldn't you like to look for him in our coal-hole?' Quite a tiff. But they made it up in the end. I suppose he did drown himself. Don't you, sir?"

"I don't suppose anything."

"You have no doubt in the matter, sir?"

"None whatever."

I left him suddenly. I felt I was producing a bad impression, but with my double down there it was most trying to be on deck. And it was almost as trying to be below. Altogether a nerve-trying situation. But on the whole I felt less torn in two when I was with him. There was no one in the whole ship whom I dared take into my confidence. Since the hands had got to know his story, it would have been impossible to pass him off for anyone else, and an accidental discovery was to be dreaded now more than ever. . . .

The steward being engaged in laying the table for dinner, we could talk only with our eyes when I first went down. Later in the afternoon we had a cautious try at whispering. The Sunday quietness of the ship was against us; the stillness of air and water around her was against us; the elements, the men were against us— everything was against us in our secret partnership; time itself—for this could not go on forever. The very trust in Providence was, I suppose, denied to his guilt. Shall I confess that this thought cast me down very much? And as to the chapter of accidents which counts for so much in the book of success, I could only hope that it was closed. For what favorable accident could be expected?

"Did you hear everything?" were my first words as soon as we took up our position side by side, leaning over my bed place.

He had. And the proof of it was his earnest whisper, "The man told you he hardly dared to give the order."

I understood the reference to be to that saving foresail.

"Yes. He was afraid of it being lost in the setting."

"I assure you he never gave the order. He may think he did, but he never gave it. He stood there with me on the break of the poop after the main topsail blew away, and whimpered about our last hope—positively whimpered about it and nothing else—and the night coming on! To hear one's skipper go on like that in such weather was enough to drive any fellow out of his mind. It worked me up into a sort of desperation. I just took it into my own hands and went away from him, boiling, and—But what's the use telling you? *You* know! . . . Do you think that if I had not been pretty fierce with them I should have got the men to do anything? Not it! The bo's'n perhaps? Perhaps! It wasn't a heavy sea—it was a sea gone mad! I suppose the end of the world will be something like that; and a man may have the heart to see it coming once and be done with it—but to have to face it day after day—I don't blame anybody. I was precious little better than the rest. Only—I was an officer of that old coal wagon, anyhow—"

"I quite understand," I conveyed that sincere assurance into his ear. He was out of breath with whispering; I could hear him pant slightly. It was all very simple. The same strung-up force which had given twenty-four men a chance, at least, for their lives, had, in a sort of recoil, crushed an unworthy mutinous existence.

But I had no leisure to weigh the merits of the matter—footsteps in the saloon, a heavy knock. "There's enough wind to get under way with, sir." Here was the call of a new claim upon my thoughts and even upon my feelings.

"Turn the hands up," I cried through the door. "I'll be on deck directly."

I was going out to make the acquaintance of my ship. Before I left the cabin our eyes met—the eyes of the only two strangers on board. I pointed to the recessed part where the little campstool awaited him and laid my finger on my lips. He made a gesture—somewhat vague—a little mysterious, accompanied by a faint smile, as if of regret.

This is not the place to enlarge upon the sensations of a man who feels for the first time a ship move under his feet to his own independent word. In my case they were not unalloyed. I was not wholly alone with my command; for there was that stranger in my cabin. Or rather, I was not completely and wholly with her. Part of me was absent. That mental feeling of being in two places at once affected me physically as if the mood of secrecy had penetrated my very soul. Before an hour had elapsed since the ship had begun to move, having occasion to ask the mate (he stood by my side) to take a compass bearing of the pagoda, I caught myself reaching up to his ear in whispers. I say I caught myself, but enough had escaped to startle the man. I can't describe it otherwise than by saying that he shied. A grave, preoccupied manner, as though he were in possession of some perplexing intelligence, did not leave him henceforth. A little later I moved away from the rail to look at the compass with such a stealthy gait that the helmsman noticed it—and I could not help noticing the unusual roundness of his eyes. These are trifling instances, though it's to no commander's advantage to be suspected of ludicrous eccentricities. But I was also more seriously affected. There are to a seaman certain words, gestures, that should in given conditions come as naturally, as instinctively as the winking of a menaced eye. A certain order should spring on to his lips without thinking; a certain sign should get itself made, so to speak, without reflection. But all unconscious alertness had abandoned me. I had to make an effort of will to recall myself back (from the cabin) to the conditions of the moment. I felt that I was appearing an irresolute commander to those people who were watching me more or less critically.

And, besides, there were the scares. On the second day out, for instance, coming off the deck in the afternoon (I had straw slippers on my bare feet) I stopped at the open pantry door and spoke to the steward. He was doing something there with his back to me. At the sound of my voice he nearly jumped out of his skin, as the saying is, and incidentally broke a cup.

"What on earth's the matter with you?" I asked, astonished.

He was extremely confused. "Beg your pardon, sir. I made sure you were in your cabin."

"You see I wasn't."

"No, sir. I could have sworn I had heard you moving in there not a moment ago. It's most extraordinary . . . very sorry, sir."

I passed on with an inward shudder. I was so identified with my secret double that I did not even mention the fact in those scanty, fearful whispers we exchanged. I suppose he had made some slight noise of some kind or other. It would have been miraculous if he hadn't at one time or another. And yet, haggard as he appeared, he looked always perfectly self-controlled, more than calm—almost invulnerable. On my suggestion he remained almost entirely in the bathroom, which, upon the whole, was the safest place. There could be really no shadow of an excuse for anyone ever wanting to go in there, once the steward had done with it. It was a very tiny place. Sometimes he reclined on the floor, his legs bent, his head sustained on one elbow. At others I would find him on the campstool, sitting in his gray sleeping suit and with his cropped dark hair like a patient, unmoved convict. At night I would smuggle him into my bed place, and we would whisper together, with the regular footfalls of the officer of the watch passing and repassing over our heads. It was an infinitely miserable time. It was lucky that some tins of fine preserves were stowed in a locker in my stateroom; hard bread I could always get hold of; and so he lived on stewed chicken, PATE DE FOIE GRAS, asparagus, cooked oysters, sardines—on all sorts of abominable sham delicacies out of tins. My early-morning coffee he always drank; and it was all I dared do for him in that respect.

Every day there was the horrible maneuvering to go through so that my room and then the bathroom should be done in the usual way. I came to hate the sight of the steward, to abhor the voice of that harmless man. I felt that it was he who would bring on the disaster of discovery. It hung like a sword over our heads.

The fourth day out, I think (we were then working down the east side of the Gulf of Siam, tack for tack, in light winds and smooth water)—the fourth day, I say, of this miserable juggling with the unavoidable, as we sat at our evening meal, that man, whose slightest movement I dreaded, after putting down the dishes ran up on deck busily. This could not be dangerous. Presently he came down again; and then it appeared that he had remembered a coat of mine which I had thrown over a rail to dry after having been wetted in a shower which had passed over the ship in the afternoon. Sitting stolidly at the head of the table I became terrified at the sight of the garment on his arm. Of course he made for my door. There was no time to lose.

"Steward," I thundered. My nerves were so shaken that I could not govern my voice and conceal my agitation. This was the sort of thing that made my terrifically whiskered mate tap his forehead with his forefinger. I had detected him using that gesture while talking on deck with a confidential air to the carpenter. It was too far to hear a word, but I had no doubt that this pantomime could only refer to the strange new captain.

"Yes, sir," the pale-faced steward turned resignedly to me. It was this maddening course of being shouted at, checked without rhyme or reason, arbitrarily chased out of my cabin, suddenly called into it, sent flying out of his pantry on incomprehensible errands, that accounted for the growing wretchedness of his expression.

"Where are you going with that coat?"

"To your room, sir."

"Is there another shower coming?"

"I'm sure I don't know, sir. Shall I go up again and see, sir?"

"No! never mind."

My object was attained, as of course my other self in there would have heard everything that passed. During this interlude my two officers never raised their eyes off their respective plates; but the lip of that confounded cub, the second mate, quivered visibly.

I expected the steward to hook my coat on and come out at once. He was very slow about it; but I dominated my nervousness sufficiently not to shout after him. Suddenly I became aware (it could be heard plainly enough) that the fellow for some reason or other was opening the door of the bathroom. It was the end. The place was literally not big enough to swing a cat in. My voice died in my throat and I went stony all over. I expected to hear a yell of surprise and terror, and made a movement, but had not the strength to get on my legs. Everything remained still. Had my second self taken the poor wretch by the throat? I don't know what I could have done next moment if I had not seen the steward come out of my room, close the door, and then stand quietly by the sideboard.

"Saved," I thought. "But, no! Lost! Gone! He was gone!"

I laid my knife and fork down and leaned back in my chair. My head swam. After a while, when sufficiently recovered to speak in a steady voice, I instructed my mate to put the ship round at eight o'clock himself.

"I won't come on deck," I went on. "I think I'll turn in, and unless the wind shifts I don't want to be disturbed before midnight. I feel a bit seedy."

"You did look middling bad a little while ago," the chief mate remarked without showing any great concern.

They both went out, and I stared at the steward clearing the table. There was nothing to be read on that wretched man's face. But why did he avoid my eyes, I asked myself. Then I thought I should like to hear the sound of his voice.

"Steward!"

"Sir!" Startled as usual.

"Where did you hang up that coat?"

"In the bathroom, sir." The usual anxious tone. "It's not quite dry yet, sir."

For some time longer I sat in the cuddy. Had my double vanished as he had come? But of his coming there was an explanation, whereas his disappearance would be inexplicable. . . . I went slowly into my dark room, shut the door, lighted the lamp, and for a time dared not turn round. When at last I did I saw him standing bolt-upright in the narrow recessed part. It would not be true to say I had a shock, but an irresistible doubt of his bodily existence flitted through my mind. Can it be, I asked myself, that he is not visible to other eyes than mine? It was like being haunted. Motionless, with a grave face, he raised his hands slightly at me in a gesture which meant clearly, "Heavens! what a narrow escape!" Narrow indeed. I think I had come creeping quietly as near insanity as any man who has not actually gone over the border. That gesture restrained me, so to speak.

The mate with the terrific whiskers was now putting the ship on the other tack. In the moment of profound silence which follows upon the hands going to their stations I heard on the poop his raised voice: "Hard alee!" and the distant shout of the order repeated on the main-deck. The sails, in that light breeze, made but a faint fluttering noise. It ceased. The ship was coming round slowly: I held my breath in the renewed stillness of expectation; one wouldn't have thought that there was a single living soul on her decks. A sudden brisk shout, "Mainsail haul!" broke the spell, and in the noisy cries and rush overhead of the men running away with the main brace we two, down in my cabin, came together in our usual position by the bed place.

He did not wait for my question. "I heard him fumbling here and just managed to squat myself down in the bath," he whispered to me. "The fellow only opened the door and put his arm in to hang the coat up. All the same—"

"I never thought of that," I whispered back, even more appalled than before at the closeness of the shave, and marveling at that something unyielding in his character which was carrying him through so finely. There was no agitation in his whisper. Whoever was being driven distracted, it was not he. He was sane. And the proof of his sanity was continued when he took up the whispering again.

"It would never do for me to come to life again."

It was something that a ghost might have said. But what he was alluding to was his old captain's reluctant admission of the theory of suicide. It would obviously serve his turn—if I had understood at all the view which seemed to govern the unalterable purpose of his action.

"You must maroon me as soon as ever you can get amongst these islands off the Cambodge[1] shore," he went on.

---

[1] Cambodian.

"Maroon you! We are not living in a boy's adventure tale," I protested. His scornful whispering took me up.

"We aren't indeed! There's nothing of a boy's tale in this. But there's nothing else for it. I want no more. You don't suppose I am afraid of what can be done to me? Prison or gallows or whatever they may please. But you don't see me coming back to explain such things to an old fellow in a wig and twelve respectable tradesmen, do you? What can they know whether I am guilty or not—or of *what* I am guilty, either? That's my affair. What does the Bible say? 'Driven off the face of the earth.'[2] Very well, I am off the face of the earth now. As I came at night so I shall go."

"Impossible!" I murmured. "You can't."

"Can't? . . . Not naked like a soul on the Day of Judgment. I shall freeze on to this sleeping suit. The Last Day is not yet—and . . . you have understood thoroughly. Didn't you?"

I felt suddenly ashamed of myself. I may say truly that I understood—and my hesitation in letting that man swim away from my ship's side had been a mere sham sentiment, a sort of cowardice.

"It can't be done now till next night," I breathed out. "The ship is on the off-shore tack and the wind may fail us."

"As long as I know that you understand," he whispered. "But of course you do. It's a great satisfaction to have got somebody to understand. You seem to have been there on purpose." And in the same whisper, as if we two whenever we talked had to say things to each other which were not fit for the world to hear, he added, "It's very wonderful."

We remained side by side talking in our secret way—but sometimes silent or just exchanging a whispered word or two at long intervals. And as usual he stared through the port. A breath of wind came now and again into our faces. The ship might have been moored in dock, so gently and on an even keel she slipped through the water, that did not murmur even at our passage, shadowy and silent like a phantom sea.

At midnight I went on deck, and to my mate's great surprise put the ship round on the other tack. His terrible whiskers flitted round me in silent criticism. I certainly should not have done it if it had been only a question of getting out of that sleepy gulf as quickly as possible. I believe he told the second mate, who relieved him, that it

---

[2] God's punishment of Cain, "driven . . . out this day from the face of the earth" (Genesis 4: 14). See page 194, note 12.

was a great want of judgment. The other only yawned. That intolerable cub shuffled about so sleepily and lolled against the rails in such a slack, improper fashion that I came down on him sharply.

"Aren't you properly awake yet?"

"Yes, sir! I am awake."

"Well, then, be good enough to hold yourself as if you were. And keep a lookout. If there's any current we'll be closing with some islands before daylight."

The east side of the gulf is fringed with islands, some solitary, others in groups. On the blue background of the high coast they seem to float on silvery patches of calm water, arid and gray, or dark green and rounded like clumps of evergreen bushes, with the larger ones, a mile or two long, showing the outlines of ridges, ribs of gray rock under the dark mantle of matted leafage. Unknown to trade, to travel, almost to geography, the manner of life they harbor is an unsolved secret. There must be villages—settlements of fishermen at least—on the largest of them, and some communication with the world is probably kept up by native craft. But all that forenoon, as we headed for them, fanned along by the faintest of breezes, I saw no sign of man or canoe in the field of the telescope I kept on pointing at the scattered group.

At noon I have no orders for a change of course, and the mate's whiskers became much concerned and seemed to be offering themselves unduly to my notice. At last I said:

"I am going to stand right in. Quite in—as far as I can take her."

The stare of extreme surprise imparted an air of ferocity also to his eyes, and he looked truly terrific for a moment.

"We're not doing well in the middle of the gulf," I continued, casually. "I am going to look for the land breezes tonight."

"Bless my soul! Do you mean, sir, in the dark amongst the lot of all them islands and reefs and shoals?"

"Well—if there are any regular land breezes at all on this coast one must get close inshore to find them, mustn't one?"

"Bless my soul!" he exclaimed again under his breath. All that afternoon he wore a dreamy, contemplative appearance which in him was a mark of perplexity. After dinner I went into my stateroom as if I meant to take some rest. There we two bent our dark heads over a half-unrolled chart lying on my bed.

"There," I said. "It's got to be Koh-ring. I've been looking at it ever since sunrise. It has got two hills and a low point. It must be inhabited. And on the coast opposite there is what looks like the mouth of a biggish river—with some towns, no doubt, not far up. It's the best chance for you that I can see."

"Anything. Koh-ring let it be."

He looked thoughtfully at the chart as if surveying chances and distances from a lofty height—and following with his eyes his own figure wandering on the blank land of Cochin-China, and then passing off that piece of paper clean out of sight into uncharted regions. And it was as if the ship had two captains to plan her course for her. I had been so worried and restless running up and down that I had not had the patience to dress that day. I had remained in my sleeping suit, with straw slippers and a soft floppy hat. The closeness of the heat in the gulf had been most oppressive, and the crew were used to seeing me wandering in that airy attire.

"She will clear the south point as she heads now," I whispered into his ear. "Goodness only knows when, though, but certainly after dark. I'll edge her in to half a mile, as far as I may be able to judge in the dark—"

"Be careful," he murmured, warningly—and I realized suddenly that all my future, the only future for which I was fit, would perhaps go irretrievably to pieces in any mishap to my first command.

I could not stop a moment longer in the room. I motioned him to get out of sight and made my way on the poop. That unplayful cub had the watch. I walked up and down for a while thinking things out, then beckoned him over.

"Send a couple of hands to open the two quarter-deck ports," I said, mildly.

He actually had the impudence, or else so forgot himself in his wonder at such an incomprehensible order, as to repeat:

"Open the quarter-deck ports! What for, sir?"

"The only reason you need concern yourself about is because I tell you to do so. Have them open wide and fastened properly."

He reddened and went off, but I believe made some jeering remark to the carpenter as to the sensible practice of ventilating a ship's quarter-deck. I know he popped into the mate's cabin to impart the fact to him because the whiskers came on deck, as it were by chance, and stole glances at me from below—for signs of lunacy or drunkenness, I suppose.

A little before supper, feeling more restless than ever, I rejoined, for a moment, my second self. And to find him sitting so quietly was surprising, like something against nature, inhuman.

I developed my plan in a hurried whisper.

"I shall stand in as close as I dare and then put her round. I will presently find means to smuggle you out of here into the sail locker, which communicates with the lobby. But there is an opening, a sort of square for hauling the sails out, which gives straight on the quarter-deck and which is never closed in fine weather, so as to give air to the sails. When the ship's way is deadened in stays and all the hands are aft at the main braces you will have a clear road to slip out and get overboard through the open quarter-deck port. I've had them both fastened up. Use a rope's end to lower yourself into the water so as to avoid a splash—you know. It could be heard and cause some beastly complication."

He kept silent for a while, then whispered, "I understand."

"I won't be there to see you go," I began with an effort. "The rest . . . I only hope I have understood, too."

"You have. From first to last"—and for the first time there seemed to be a faltering, something strained in his whisper. He caught hold of my arm, but the ringing of the supper bell made me start. He didn't though; he only released his grip.

After supper I didn't come below again till well past eight o'clock. The faint, steady breeze was loaded with dew; and the wet, darkened sails held all there was of propelling power in it. The night, clear and starry, sparkled darkly, and the opaque, lightless patches shifting slowly against the low stars were the drifting islets. On the port bow there was a big one more distant and shadowily imposing by the great space of sky it eclipsed.

On opening the door I had a back view of my very own self looking at a chart. He had come out of the recess and was standing near the table.

"Quite dark enough," I whispered.

He stepped back and leaned against my bed with a level, quiet glance. I sat on the couch. We had nothing to say to each other. Over our heads the officer of the watch moved here and there. Then I heard him move quickly. I knew what that meant. He was making for the companion; and presently his voice was outside my door.

"We are drawing in pretty fast, sir. Land looks rather close."

"Very well," I answered. "I am coming on deck directly."

I waited till he was gone out of the cuddy, then rose. My double moved too. The time had come to exchange our last whispers, for neither of us was ever to hear each other's natural voice.

"Look here!" I opened a drawer and took out three sovereigns.[3] "Take this anyhow. I've got six and I'd give you the lot, only I must keep a little money to buy some fruit and vegetables for the crew from native boats as we go through Sunda Straits."

He shook his head.

"Take it," I urged him, whispering desperately. "No one can tell what—"

He smiled and slapped meaningly the only pocket of the sleeping jacket. It was not safe, certainly. But I produced a large old silk handkerchief of mine, and tying the three pieces of gold in a corner, pressed it on him. He was touched, I supposed, because he took it at last and tied it quickly round his waist under the jacket, on his bare skin.

Our eyes met; several seconds elapsed, till, our glances still mingled, I extended my hand and turned the lamp out. Then I passed through the cuddy, leaving the door of my room wide open. . . . "Steward!"

He was still lingering in the pantry in the greatness of his zeal, giving a rub-up to a plated cruet stand the last thing before going to bed. Being careful not to wake up the mate, whose room was opposite, I spoke in an undertone.

He looked round anxiously. "Sir!"

"Can you get me a little hot water from the galley?"

"I am afraid, sir, the galley fire's been out for some time now."

"Go and see."

He flew up the stairs.

"Now," I whispered, loudly, into the saloon—too loudly, perhaps, but I was afraid I couldn't make a sound. He was by my side in an instant—the double captain slipped past the stairs—through a tiny dark passage . . . a sliding door. We were in the sail locker, scrambling on our knees over the sails. A sudden thought struck me. I saw myself wandering barefooted, bareheaded, the sun beating on my dark poll. I snatched off my floppy hat and tried hurriedly in the dark to ram it on my other self. He dodged and fended off silently. I wonder what he thought had come to me before he understood and suddenly desisted. Our hands met gropingly, lingered united in a steady, motionless clasp for a second. . . . No word was breathed by either of us when they separated.

[3] A sovereign is a £1 gold coin.

I was standing quietly by the pantry door when the steward returned.

"Sorry, sir. Kettle barely warm. Shall I light the spirit lamp?"

"Never mind."

I came out on deck slowly. It was now a matter of conscience to shave the land as close as possible—for now he must go overboard whenever the ship was put in stays. Must! There could be no going back for him. After a moment I walked over to leeward and my heart flew into my mouth at the nearness of the land on the bow. Under any other circumstances I would not have held on a minute longer. The second mate had followed me anxiously.

I looked on till I felt I could command my voice.

"She will weather," I said then in a quiet tone.

"Are you going to try that, sir?" he stammered out incredulously.

I took no notice of him and raised my tone just enough to be heard by the helmsman.

"Keep her good full."

"Good full, sir."

The wind fanned my cheek, the sails slept, the world was silent. The strain of watching the dark loom of the land grow bigger and denser was too much for me. I had shut my eyes—because the ship must go closer. She must! The stillness was intolerable. Were we standing still?

When I opened my eyes the second view started my heart with a thump. The black southern hill of Koh-ring seemed to hang right over the ship like a towering fragment of everlasting night. On that enormous mass of blackness there was not a gleam to be seen, not a sound to be heard. It was gliding irresistibly towards us and yet seemed already within reach of the hand. I saw the vague figures of the watch grouped in the waist, gazing in awed silence.

"Are you going on, sir?" inquired an unsteady voice at my elbow.

I ignored it. I had to go on.

"Keep her full. Don't check her way. That won't do now," I said warningly.

"I can't see the sails very well," the helmsman answered me, in strange, quavering tones.

Was she close enough? Already she was, I won't say in the shadow of the land, but in the very blackness of it, already swallowed up as it were, gone too close to be recalled, gone from me altogether.

"Give the mate a call," I said to the young man who stood at my elbow as still as death. "And turn all hands up."

My tone had a borrowed loudness reverberated from the height of the land. Several voices cried out together: "We are all on deck, sir."

Then stillness again, with the great shadow gliding closer, towering higher, without a light, without a sound. Such a hush had fallen on the ship that she might have been a bark of the dead floating in slowly under the very gate of Erebus.[4]

"My God! Where are we?"

It was the mate moaning at my elbow. He was thunderstruck, and as it were deprived of the moral support of his whiskers. He clapped his hands and absolutely cried out, "Lost!"

"Be quiet," I said, sternly.

He lowered his tone, but I saw the shadowy gesture of his despair. "What are we doing here?"

"Looking for the land wind."

He made as if to tear his hair, and addressed me recklessly.

"She will never get out. You have done it, sir. I knew it'd end in something like this. She will never weather, and you are too close now to stay. She'll drift ashore before she's round. O my God!"

I caught his arm as he was raising it to batter his poor devoted head, and shook it violently.

"She's ashore already," he wailed, trying to tear himself away.

"Is she? . . . Keep good full there!"

"Good full, sir," cried the helmsman in a frightened, thin, child-like voice.

I hadn't let go the mate's arm and went on shaking it. "Ready about, do you hear? You go forward"—shake—"and stop there"—shake—"and hold your noise"—shake—"and see these head-sheets properly overhauled"—shake, shake—shake.

And all the time I dared not look towards the land lest my heart should fail me. I released my grip at last and he ran forward as if fleeing for dear life.

I wondered what my double there in the sail locker thought of this commotion. He was able to hear everything—and perhaps he was able to understand why, on my conscience, it had to be thus

---

[4] In classical mythology, the entrance to the underworld abode of the dead; also the name of a ship in Sir John Franklin's expedition, 1845, in search of the Northwest passage to the Pacific Ocean, a venture in which all perished.

close—no less. My first order "Hard alee!"[5] re-echoed ominously under the towering shadow of Koh-ring as if I had shouted in a mountain gorge. And then I watched the land intently. In that smooth water and light wind it was impossible to feel the ship coming-to. No! I could not feel her. And my second self was making now ready to ship out and lower himself overboard. Perhaps he was gone already . . .?

The great black mass brooding over our very mastheads began to pivot away from the ship's side silently. And now I forgot the secret stranger ready to depart, and remembered only that I was a total stranger to the ship. I did not know her. Would she do it? How was she to be handled?

I swung the mainyard and waited helplessly. She was perhaps stopped, and her very fate hung in the balance, with the black mass of Koh-ring like the gate of the everlasting night towering over her taffrail. What would she do now? Had she way on her yet? I stepped to the side swiftly, and on the shadowy water I could see nothing except a faint phosphorescent flash revealing the glassy smoothness of the sleeping surface. It was impossible to tell—and I had not learned yet the feel of my ship. Was she moving? What I needed was something easily seen, a piece of paper, which I could throw overboard and watch. I had nothing on me. To run down for it I didn't dare. There was no time. All at once my strained, yearning stare distinguished a white object floating within a yard of the ship's side. White on the black water. A phosphorescent flash passed under it. What was that thing? . . . I recognized my own floppy hat. It must have fallen off his head . . . and he didn't bother. Now I had what I wanted—the saving mark for my eyes. But I hardly thought of my other self, now gone from the ship, to be hidden forever from all friendly faces, to be a fugitive and a vagabond on the earth, with no brand of the curse on his sane forehead to stay a slaying hand[6] . . . too proud to explain.

And I watched the hat—the expression of my sudden pity for his mere flesh. It had been meant to save his homeless head from the dangers of the sun. And now—behold—it was saving the ship, by serving me for a mark to help out the ignorance of my strangeness. Ha! It was drifting forward, warning me just in time that the ship had gathered sternaway.

---

[5] Toward land.

[6] A final echo of the curse on Cain (Genesis 4).

"Shift the helm," I said in a low voice to the seaman standing still like a statue.

The man's eyes glistened wildly in the binnacle light as he jumped round to the other side and spun round the wheel.

I walked to the break of the poop. On the over-shadowed deck all hands stood by the forebraces waiting for my order. The stars ahead seemed to be gliding from right to left. And all was so still in the world that I heard the quiet remark, "She's round," passed in a tone of intense relief between two seamen.

"Let go and haul."

The foreyards ran round with a great noise, amidst cheery cries. And now the frightful whiskers made themselves heard giving various orders. Already the ship was drawing ahead. And I was alone with her. Nothing! no one in the world should stand now between us, throwing a shadow on the way of silent knowledge and mute affection, the perfect communion of a seaman with his first command.

Walking to the taffrail, I was in time to make out, on the very edge of a darkness thrown by a towering black mass like the very gateway of Erebus—yes, I was in time to catch an evanescent glimpse of my white hat left behind to mark the spot where the secret sharer of my cabin and of my thoughts, as though he were my second self, had lowered himself into the water to take his punishment: a free man, a proud swimmer striking out for a new destiny.

Joseph Conrad's
Letters on *The Secret Sharer*[1]

To John Galsworthy, 28 October (?)1912

Ten years Conrad's junior, John Galsworthy (1867–1933) published his first collection of stories, From the Four Winds, *in 1897, under the pen-name John Sinjohn; the first work to appear under his own name was* The Island Pharisees *(1904). With the success in 1906 of his play,* The Silver Box, *and in quick succession* Strife *(1909) and* Justice

---

[1] From *The Collected Letters of Joseph Conrad*, ed. Frederick R. Karl and Laurence Davies, vol. 5 (Cambridge UP, 1996); punctuation and spelling are unchanged; italics appear as underlines.

(1910), his claim to importance in 1912 was as a playwright on themes of class antagonisms and social inequality. Justice *prompted prison reform in England. His novel,* The Man of Property *(1906), would become the first of the Forsyte saga, to which he would not return until after World War I.*

I can't tell you what pleasure you have given me by what you say of the Secret Sharer—and especially of the swimmer. I havent seen many notices—3 or 4 in all; but in one of them he is called a murderous ruffian—or something of that sort. Who are those fellows who write in the Press? Where do they come from? I was simply knocked over—for indeed I meant him to be what you have seen at once he was. And as <u>you</u> have seen I feel altogether comforted and rewarded for the trouble he has given me in the doing of him. For it wasn't an easy task. It was extremely difficult to keep him true to type first as modified to some extent by the sea-life and further as affected by the situation.

To Edward Garnett, 5 November 1912

As editor and reader for publisher T. F. Unwin, Edward Garnett (1868–1937) championed and mentored both Conrad and Galsworthy. Like Galsworthy, who dedicated The Man of Property *to him, Garnett was a playwright on controversial themes.* The Breaking Point, *which featured an unmarried mother, was denied a license for performance in London, though it did get published in 1907, with an open letter to the censor.*

Thanks for your letter on the 3 tales—very much of sorts. I dare say Freya[2] is pretty rotten. On the other hand the Secret Sharer, between you and me, is <u>it</u>. Eh? No damned tricks with girls there. Eh? Every word fits and there's not a single uncertain note. Luck my boy. Pure luck. I knew you would spot the thing at sight. But I repeat: mere luck.

To Edith Wharton, 24 December 1912

In 1905, poet, story-writer, and writer on interior decoration Edith Wharton (1862–1937) achieved international fame with her brilliant

---

[2] *Freya of the Seven Isles* is another one of the tales with which *The Secret Sharer* was published in *'Twixt Land and Sea* (1912).

novel, The House of Mirth. *Born to a New York family whose wealth produced the phrase "Keeping up with the Joneses," 23-year-old Edith Jones married Teddy Wharton, 12 years her senior. By the time of this letter, the marriage was foundering on the rocks of Teddy's philandering, and his deteriorating mental and physical health (they would divorce in 1913), as well as Edith's own affair in Paris (from 1908) with Morton Fullerton, journalist for the* London Times, *bisexual, and friend of Henry James. Conrad's bantering in French (he and Wharton are fluent) is relevant to the subject of translation.*

I am very much touched by your infinitely kind and delightful letter. The appreciation of a fellow worker of such great and distinguished gifts can't be but very precious to me; and I am very glad that you like that particular story.

Yes. I admit that I owe a debt of gratitude to Mr Marcel Proust[3] for procuring me the pleasure of your generous letter. But I am bound to be perfectly open with you. The idea of translating the S S into French, fascinating as it is, frightens me. C'est que, voyez-vous, je ne me connais que trop.[4] I would try to re-write it; and really and truly I can't afford the time for the experiment. After sixteen years of most painful scribbling I am still living from day to day by my pen. Voilà, Madame, la verité toute nue.[5]

And the thing (I need not point out to you) is so particularly English, in moral atmosphere, in feeling and even in detail—n'est-ce pas?[6] But still if you think a rendering practicable why should not M. Prevost come to some understanding with Henry Darvay (of the <u>Mercure</u>[7]) who is the official translator of my work into French. [. . .] Well, all I can say is that if I get (by some means) a mere mot-à-mot[8] rendering I'll find time to give it a tournure[9] on individual character, which no doubt won't be french style in any sense but which will be Conrad's diction, his note personelle.

---

[3] Proust would publish the first of his acclaimed novels in the series *À la recherche du temps perdu* in 1913. At the time he was working, not too successfully, as a translator.

[4] *It's that, you see, I know myself too well.*

[5] *There, Madame, the whole naked truth.*

[6] *Is it not?* (the wit is declaring Englishness in French).

[7] *Le Mercure de France,* a review.

[8] *Word-by-word.*

[9] *A shaping.*

From "Author's Note"

on "the basic fact of the tale" ('*Twixt Land and Sea* 1920)

The Secret Sharer was collected with two other tales in 1912 in 'Twixt Land and Sea. In a prefatory retrospect for the 1920 edition, Conrad comments on the relevance of the Cutty Sark *scandal of 1880, in which Sidney Smith, first mate of this legendary sea-clipper and a reputed bully, violently beat a black crewman, John Francis, who had refused an order in the midst of a hurricane. Francis fell into a coma and died three days later. Smith, confined to his quarters, was allowed by Captain James S. Wallace to slip away and join the crew of an American ship. On learning this, the crew of the* Cutty Sark *refused orders, and four days out of port Wallace jumped overboard into the shark-infested waters of the Java Sea. Smith was subsequently apprehended, and tried in the summer of 1882.*

The basic fact of the tale I had in my possession for a good many years. It was in truth the common possession of the whole fleet of merchant ships trading to India, China, and Australia: a great company the last years of which coincided with my first years on the wider seas. The fact itself happened on board a very distinguished member of it, *Cutty Sark* by name and belonging to Mr. Willis, a notable shipowner in his day, of the kind (they are all underground now) who used personally to see his ships start on their voyages to those distant shores where they showed worthily the honoured house-flag of their owner. I am glad I was not too late to get at least one glimpse of Mr. Willis on a very wet and gloomy morning watching from the pier-head of the New South Dock one of his clippers starting on a China voyage—an imposing figure of a man under the invariable white hat so well known in the Port of London, waiting till the head of his ship had swung downstream before giving her a dignified wave of a big gloved hand. For all I know it may have been the *Cutty Sark* herself, though certainly not on that fatal voyage. I do not know the date of the occurrence on which the scheme of "The Secret Sharer" is founded; it came to light and even got into newspapers about the middle eighties, though I had heard of it before, as it were privately, among the officers of the great wool fleet in which my first years in deep water were served. It came to light under circumstances dramatic enough, I think, but which have nothing to do with my story. In the more specially maritime part of my writing this bit of presentation may take its place as one of my two Calm-pieces. For, if there is to be any classification by subjections, I have done two Storm-pieces, in *The Nigger of the*

Narcissus and in *Typhoon;* and two Calm-pieces: this one and *The Shadow-Line,* a book which belongs to a later period.

Notwithstanding their autobiographical form the above two stories are not the record of personal experience. Their quality, such as it is, depends on something larger if less precise: on the character, vision, and sentiment of the first twenty independent years of my life.

Joseph Conrad on the art of fiction

from *Henry James, An Appreciation* (1905)

Novelist Henry James (1843–1916) revolutionized fiction with his language of the minute and subtle turns of subjective perception and the interior life. From Notes on Life and Letters *(London: J. M. Dent, 1921).*

All creative art is magic, is evocation of the unseen in forms persuasive, enlightening, familiar and surprising, for the edification of mankind, pinned down by the conditions of its existence to the earnest consideration of the most insignificant tides of reality.

Action in its essence, the creative art of a writer of fiction may be compared to rescue work carried out in darkness against cross gusts of wind swaying the action of a great multitude. It is rescue work, this snatching of vanishing phases of turbulence, disguised in fair words, out of the native obscurity into a light where the struggling forms may be seen, seized upon, endowed with the only possible form of permanence in this world of relative values—the permanence of memory. And the multitude feels it obscurely too; since the demand of the individual to the artist is, in effect, the cry, "Take me out of myself!" meaning really, out of my perishable activity into the light of imperishable consciousness. But everything is relative, and the light of consciousness is only enduring, merely the most enduring of the things of this earth, imperishable only as against the short-lived work of our industrious hands. [. . .]

[F]rom the duality of man's nature and the competition of individuals, the life-history of the earth must in the last instance be a history of a really very relentless warfare. Neither his fellows, nor his gods, nor his passions will leave a man alone. In virtue of these allies and enemies, he holds his precarious dominion, he possesses his fleeting significance; and it is this relation in all its manifestations, great and little, superficial or profound, and this relation alone, that is commented upon, interpreted, demonstrated by the art of the novelist in the only possible way in which the task can be performed: by the independent creation of circumstance and character, achieved against all the difficulties of expression, in an imaginative effort finding its inspiration from the reality of forms and sensations.

from "Author's Note" (1920) to *The Shadow Line*

The Shadow Line was first published in 1917. Conrad added this note to the 1920 publication to explain his aversion to "the supernatural."

This story, which I admit to be in its brevity a fairly complex piece of work, was not intended to touch on the supernatural. Yet more than one critic has been inclined to take it in that way, seeing in it an attempt on my part to give the fullest scope to my imagination by taking it beyond the confines of the world of the living, suffering humanity. But as a matter of fact my imagination is not made of stuff so elastic as all that. I believe that if I attempted to put the strain of the supernatural on it it would fail deplorably and exhibit an unlovely gap. But I could never have attempted such a thing, because all my moral and intellectual being is penetrated by an invincible conviction that whatever falls under the dominion of our senses must be in nature and, however exceptional, cannot differ in its essence from all the other effect of the visible and tangible world of which we are a self-conscious part. The world of the living contains enough marvels and mysteries as it is; marvels and mysteries acting upon our emotions and intelligence in ways so inexplicable that it would almost justify the conception of life as an enchanted state. No, I am too firm in my consciousness of the marvellous to be ever fascinated by the mere supernatural, which (take it any way you like) is but a manufactured article, the fabrication of minds insensitive to the intimate delicacies of our relation to the dead and to the living, in their countless multitudes; a desecration of our tenderest memories; an outrage on our dignity.

Reviews of *The Secret Sharer* in *'Twixt Land and Sea*

The Secret Sharer received fresh notice when it was published with two other tales, A Smile of Fortune and Freya of the Seven Isles, in this collection of 1912.

ROBERT LYND, *Daily News,* 14 OCTOBER 1912, p. 8

> *Essayist and Irish Republican activist Robert Lynd (1879–1945) was a*
> *close friend of Roger Casement, who, like Conrad, wrote about the*
> *abuses by the Belgian corporation in the Congo.*

If anyone has any doubts of Mr. Conrad's genius he will do well
to read "The Secret Sharer," the second story in this volume. I confess repentantly that I once had such doubts. But I had not read
"Typhoon" then.[1] None of the three stories in *'Twixt Land and Sea*
possesses the cosmic, or rather the infernal, energy of "Typhoon."
In reading "Typhoon" one has constantly, as it were, to catch hold
of something solid in order to keep oneself from being swept off
one's feet by the fury of the author's sensitive and truthful genius.
"The Secret Sharer" is work of a quieter mood. It is as different
from "Typhoon" as still water is from a storm. But it is to an equal
extent a mastering vision of a world which Mr. Conrad knows and
nobody else knows—a world of artistically uncharted seas—a
world the seas of which have at once the reality of the seas we
know, and something of the still intenser reality of the phantom
seas of "The Ancient Mariner."[2]

Everyone who has read Mr. Conrad's stories knows how sensi-
tively and how surely he can create a living atmosphere as he adds
nervous sentence to nervous sentence. Every sentence has a nerve;
that is one of the distinguishing features of his writing. It is not
clever writing—at least, not deliberately so. If his genius fails
him, he has none of those glittering reserves of cleverness to fall
back upon, such as enable Mr. Kipling always to achieve vividness
even when he does not achieve life. But in what has been called
the sense of life, Mr. Conrad is, within his limits, far richer than
Mr. Kipling.[3]

---

[1] Also about a captain in crisis, this novel, begun in 1899, appeared in *Pall Mall
Magazine* in 1902.

[2] Samuel Taylor Coleridge's haunting ballad, *The Rime of the Ancient Mariner* (in
various forms, 1798–1834), features a strange mariner who fascinates, or mysteri-
ously compels, his audience with his narrative of supernatural events at sea.

[3] Joseph Rudyard Kipling (1865–1936), born in India, was widely admired for his
children's books, *The Jungle Book* (1894), *The Second Jungle Book* (1895), *Just So
Stories* (1902), and the novel, *Kim* (1901); for his poems, including *Mandalay*
(1890), *Gunga Din* (1890), and *If—* (1895), and many short stories, among them
The Man Who Would Be King (1888), in David Damrosch's Longman Cultural
Edition. He was the first Briton to receive the Nobel Prize for Literature, in 1907.

It is true that he expresses his sense of life rather through his winds and seas and ships than through his human beings. His human beings are, on the whole, small and eccentric creatures compared to those elements which spring upon them and lie in wait for them like the messengers of gods and devils. His characters, in other words, do not belong to that aristocracy of passion of which Pater wrote.[4] Even though they perform miracles of endurance in their warfare against wind and wave, it is the latter who are the mighty characters of his books. Compared with them, the captains and the sailors seem at times to be just a sort of odd playthings.

Thus his characters have frequently something of the quality of victims. One is very conscious of this as one reads 'Freya of the Seven Isles,' in the present book. This is a wonderful pitiless story of revenge in the Dutch East Indies. It tells how a Dutch naval lieutenant, an ugly, surly, thick-bodied man, was enabled to get his rival, a young English trading captain, into his clutches in a manner that cost a charming and generous young man his reason, and a charming and high-hearted girl her life. The especial pitilessness of the story arises from the fact that the Dutchman's bitterness would hardly have been able to plan the destruction of his rival unaided. It was fate that struck the young man down—struck him down, too, not through his vices, but his virtues. For a man to whom he had done a service stole, in a moment of drunken weakness, the firearms belonging to his ship, and sold them to the natives on one of the Dutch islands, with the result that the young trader was delivered into the lieutenant's power. No one but Mr. Conrad could have described with such intense imaginative excitement—excitement free from every trace of melodrama and rhetoric—that calculated devilish tragedy when the lieutenant manoeuvred Jasper Allen's beautiful white ship to its doom upon the reef where it would lie long afterwards, a grey ghost, haunting the insane eyes of its owner as he watched it, the ghost of a man, from the shore.

In his description of human beings subjected to some terrible fascination Mr. Conrad excels. "Studies in fascination" would be a not inapt description of the three stories in this book. The first of the three, "A Smile of Fortune," which also has its scene among tropical seas, is a study of the spell cast on the captain of a ship by a

---

[4] Influential critic Walter Pater (1839–1894), refusing the Victorian moral imperative for art, championed "art for art's sake" and the "spirit of general elevation and enlightenment" that binds the passions of artists to one another (*The Renaissance*, 1873).

mysterious outcast, shy, untamed, animal of a woman. It is good, but not supremely good. "The Secret Sharer," on the other hand, which tells of the spell cast upon another captain by a mate charged with murder, who has taken refuge in his ship, is surely a masterpiece. Here Mr. Conrad himself casts a spell.

Ever from that midnight moment, when the captain, lonelily pacing the deck of his anchored ship in islanded eastern seas, looks over the side and beholds the apparently headless body of a man in the phosphorescent water at the foot of the ladder, the story grips one in its quiet, inevitable sentences. There is marvellous psychological insight shown in the way in which the captain, having clothed the man in his clothes and hidden him in his room and heard his strange story, like a secret, in intimate whispers, gradually comes to associate his own identity with the identity of the fugitive. It is the captain and not the fugitive who jumps at sudden sounds and at chances of discovery. The great elation of the story, however, does not arise from its study of the psychology of fascination or curious sense of identity or alarm. All this is necessary to produce it, but all this alone would not produce it. In his eagerness for the escape of his double, who insists upon dropping over the ship's side at night and swimming to one of the islands where he can live as one dead, a marooned and forgotten man, the captain compels his crew, almost still with horror, to bring the ship right up under the shadow of the land on a pretence of looking for land winds. That scene gives us one of the great thrills of modern literature.

> Such a hush had fallen on the ship that she might have been a bark of the dead floating in slowly under the very gate of Erebus.
>
> "My God! Where are we?"
>
> It was the mate moaning at my elbow.

As the helmsman gives his answers to the captain's orders "in a frightened, thin, childish voice" we, too, are still and tense like the horror-stricken crew. Then comes the fugitive's escape in the dark water. After that, the escape of that fine ship herself from the shadow, as it were, of the everlasting night—an escape that is one of the wonderful things of the literature of the sea. The elation that we get from this story is the elation which all great literature, even tragic literature, ought to give. Let all the bells of praise ring for so fine a piece of work.

John Masefield, *Manchester Guardian*, 16 October 1912, p. 7

Like the Captain and Leggatt in The Secret Sharer, *English poet and writer Masefield (1878–1967) was a "Conway boy," spending several years of his youth aboard this training ship, where in addition to learning seamanship and reveling in the excitements of the seafaring life and the beauties of the ocean, he fell in love with sea-lore stories, and determined to become a writer. By 1902, he was publishing poetry; two novels followed in 1908 and 1909; but it was three subsequent narrative poems, appearing in 1911 and 1912, that catapulted him to fame.*

'Twixt Land and Sea, by Joseph Conrad, contains three stories, written in the new and handy form (about a third the length of the ordinary novel) which will perhaps be the usual literary form in the decade after this. Mr. Conrad has always used this form with fine effect, and he uses it again here finely, with a complete mastery of his art and with his old colours of mystery, romance, and the strangeness of life. His three new stories illustrate the three kinds of creative writing for which he is best known. The first tale, "A Smile of Fortune," is another study in the manner of "Heart of Darkness."[5] The suggestion of a strange and rather great character through a veil of mystery, which is plucked away, as it were, thread by thread, by a multitude of clever pickings, till the character behind it stands out, bigger perhaps than we had expected, but also stranger although revealed. The second story, "The Secret Sharer," is a new romance of the sea, a second "Youth," beautiful like that fine tale, with the suggestion that something done with difficulty and perhaps unavailingly has, after all, brought something into life, bigger than one thought, something to count as significant later on when the play is considered as a whole. The third story, "Freya of the Seven Isles," ends the symphony of the book with a study of blindness, mental this time, not physical, as in the tale at the end of "Youth," but not less tragical, being the blindness of an old, kindly father to the depths of emotion in his tragically placed daughter.

Of the three tales the first two have most of that particular art and personal way of looking at life which give Mr. Conrad's books their new and fine flavour in the mind. All three are written in a firm

---

[5] Conrad's extraordinary novella, drawing on his experience in the Congo, appeared in *Blackwood's Edinburgh Magazine* in 1899, then in 1902 with the novella *Youth*, which drew on his experiences on the sailing-ship *Palestine*.

and beautiful prose, at once precise and supple, good both in dialogue and in description. There is quality in the prose as in the subjects, difficult to define exactly, except as a personal quality of the kind sometimes got in loneliness by a strong and strange temperament who is more sensitive to impressions than his way of life gives warrant for. This quality in the choice of subjects and in the way of handling them is Mr. Conrad's own special quality. There is not and never has been anything in the least like it. Given an unusual temperament placed in a rough-and-ready way of life which leads men into those unusual places unusual traits in character are called out, a quality of this kind is likely to develop; a quality of great mental sensitiveness, which is the real man, hidden behind the mask of the activity of the occupation. Having this special gift of sensitiveness, and having as a master mariner little occasion to use it in his daily work, it seems to have developed in Mr. Conrad a deep, never-sated curiosity about life, mostly about the life known to him, the life of sailors and of the men who deal with sailors, traders, charterers, consignees, consuls, and ship's chandlers, natives of various colours, and so on, and his main achievement is this—that he has brought these people into the imaginative kingdom in all the sincerity of their simplicity. His is not a vision of the world, like Shakespere's, nor of a society, like Chaucer's; but of unusual people outside the settled orders, and his vision is all the more intense from being focussed on individuals.

His power of focussing upon the out-of-the-way gives an uncanny flavour to the first of these three tales, told in the first person of a sea captain newly arrived at an island, where he is served by a profound and single being with a kind of elemental greatness in his singleness, who has an inexplicable daughter and a home like a private madhouse. Little by little one is made more intimate with the man and his home, one comes almost to dread him and it, then one changes to dislike him or despise him, and ends by thinking him rather great, rather sinister, but quite mysterious one way or the other, in the end (like life itself, sanely looked at). The second story is not less wonderful in its atmosphere; a captain newly come to a ship in a far-away Eastern road, with the masts of another ship (waiting to be towed up the river) just visible over an island, and night coming down, and a murderer, flying from the law, in the water alongside, having swum out on a last chance. This tale, made perhaps a little petty by some of its intrigue, gets a great lift of romantic beauty towards the end, and finishes with what musicians call a full close. . . .

Standard, 25 OCTOBER 1912, p. 7

No volume that Mr. Conrad has ever published could offer more unmistakable proof of his genius than does this collection of three stories. In his greatest things—in "Typhoon," in "Youth," in *Lord Jim,* in *Nostromo*[6]—he had big themes, motifs that lent themselves readily in his hands to great results. In two of the stories here presented to us there would seem to the ordinary writer scarcely any theme at all; never before have we realised so vividly the things that Mr. Conrad can do.

We may acclaim him perhaps as the first king of a new country—that country of story-tellers who will combine the sense of life proclaimed by the great mid-Victorians with the sense of form discovered here in England somewhere about 1890. He is as enthralled by the actual world that he beholds as were ever Dickens or Thackeray; his prose is as singing and haunting a melody as was ever Meredith's or Stevenson's. It is when he is concerned with the mean things of life, as, for instance, the little paper-shop in *The Secret Agent,* or Jim's fellow criminals on the pilgrim ship in *Lord Jim,* that this startling welding of vision and matter-of-fact is most plainly to be discerned. [. . .] "The Secret Sharer" [may be] the most perfect of all Mr. Conrad's stories, although we have not forgotten "Youth" nor "The Duel," nor "Typhoon." It tells of a captain of a ship walking his decks at night. He sees a swimmer approach him out of the darkness. He helps him on board, discovers that he is a murderer escaping from justice, hides him in his cabin until his vessel approaches the coast, when he assists him again to escape. That is all. You are presented with the effect on the captain's mind of the silent and secret presence of this other man. You are made to feel the rising of that secret presence through the very boards of the ship, so that the reader himself, as the ship moves and the tension grows, is almost impelled, as though he were himself a secret watcher there, to cry out, "Take care! Take care!" to the other passengers on the boat. Mr. Conrad places these sensations in the mind of a quite ordinary matter-of-fact man, so that immediately the experience is brought into relation with us all—for all of us that moment may come when the prevailing menace of that Other Self, concealed as we think from the world, threatens us with instant disaster. . . .

---

[6] These novels were first published, respectively, in 1900 and 1904; *The Secret Agent* appeared in 1907.

Spectator, 16 NOVEMBER 1912, p. 815

In one or two of the latest of Mr. Conrad's books some of his admirers have noticed with consternation signs of new and by no means happy developments both in his matter and style. [. . .] the most marked element in the new manner seemed to be the influence of a writer as far removed as possible in his inspiration from that of Mr. Conrad—the influence, we mean, of Mr. Henry James. Much might be written of the effects of Mr. Henry James upon contemporary English fiction. [. . .] And, whatever may be the value of Mr. James's surreptitious permeations into English literature in general, upon Mr. Conrad the effect was entirely lamentable. It is with deep satisfaction therefore that we see that in his new book he has once more shaken himself free. He has returned with fresh vigour to his earlier course, and is as triumphantly successful in it as he has ever been in the past. . . .

Further Reading and Viewing

Mary Wollstonecraft Shelley

The Journals of Mary Shelley, 1814–1844. Eds. Paula R. Feldman and Diana Scott-Kilvert. 1987; Johns Hopkins UP, 1995.

The Letters of Mary Wollstonecraft Shelley. Ed. Betty T. Bennett. 3 vols. Johns Hopkins UP, 1980–1988.

Mellor, Anne K. *Mary Shelley: Her Life, Her Fiction, Her Monsters*. Methuen, 1988.

Sunstein, Emily. *Mary Wollstonecraft Shelley: Romance and Reality*. Little, 1989.

Walling, William. *Mary Shelley*. Twayne, 1972.

Frankenstein, A Longman Cultural Edition. Ed. Susan J. Wolfson. 2d edition. Pearson/Longman, 2006. Kin to *Transformation*, not only by publication close to the 1831 version of this novel, but also conceptually: Frankenstein and his Creature begin as a dyad of socially acceptable body and abject monstrosity, the difference then destabilizing over the course of the tale, with Frankenstein becoming more monstrous and the Creature mastering human language and rhetoric. This edition includes a fuller bibliography on Mary Shelley.

Transformation

Cantor, Paul A. "Mary Shelley and the Taming of the Byronic Hero: *Transformation* and *The Deformed Transformed*," in *The Other Mary Shelley*. Eds. Audrey A. Fisch, Anne K. Mellor, and

Esther H. Schor. Oxford UP, 1993. 89–106. Shelley's tale as a feminist revision of Byron's unfinished play of exchanged bodies.

Hofkosh, Sonia. "Disfiguring Economies: Mary Shelley's Short Stories." In *The Other Mary Shelley*, 204–19, esp. 213–15. Attending to annuals-culture and the plate of Juliet, Hofkosh reads the feminine and feminizing trajectory of transformation, proposing Juliet as the visible locus of interest, not only in the tale but also for readers of *The Keepsake*.

Robinson, Charles E., ed. *Mary Shelley: Collected Tales and Stories, with original engravings*. Johns Hopkins UP, 1976. Good textual notes on *Transformation*, 381–82.

Sussman, Charlotte. "Stories for the *Keepsake*," in *The Cambridge Companion to Mary Shelley*, ed. Esther Schor. Cambridge UP, 2003; 163–79, esp. 168–70. The exchange of bodies and identities is related to the exchanges of the economic marketplace, in which everything and everyone proves fungible.

Robert Louis Stevenson

Biography and Letters

The Letters of Robert Louis Stevenson. Ed. Bradford A. Booth and Ernest Mehew. Yale UP, 1994.

Balfour, Graham. *The Life of Robert Louis Stevenson*. Charles Scribner's Sons, 1901.

Bell, Ian. *Dreams of Exile: Robert Louis Stevenson, A Biography*. Henry Holt, 1992.

Calder, Jenni. *RLS: A Life Study*. Oxford UP, 1980.

———.*The Robert Louis Stevenson Companion*. P. Harris, 1980.

Chesterton, G. K. *Robert Louis Stevenson*. Dodd, Mead, 1928.

Daiches, David. *Robert Louis Stevenson: A Revaluation*. New Directions, 1947.

Davies, Hunter. *Robert Louis Stevenson: A Life Study*. Hamish Hamilton, 1980.

Harman, Claire. *Myself and the Other Fellow: A Life of Robert Louis Stevenson*. HarperCollins, 2005.

Lapierre, Alexandra. *Fanny Stevenson: A Romance of Destiny*. Graf, 1995.

McLynn, Frank J. *Robert Louis Stevenson: A Biography*. Random House, 1993.

Stevenson and the Victorian Era

Stevenson and Victorian Scotland. Ed. Jenni Calder. Edinburgh UP, 1981.

Brantlinger, Patrick. *The Reading Lesson: The Threat of Mass Literacy in Nineteenth-Century British Fiction*. Indiana UP, 1998.

Daiches, David. *Robert Louis Stevenson and His World*. Thames and Hudson, 1973.

Dryden, Linda. *The Modern Gothic and Literary Doubles*. Palgrave Macmillan, 2003.

Elwin, Malcolm. *The Strange Case of Robert Louis Stevenson*. Macdonald, 1950.

Eigner, Edwin M. *Robert Louis Stevenson and Romantic Tradition*. Princeton UP, 1966.

Honaker, Lisa. *Revising Romance: Gender, Genre, and the Late-Victorian Anti-Realists*. Rutgers University dissertation, 1993.

Hughes, Winifred. *The Maniac in the Cellar: Sensation Novels of the 1860s*. Princeton UP, 1980.

Jackson, Rosemary. *Fantasy: The Literature of Subversion*. Methuen, 1981.

Kiely, Robert. *Robert Louis Stevenson and the Fiction of Adventure*. Harvard UP, 1964.

Levine, George. *Darwin and the Novelists: Patterns of Science in Victorian Fiction*. Harvard UP, 1988.

H. L. Malachow. *Gothic Images of Race in Nineteenth-Century Britain*. Stanford UP, 1996.

Saposnik, Irving S. *Robert Louis Stevenson*. Twayne, 1974.

The Strange Case of Dr. Jekyll and Mr. Hyde

Robert Louis Stevenson: The Critical Heritage. Ed. Paul Maixner. Routledge and Kegan Paul, 1981.

The Definitive Dr. Jekyll and Mr. Hyde Companion. Ed. Henry Geduld. Garland, 1983.

Dr. Jekyll and Mr. Hyde after One Hundred Years. Ed. William Veeder and Gordon Hirsch. U Chicago P, 1988. Especially: Patrick Brantlinger and Richard Boyle, "Stevenson's 'Gothic Gnome' and the Mass Readership of Late Victorian England"; Peter K. Garrett, "Cries and Voices: Reading *Jekyll and Hyde*"; Gordon Hirsch, "*Frankenstein,* Detective Fiction, and *Jekyll and*

Hyde"; Ronald R. Thomas, "The Strange Voices in the Strange Case: Dr. Jekyll, Mr. Hyde, and the Voices of Modern Fiction"; William Veeder, "The Questions of Text," and "Children of the Night: Stevenson and the Patriarchy"; Virginia Wright Waxman, "Horrors of the Body: Hollywood's Discourse on Beauty and Rouben Mamoulian's *Dr. Jekyll and Mr. Hyde.*"

Arata, Stephen. *Fictions of Loss in the Victorian Fin de Siècle.* Cambridge UP, 1996.

Block, Ed, Jr. "James Sully, Evolutionary Psychology, and Late Victorian Gothic Fiction." *Victorian Studies* 25 (Summer 1982): 44–67.

Borges, Jorge Luis. *Borges On Writing.* Ed. Norman Thomas di Giovanni, Daniel Halpern, and Frank MacShane. E.P. Dutton, 1973.

Cohen, Ed. "The Double Lives of Men: Narration and Identification in the Late Nineteenth-Century Representation of Ex-Centric Masculinities." *Victorian Studies* 36 (Spring 1993): 353–76.

Fiedler, Leslie. *No! In Thunder.* Eyre and Spottiswoode, 1963.

Heath, Stephen. "Psychopathia sexualis: Stevenson's *Strange Case.*" *Critical Quarterly* 28 (1986): 93–108.

Martin, Valerie. *Mary Reilly: The Untold Story of Dr. Jekyll and Mr. Hyde.* Simon and Schuster, 1990.

Miller, Karl. *Doubles: Studies in Literary History.* Oxford UP, 1985.

Miyoshi, Masao. *The Divided Self: A Perspective on the Literature of the Victorians.* New York UP, 1969.

Nabokov, Vladimir. "The Strange Case of Dr. Jekyll and Mr. Hyde." In *Lectures on Literature,* ed. Fredson Bowers. Harcourt Brace Jovanovich, 1980.

Oates, Joyce Carol. "Foreword," *The Strange Case of Dr. Jekyll and Mr. Hyde.* U Nebraska P, 1990.

Rogers, Robert. *Psychoanalytic Study of the Double in Literature.* Wayne State UP, 1970.

Showalter, Elaine. *Sexual Anarchy: Gender and Culture at the Fin de Siècle.* Viking, 1990.

Stewart, Garrett. *Dear Reader: The Conscripted Audience in Nineteenth-Century British Fiction.* Johns Hopkins UP, 1996.

Stone, Donald. *Novelists in a Changing World.* Harvard UP, 1972.

Thomas, Ronald R. *Dreams of Authority: Freud and the Fictions of the Unconscious.* Cornell UP, 1990.

Twitchell, James B. *Dreadful Pleasures: An Anatomy of Modern Horror*. Oxford UP, 1985.
Walkowitz, Judith. *City of Dreadful Delight: Narratives of Sexual Danger in Victorian London*. U Chicago P, 1992.

Films

Dr. Jekyll and Mr. Hyde, dir. John S. Robertson (1920), with John Barrymore and Nita Naldi.
Dr. Jekyll and Mr. Hyde, dir. Rouben Mamoulian (1932), with Fredric March, Miriam Hopkins, and Rose Hobart.
Dr. Jekyll and Mr. Hyde, dir. Victor Fleming (1941), with Spencer Tracy, Ingrid Bergman, and Lana Turner.

Joseph Conrad
Biography and Letters

The Collected Letters of Joseph Conrad. Eds. Frederick R. Karl and Laurence Davies. Cambridge UP, 1990.
Batchelor, John. *The Life of Joseph Conrad*. Blackwell, 1994.
Karl, Frederick R. *Joseph Conrad: The Three Lives, A Biography*. Farrar, 1979.
Meyers, Jeffrey. *Joseph Conrad: A Biography*. Scribner's, 1991.
Watt, Ian. *Conrad in the Nineteenth Century*. U California P, 1979.
Watts, Cedric. *Joseph Conrad: A Literary Life*. St. Martin's P, 1989.
Sherry, Norman, ed. *Conrad: The Critical Heritage*. Routledge and Kegan Paul, 1973.

The Secret Sharer

Conrad's Secret Sharer and the Critics. Ed. Bruce Harkness. Wadsworth, 1962. Includes: Jocelyn Baines, "Conrad's Biography and *The Secret Sharer*"; Carl Benson, "Conrad's Two Stories of Initiation"; Daniel Curley, "Legate of the Ideal"; Royal Gettman and Bruce Harkness, "Morality and Psychology in *The Secret Sharer*"; Albert Guerard, "The Journey Within"; Louis Leiter, "Echo Structures: Conrad's *The Secret Sharer*"; Marvin Murdick, "Conrad and the Terms of Modern Criticism"; R. W. Stallman, "Conrad and *The Secret Sharer*"; Walter Wright, "*The Secret Sharer* and Human Pity."
Approaches to Teaching Conrad's "Heart of Darkness" and "The Secret Sharer." Ed. Hunt Hawkins and Brian Shaffer. MLA,

2003. Bibliography and essays, including: Brian Richardson, "'He Was Not a Bit like Me, Really': Narrators and Audiences in *The Secret Sharer*"; Daniel Schwarz, "Creating a Self: Transference as Narrative Form in *The Secret Sharer*"; Andrea White, "Conrad and the Adventure Tradition."

Barnett, Louise K. "'The Whole Circle of the Horizon': The Circumscribed Universe of *The Secret Sharer*." *Studies in the Humanities* 8.2 (1981): 46–56.

Benson, Carl. "Conrad's Two Stories of Initiation." *PMLA* 69 (March 1954): 45–56.

Cox, C. B. "Mirrors in *The Secret Sharer* and *The Shadow-Line*." In *Joseph Conrad: The Modern Imagination*. J. M. Dent, 1974, esp. 137–50.

Dawson, Arthur B. "In the Pink: Self and Empire in *The Secret Sharer*." *Conradiana* 22 (1990): 185–96.

Dazey, Mary Ann. "Shared Secret or Secret Sharing in Joseph Conrad's *The Secret Sharer*." *Conradiana* 18.3 (1986): 201–03.

Dussinger, Gloria R. "*The Secret Sharer*. Conrad's Psychological Study." *Texas Studies in Literature and Language* 10 (1968–69).

Facknitz, Mark A. R. "Cryptic Allusions and the Moral of the Story: The Case of Joseph Conrad's *The Secret Sharer*." *The Journal of Narrative Technique* 17.1 (Winter 1987): 115–30.

Guerard, Albert. *Conrad the Novelist*. Harvard UP, 1958.

Guetti, James. *The Limits of Metaphor*. Cornell UP, 1967.

Harkness, Bruce. "The Secret of *The Secret Sharer* Bared." *Joseph Conrad: Critical Assessments*. Vol. 3, ed. Keith Carabine. Helm Information, 1992; 301–8.

Haugh, Robert F. *Joseph Conrad: A Discovery in Design*. U Oklahoma P, 1957.

Hodges, Robert. "Deep Fellowship: Homosexuality and Male Bonding in the Life and Fiction of Joseph Conrad." *Journal of Homosexuality* 4.4 (1979): 379–87.

Johnson, Barbara and Marjorie Garber. "Secret Sharing: Reading Conrad Psychoanalytically." *College English* 49.6 (1987): 628–40.

Miller, J. Hillis. "Sharing Secrets." *The Secret Sharer: Case Studies in Contemporary Criticism*. Ed. Daniel R. Schwarz. Bedford, 1997. 232–52.

Murphy, Michael. "*The Secret Sharer*: Conrad's Turn of the Winch." *Conradiana* 18.3 (1986): 193–200.

Paccaud, Josiane. "Under the Other's Eyes: Conrad's *The Secret Sharer.*" *Conradiana* 12.1 (1987): 59–73.

Said, Edward. *Joseph Conrad and the Fiction of Autobiography.* Harvard UP, 1966; esp. 120–32, 156–57.

Schwartz, Daniel. *Conrad: The Later Fiction.* Macmillan, 1982.

Sherry, Norman. "*The Secret Sharer*: The Basic Fact of the Tale." In *Conrad's Eastern World.* Cambridge UP, 1966. 253–69. On the *Cutty Sark* incident of 1880 (see Author's Note on *The Secret Sharer,* above).

Stallman, R. W. "Life, Art, and *The Secret Sharer.*" *Forms of Modern Fiction.* Ed. William Van O'Connor. U Minnesota P, 1948. 229–42.

Troy, Mark. "'. . . of not particular significance except to myself': Narrative Posture in Conrad's *The Secret Sharer.*" *Studia Neophilogica* 56 (1984): 35–50.

Wexler, Joyce. "Conrad's Dream of a Common Language: Lacan and *The Secret Sharer.*" *Psychoanalytic Review* 78.4 (1991): 599–606.

White, Andrea. *Joseph Conrad and the Adventure Tradition.* Cambridge UP, 1993.

White, James F. "The Third Theme in *The Secret Sharer.*'" *Conradiana* 21:1 (1989): 37–46.

Wiley, Paul L. *Conrad's Measure of Man.* U Wisconsin P, 1955.

Wollager, Mark. *Joseph Conrad and the Fictions of Skepticism.* Stanford UP, 1990.

Wyatt, Robert D. "Joseph Conrad's *The Secret Sharer.*" *Conradiana* 5:1 (1973): 12–26.

Films

Face to Face (RKO 1952), a double-feature produced by Huntington Hartford. The first story is *The Secret Sharer*: screenplay, Aeneas MacKenzie; dir. John Brahm; James Mason as the Captain and Michael Pate as the Swimmer. "By jettisoning the inner probing and the moral preoccupation of the original, the film emerges as a becalmed, dialogue-ridden mood piece," said *Time Magazine* (Dec. 15, 1952); Pauline Kael called it "an intense, eerie mood piece" (*5001 Nights at the Movies*).

The Secret Sharer, directed by Larry Yust (1972), with David Soul.